HARD
ROAD

HARD ROAD

BERNIE GUINDON
AND THE REIGN OF THE
SATAN'S CHOICE MOTORCYCLE CLUB

PETER EDWARDS

RANDOM HOUSE CANADA

PUBLISHED BY RANDOM HOUSE CANADA

Copyright © 2017 Peter Edwards

www.penguinrandomhouse.ca

Random House Canada and colophon are registered trademarks.

(All photos are property of Bernie Guindon or the author, unless otherwise noted.)

Library and Archives Canada Cataloguing in Publication

Edwards, Peter, 1956–, author
Hard road : Bernie Guindon and the reign of the Satan's
Choice Motorcycle Club / Peter Edwards.

Includes bibliographical references and index.
Issued in print and electronic formats.

ISBN 978-0-345-81608-5
eBook ISBN 978-0-345-81610-8

1. Guindon, Bernie. 2. Satan's Choice Motorcycle Club.
3. Gang members—Ontario—Biography 4. Motorcycle clubs—
Ontario. 5. Organized crime—Ontario. I. Title.

HV6491.C3E39 2017   364.106'6092   C2016-906069-1

Book design by Andrew Roberts

Cover images: (biker) © Glyn Jones/Corbis/VCG;
(tire tracks) © Rustamank / Dreamstime.com

Printed and bound in the United States of America

2 4 6 8 9 7 5 3 1

Penguin
Random House
RANDOM HOUSE CANADA

To Winona and Kenneth Edwards

Thanks a million

Contents

The sins of the father are to be laid upon the children.

WILLIAM SHAKESPEARE, *The Merchant of Venice* (3.5.1)

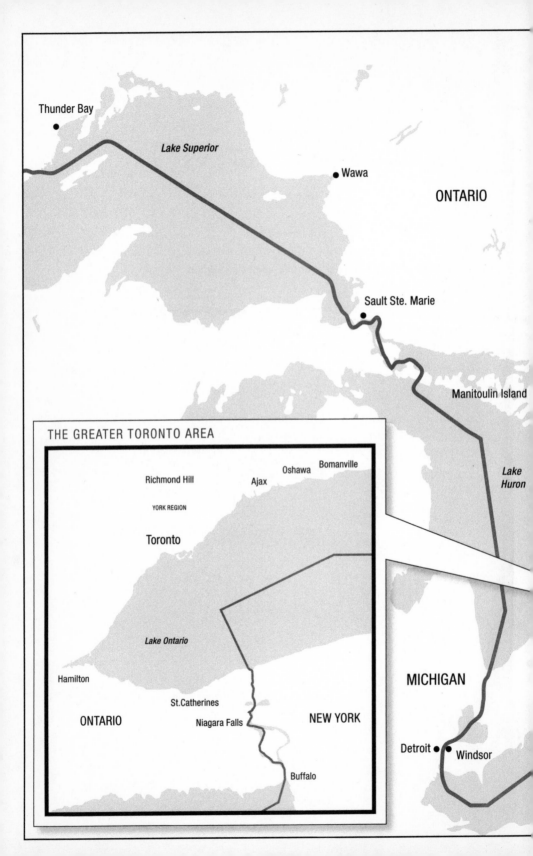

The Hard Roads of Bernie Guindon

QUEBEC

Sudbury

Sorel

Ottawa

Montreal

Georgian Bay

Lake Simcoe

Peterborough

Kingston

Rice Lake

Port Hope ● ● Cobourg

Toronto

Lake Ontario

Kitchener

London

NEW YORK

Lake Erie

N

INTRODUCTION

The first time I met Bernie Guindon, he was swearing at a string of Christmas tree lights. We were in the house of Lorne Campbell, one of his former clubmates from the Satan's Choice and Hells Angels motorcycle clubs. I was writing a book about Campbell called *Unrepentant: The Strange and (Sometimes) Terrible Life of Lorne Campbell, Satan's Choice and Hells Angels Biker,* when Guindon paid a visit. It was December, and soon he was trying to help his old friend put the lights on his Christmas tree. He clearly wanted them just right, but they kept getting tangled and were not lighting up as they should.

If the uncooperative lights had been uncooperative human beings, the situation wouldn't have been so tricky for Guindon. Though in his seventies now, he was a former world class boxer and head of a major outlaw motorcycle club. He could have settled things as he had many times before, with a crisp left hook. It would have been lights out.

I noticed during his visit to Campbell's house that Guindon didn't drink any liquor, even though plenty was available. I have met with him scores of times since and have never seen him touch alcohol or use any kind of drug, prescription or otherwise. He's a confirmed teetotaller and strongly opposed to drug use, which doesn't jibe with his image as an old-school, big-time outlaw biker who served prison time for his role in an international drug trafficking ring.

Guindon impressed me that day as a polite, complex man who had lived a hard life and had probably seen and done some truly horrifying things. That initial impression only deepened after he decided that he, too, would like to co-operate on a book about his life and we began getting to know one another.

This book is based on hundreds of hours of interviews with Guindon and those around him, including family members, bikers, former bikers, police and former police, boxers, a former bitter rival, and a couple of people who have had murder contracts on their lives. (I'm not sure when an unfulfilled murder contract expires. I'm not sure it does.) The book also draws upon various written and online archives as well as my three decades of reporting on outlaw motorcycle gangs.

Throughout my research, Guindon never told me what to write or whom I could and couldn't speak with. He only asked that I not go out of my way to stir up trouble with the Hells Angels, but that's generally a wise philosophy. He never missed or was late for an interview. If a book was going to be written on his life, he clearly wanted it done right, so his place in outlaw biker history would be properly recorded before the memories totally fade or too many participants die off.

Guindon's memory is not what it once was, which made the supporting interviews all the more necessary. The perspectives of others proved to be a good thing. I heard the full spectrum of opinions about him, from reverential to damning. Some of the people who know him best have the most nuanced views of him, blending strong positives and negatives. Several of the people interviewed for this book can't stand each other for reasons that will become evident. (I have actually wondered how we can have an inclusive book launch that doesn't end in a punch-up or shootout.) Undoubtedly, some of my interview subjects will be upset with me for giving space to their rivals and enemies, but I hope they will respect my effort to get as close to the truth as I can.

I was surprised to find that Guindon can be quite critical of himself, which may also surprise some who knew him in his heyday. And so this book is not an attempt to either glamorize or demonize Bernie Guindon. That he was a major figure in Canadian biker history is beyond dispute. As the leader of Satan's Choice, once the second-largest club in the world after only the Hells Angels and exemplars of the old-school biker lifestyle, he is arguably a major figure in the global history of biker clubs, too. My goal, however, is to humanize him, with all of the good and bad that goes with that—to learn what kind of a man makes a biker club, and what club life ultimately makes of a man.

I have learned some things through my research that go far beyond Bernie Guindon's personal story. Some of what I have learned, obviously, is about the development of outlaw motorcycle clubs in Canada, from their beginning to the present day. But the more I worked on this book, the more I realized it's also about something far bigger and wider reaching than how outlaws on motorcycles organize themselves in one country. The further I got into the research, the more I was pushed to think about the vital role of fathers. In particular, I understood the devastating multi-generational effects of domestic violence. The prolonged and intense cruelty inflicted upon Guindon, his mother and his brother in their home has had a painful ripple effect that's still being felt today throughout their families and communities.

There is a recurring pattern in this book of boys witnessing their mothers getting beaten, and then eventually, between the ages of fifteen and seventeen, defending their mothers against their fathers. I didn't seek out this pattern but I kept finding it. After a while, I came even to expect it.

Small wonder that these boys often grew into men who have little respect for authority. The system didn't protect them or their mothers, so why should they respect it? Also, small wonder that those boys often grew into men who greatly value violence as a way to solve problems.

That said, much of my research has been fun and some has even been inspiring. A true hero in this narrative is the stepmother of Guindon's son, Harley Davidson Guindon. (The fact that he would name his son after what he considers the world's best motorcycle speaks volumes about the man.) She has selflessly nurtured a sense of family under extremely difficult conditions. Out of respect for her request that her name not be included in these pages to protect her professional life, I have referred to her as simply "Harley's stepmother."

I have also benefited from the unpublished writing of Harley Guindon and his father's former clubmates Verg Erslavas and Frank Hobson. I am extremely grateful to them for sharing their work with me and allowing me to quote from it.

Most of the comments from Harley Guindon in this book come from his own writing, which impressed me. I think he has the potential to develop along the lines of Roger Caron, the former inmate who won a Governor General's Literary Award for (English) Non-Fiction. I hope that one day Harley will write his own book and I can write its introduction.

Conversations in these pages are taken from the memories of participants. Obviously, they are not reproduced precisely word for word. What appears in these pages is solely my responsibility. I have included endnotes for those who want to check sources or take some of the many Dickensian side roads that spin off from the main story. Nothing you are about to read has been made up. The true story of Bernie Guindon's life is more interesting than anything I could imagine.

CHAPTER 1

Beginnings

My old man was a good boot man. I knew when to shut the fuck up
and get away.

BERNIE GUINDON

L ucienne Guindon gave his youngest son a twenty-five-cent weekly
allowance when he was growing up in the early 1950s, but there
was a catch. Bernie could only collect it if he punched out his older
brother, Jack, in front of often-drunk customers of the family bootlegging
business. Lucienne peddled his booze from the Guindon family home
on Simcoe Street South for double the going price after Oshawa's bars
and liquor stores had closed. "Bootleggers have to be available at all
hours," Bernie recalls. "He'd get woken up early in the morning and late
at night."

Punching out Jack with his bare knuckles wasn't that tough a chore for
young Bernie, even though Jack was ten months older and scrappy. Bernie
had a natural grasp of the footwork, balance and leverage that help make
a great fighter, which contributed to his paralyzing left hook. He also possessed a fighter's inborn desire to be the last one standing, so it wasn't a
particularly emotional thing to put a beating on his only sibling.

Jack was hobbled by a short leg that had never healed correctly after
a bad break. He also wasn't a fighter at heart. In Jack's perfect world, he

would be an altar boy in a grand cathedral and a recreational body-builder. No part of him took joy in trading punches with his younger brother for the promise of a coin he never won.

The spectacle of the battling Guindon brothers helped draw paying customers to the family's living room, and there was never a time when the Guindons didn't sorely need the money. Their mother, Albini (Lucy), didn't like the family business but she didn't really have a say in the matter. "She didn't like us fighting too much," Bernie recalled. "The old man would love it, and the people drinking with him would like it. Give them some entertainment."

Lucy Guindon was illiterate, having completed only Grade 1 in French school, and spoke virtually no English. Guindon later heard that she had some Métis blood, although he wasn't clear on how much or whom exactly it was from. Isolated and far from where she'd grown up in the Gatineau district of rural Quebec, she could only find work as a housekeeper.

Her husband was a scholar by comparison, with a Grade 5 education and the ability to read and write in English as well as his native French. Lucienne Guindon was a smallish man but a commanding presence, who supplemented his bootlegging income by fencing stolen goods, sometimes working with crooked Oshawa cops. As much as he enjoyed a rare quiet day spent fishing, his sons remember their father more as a merciless and efficient fighter and a tyrant about the home. "I saw my old man kick a few guys in the head," Bernie Guindon said. "He could really kick. He could jump up and kick the ceiling. I saw my old man kick a guy in the face once and boot him down the stairs. He wouldn't take shit from nobody. He was maybe 135 pounds."

The Guindon brothers didn't fight just for the twenty-five cents. They also exchanged punches to keep their dad happy. "Being that he was a bootlegger, he'd be in a bad mood if he didn't get many customers. He'd use his fists and his boots on us. My old man was a good boot man. I knew when to shut the fuck up and get away."

Bernie didn't know too much about his father's father, except that he was also a violent man from Buckingham, Quebec, who also liked his liquor. Bernie's father was a twin, and Bernie heard rough things about his father's brother Denis. "He was a drunk. That's how I knew him. 'He's your uncle the drunk.'" Bernie's uncle Denis was also a police officer for a short period of time, something that wasn't bragged about in the Guindon household. "I think they fired him. Then he ended up driving a cement truck." That career came to an even worse end when the cement truck got stuck on a train line in Angers, Quebec, and was cut in half by a train, killing Denis.

Guindon didn't talk much about his father, but stories circulated about him nonetheless. There was one about how he threw Guindon's mother through a plate-glass window. He put her in the hospital more than once. There was another story about Bernie and Jack coming home dirty once, from an afternoon of play. They were placed in a tub of near scalding water and then scrubbed with the cleaner Comet until their skin felt like it might peel off. "He had a terrible temper. He had a worse temper than I did. It must have rubbed off on me."

Authorities in Oshawa must have known about the violence in the Guindon household, but they didn't interfere. Everybody looked the other way.

Personal shortcomings aside, Lucienne did attempt to provide his boys with direction, summarized by Bernie as: "Shut your goddamn mouth and keep your ears open."

Coming from their mother, the same message was less direct and more affectionate. "She tried to keep me on the straight and narrow," Bernie said. "She didn't want me to take after my dad . . . She didn't drink. I don't drink. She was sort of quiet. Tried to take care of business her own way. That's how I usually like doing it."

Not surprisingly, considering the regular bouts in the family living room, the Guindon boys developed a nasty case of sibling rivalry that never really went away. Jack blamed Bernie in part for his weakened, shortened leg, which was severely broken in a childhood rumble. Bernie maintained this was a bum rap, since he was only one of several people who played a role in Jack's frequent leg injuries.

Before they landed on Simcoe Street South, the roughest part of a tough town, the Guindons bounced from town to town as Lucienne scrounged about for money, which he seldom found. Jack was born on

January 8, 1942, in Buckingham, the birthplace of their mother. She had precious little time to rest up after Jack's birth, as Bernie was born on November 19 of the same year in nearby Hull. His mother was just nineteen when she gave birth to her second boy in ten months.

Being unsettled was a family tradition for the Guindons. Lucy had been raised in Montreal by her grandmother because her own mother was unable to raise a child. The first time Lucy spoke with her mother, she was fifteen or sixteen. "She [grandmother] just couldn't keep my mom, I guess," Jack said. Family relationships were a bit hard to explain to an outsider and confusing enough even for insiders. "My mom's mother was an aunt," Jack said. "My aunt was my grandmother, but nobody ever told me that." It all made sense to a point, and no one outside the family particularly cared. For all of the complexity of their relationships, Bernie said he had no doubt exactly where he stood in relation to Jack. "He was the favourite. I was the little bastard."

Lucienne always seemed on the run from poverty and alcoholism. He supported his young family for a time in Quebec as a log-roller on the Ottawa River, hopping from log to log and using a hook to break up logjams. That's a tough occupation at the best of times and particularly demanding when you can't swim. "He was afraid of water. In those days, you did what you had to do," Bernie said.

Lucienne's fear of water helped explain why he next tried his hand on dry land as a lumberjack in the hamlet of Red Rock, fifty-six miles east of Thunder Bay, on the shore of Lake Superior. The Guindons arrived shortly after the closure of Camp R, a prisoner-of-war camp for a diverse population that included captured Nazis, merchant seamen and even German Jews in the early 1940s. It was a prime location for isolating prisoners, since the camp wasn't reachable by any sort of road. Anyone wanting to shop had to be game for a five-mile walk along the railway tracks to the town of Nipigon, while mailing a letter at the post office meant a three-mile hike to Everard.

It was in this isolated corner of Canada where young Jack and Bernie each almost died as toddlers. One day, Jack wandered out onto the frozen lake and refused to come back no matter how loudly and frantically his mother shouted. A slip through the ice would have meant certain death, and so his parents ventured carefully onto the ice to retrieve him. Young Bernie almost went to an early grave when he drank Javex bleach by mistake. The closest doctor was seventy-five miles away—too far to be an option. Somehow, he rebounded.

The worst of the boys' mishaps in Red Rock came when Bernie was about four and his mother was boiling a tub of laundry water on a wood-burning stove. The wood floor collapsed and the tub spilled onto Bernie's chest and neck. "They didn't think I was going to live," Bernie said. "The skin peeled away. You could see my collarbone. One of the guys my dad knew put cattails and bear grease on the scar."

"Mom felt horribly," Jack recalled.

Lucy Guindon was God-fearing and tried to pass her faith on to her boys. The name Bernie isn't in honour of anyone in particular, but Guindon's middle name is Dieudonne, which is French for "God given." Both of the boys were exposed to the Roman Catholic religion at a young age. Jack was naturally good at Latin and the ways of the Church. Bernie was less taken by the mysteries of theology. "There's somebody up there but I don't know who the fuck He is," Bernie reflected. "Sometimes you swear at Him and sometimes you say thank you. I'm not all that religious. I used to hate being on my knees all the time, saying prayers and losing a couple of hours on Sunday."

After Red Rock, the family's next stop was in Sault Ste. Marie, where they lived with Lucy's mother. Lucienne tried his hand again in the lumber industry and then truck driving, failing at both. Yet he and Lucy somehow scraped together enough money to outfit their boys in new suits for their First Communion. Bernie and Jack never looked tidier or more civil than on that day, posing for a photo in their matching double-breasted jackets.

The boys' fondest early memories include going to the movies, where they'd lose themselves in the action adventures of Roy Rogers, Gene Autry, Randolph Scott and Superman. They loved tales of brotherhood and power, which contrasted sharply with real life at home. "It was tough," Jack recalled. "My dad was kind of a mean guy. We'd get lickings, that's for sure."

Next, they moved to Oshawa, an industrial city less than an hour by car east of Toronto. The kids had lived there briefly before, when they were preschoolers. There had also been a brief stop in Buckingham before the second move to Oshawa. Exactly why each move was made wasn't explained to the boys and, in time, this constant state of motion had become the norm.

They settled for about four years at 552 Simcoe Street South, just across the street from the Simcoe Street elementary school, in an old farmhouse behind a dry cleaner's, clothing store, variety store and beauty salon. The Guindon boys discovered a tunnel from the basement that brought them into the dry cleaner's. They would steal bobby pins and, at home, incorporate them into the kinds of rough games young brothers play. "We used to shoot at each other with elastics around the house," Bernie said. "I got him in the dick once."

They also lived in a house on Ritson Road, across from a brewery. Jack recalled an evening there when his parents had planned a night out. Before they could leave, a group of strangers dropped by for booze. There was a sudden commotion outside, and next thing Jack knew their father had knocked a man out and left him lying motionless on the road. Lucienne and Lucy got into a cab and sped off to enjoy their night. The man's friends dragged him away. "We didn't know if he was dead or not," Jack said. "Thank goodness he came out of it."

The boys were expected to do the dishes, pile wood in the basement, refrain from swearing and never argue with their mother. Lucienne demanded that the boys respect their mother, but he still beat her mercilessly in front of them. Those beatings were a sad constant throughout their early years. The boys witnessed one particularly ugly incident when they lived at an apartment on Drew Street. "Bernie jumped on my dad one time because my mom was getting beaten up," Jack recalled. "I jumped in there too, the two of us. Then the cops came and Bernie and I were thrown out of the house." The police said the brothers could stay at the station overnight and the boys thought that sounded okay. The next day, they went to stay with some relatives but felt out of place. They returned to the police station. "When we got there, they put us where the lost articles were," Jack said. "A cement floor in the basement.

I'll never forget that. Was Bernie ever pissed off!" They went home the next morning. Lucienne was sporting a black eye, courtesy of his eldest son. There would be other nights spent fleeing the violence at home, one spent in an abandoned car. "We went to a scrapyard to sleep," Bernie recalled matter-of-factly, as if it was just a normal part of growing up.

In the summertime, Bernie and Jack were dispatched to rural Gatineau Mills, Quebec, where they stayed with their aunt and uncle, who had sixteen children, two of whom died young. Bernie remembers his father saying, "Learn your French," as he sent them off to help out on their aunt and uncle's farm. "They never spoke English. I'd have to really listen well in order to know what they were saying." There were just a few beds for so many kids, and they slept head to toe so they could pack in as many as possible. Bernie and Jack were dressed well when they arrived at the farm so that the family appeared wealthier than they really were. "We'd get there in suits," Bernie said. "The old man showed us off . . . They got all hand-me-downs and they were lucky to get fed. They'd stare at us."

The Guindon boys had adventures of their own during their visits to Quebec. Once, one of their older cousins sent Bernie off in a field to chase after some horses, not warning him that those horses didn't like people. "The horse kicked me in the leg," Bernie said, but it didn't get a good shot at him. A kick from another horse gave Bernie his first broken nose of many.

Summers in Quebec proved rougher for Jack. The first time he broke his left leg was at their grandmother's. When the boys wanted to play baseball, she said no, but the boys went off anyway. "I ran to first base," Jack recalled. "My cousin was on first base. I collided with him . . . it snapped the leg in both places. It was just hanging there. I'll never forget that. It was painful." Jack broke that leg another six times as a boy. Doctors tried implanting a steel rod, steel plates and lamb's bone, all with limited success. "His leg didn't grow," Bernie said. "He always walked with his heel up." Perhaps that explained Jack's woeful record against Bernie in their living room brawls.

A youth as rough as the Guindon boys' was bound to leave Bernie with medical issues of his own. He had a punctured eardrum, most likely a result of too many shots to the head from his father and kids in the schoolyard, and needed an operation at the Hospital for Sick Children in Toronto. He continued to have hearing problems for the rest of his life. (In later years, he liked to keep his bad ear turned toward any particularly chatty company.)

Christmases for the Guindon boys weren't spectacular, but they definitely were better than what was experienced by their Quebec cousins. "They were lucky to get fed at Christmas," Bernie said. "Sometimes we'd only get one present, but you got a present. I got my double cap guns one year with holsters. Jack got them too. That was pretty exciting. The old man must have sold quite a bit of beer."

No matter where they were living in Oshawa, Bernie always knew where to find his father when he wasn't at home. He'd be up the street at the Cadillac Hotel, and he would likely be slumped at a table, his senses dulled by beer. The Cadillac was a bucket of blood hotel with loud, live country music on the weekends, and Lucienne was one of the men who contributed to its rough reputation. "My old man used to be in there all of the time," Bernie recalled. "My old man used to bounce there. After the bar, they'd all go to my dad's house. He'd have them there until five or six in the morning."

Lucienne did try, in his own way, to steer his boys in the right direction. Once, he took the boys to see Kingston Penitentiary. Since 1835, it had housed generations of the country's most desperate, violent criminals behind its thick limestone walls. Lucienne pointed to its heavy front gates and told his sons, "This is where you're going to go when you're bad."

CHAPTER 2

Local Celebrity

My parents didn't give me shit about homework. My mother couldn't read or write. My dad was busy with bootlegging.

BERNIE GUINDON on his early education

T he Guindon family home on Simcoe Street South was in the centre of Oshawa's old southern immigrant neighbourhood. It was much poorer than the northern, suburban area that later attracted Toronto's commuting class. Directly across the street from the Guindons' rented house was the Simcoe Street elementary school, and students there quickly made it clear they didn't want Catholics—who they called "Cat-lickers"—on their playground. "I used to go across the street and fight all of the Protestants," Bernie Guindon said. "I was a 'cat-licker.' I fought a lot of the big guys. I did good. I held my own. That's how I got into boxing."

At the Holy Cross Catholic Elementary School just up the street, Guindon was constantly in trouble for fighting, talking and not doing his homework. Jack was better behaved, but he fell behind too. Jack had lost about two years of schooling because of his leg operations, and neither parent was pushing the boys to catch up. "My parents didn't give me shit about homework," Guindon said. "My mother couldn't read or write. My dad was busy with bootlegging."

Guindon's lack of academic production led him frequently to the principal's office, where a nun he nicknamed "Dirty Gertie" cut an imposing figure with a leather strap in hand. "That strap looked pretty goddamned big. I used to have welts on my hands all of the time."

In class Bernie listened to a priest say God knew everything past, present and future. That didn't settle much in Guindon's mind. He raised his hand and asked, "If God knows all of this, then he already knows if I'm going to heaven or hell, and if I'm going to hell, why would he want anything to do with me?"

The bright spot in Guindon's days came after school, when he boxed at the Simcoe Hall Boys' Club on Simcoe Street South. He often tried to drag Jack along and sometimes he succeeded. Their parents weren't home after school, and young Bernie had plenty of aggression to vent. "At that time, I never thought about boxing," Jack said. "I went to the Y and took up bodybuilding, which I should have stuck to. Bernie wanted me to get into the boxing. I was his sparring partner. Oh boy."

Experienced boxers taught Guindon a lesson his father began years before: if you're in a fight, it's vastly preferable to give out the punches than receive them. "When you're young, you're not that vicious. When I first started, I used to do a lot of playing around. As you got a little older, you knew the guys are out there to hurt you. It's no longer a fun game."

His father enjoyed watching Bernie fight, although he didn't praise him. "He thought I was pretty lucky, pretty good." His mother cheered him on. "Whenever she had the opportunity, she'd come watch, if it was around town. She didn't mind me boxing. She knew it kept me out of shit."

Shit still came at home, where the fighting was never fun and no one cheered. But by the age of fifteen, Bernie could fight back. "I slapped him for beating my mother once. I gave him a shot in the head. He left shortly after that."

The same year that his father moved out, Bernie was expelled for truancy, which gave him more time to train. He was now in his third year of boxing and starting to make a name for himself, headlining boxing cards at places like the Avalon dance hall on King Street West. He ran up an amateur record of twelve wins and no losses and was clearly a kid to watch. For all of its brutality, boxing offers a basic fairness that appealed to him. It doesn't matter, once you step into the ring, whether you're rich and snooty or poor white trash from the wrong side of the tracks. All that matters is what you do with your fists. "The thing in boxing is the better man wins."

His mother found a boyfriend who liked motorcycles. He took Guindon for a ride. "It was unbelievable. He asked me if I wanted to drive. I said yes, so he sidesaddles the bike and makes me change positions without even stopping." Guindon was hooked and soon bought a 1948 Matchless G80.

He began hanging around the newly formed Golden Hawks Motorcycle Club. Clubs were a new and exhilarating thing in the 1950s, especially after Marlon Brando and Lee Marvin appeared as bikers in the movie *The Wild One*. The Hawks were the largest bike club in the province east of Toronto, with several Korean War and World War II veterans in their ranks. When they admitted seventeen-year-old Guindon as a full member, his initiation consisted of chugging a bottle of red wine, something he found particularly unpleasant. The parade of drunks through his family's living room had already killed any notion that drinking was glamorous, and he soon quit drinking altogether.

Guindon was quickly promoted to Hawks road captain, which put him in charge of mapping out runs and making sure no one got lost or in trouble on the way to events. When they rode together smoothly as a group, the Hawks were impossible to ignore. Individually, members of the club might be forgettable, but everything changed when they rode down the highway together in a tight, loud formation, like a fighter squadron. They felt free and dangerous and it was intoxicating. "It gave you a sense of power, when you were in a pack. You could hear the rumble. You could hear it for a long ways. They knew you were coming."

At the start of a run, Guindon loved to growl, "Come on, you criminals." It was his responsibility to make sure the bikes assumed a proper formation, neither too close nor too far apart, as they raced along at over sixty miles an hour. Colliding at a high speed wouldn't be just embarrassing, someone could die. "I'd run a few off the road. They're not just fucking things up for themselves. There's going to be a major accident and I don't want to be one of them." Guindon was promoted again, to sergeant-at-arms, which put him in charge of discipline. He kept order at meetings and made sure everyone paid their dues.

He wore a helmet back then, even though they didn't become mandatory in Ontario until 1969. It wasn't for the safety. He used helmets as a government-approved punch enhancer. At first he wore a small one, called a "half casket," which didn't go down over the ears and doubled as a nice, light boxing glove during a rumble with a rival club. He then shifted to a full helmet when he realized he could punch even harder with more helmet. "They're even better. You've got more plastic to hit them with."

Guindon still lived in Oshawa with his mother, but he worked at the BIA gas station at the corner of Simcoe and Gibb Streets, which was owned by former motorcycle racer Monty Cranfield. As Guindon dashed back and forth, filling cars, he caught the eye of a new girl in the neighbourhood. Suzanne Blais, who went by the nickname "Nicky," and her mother had moved from Toronto in August 1958, settling into an apartment building looking over the gas station.

Suzanne was three years younger and liked something about how Guindon looked as he handled the pumps. She was smitten by his slim build, kind smile and "gorgeous eyes."

"Who's that cute guy pumping gas?" she asked her mother.

"I don't know. Why don't you ask him?"

The next day, on her way to school, Suzanne walked up to the stranger.

"I don't need gas, but I would love to know your name."

"I'm Bernie, and you are . . . ?"

"Suzanne."

He asked where she lived and she pointed to the apartment building.

"Up there."

He said he hadn't seen her before. The conversation shifted to school and she said she went to Holy Cross. That was his old school, he told her. He could tell by her accent that she was French and said he was French too. They had so many things in common, Suzanne noted, as her interest increased. It didn't escape her notice that several other girls enjoyed stopping by the pumps to speak with Bernie, as well.

That night, Suzanne told her mother his name and that he was French. Her mother wanted to get in touch with his parents because she only knew a few French-speaking people in the area.

This is a guy I would really like to know forever, Suzanne thought that night.

She arrived in Guindon's life with a tangled back story that rivalled his own. Suzanne's parents had grown up two farms away from each other in Quebec, but after Suzanne was conceived, her father left his wife for a woman named Alma. Her mother vowed she would never let him see their baby girl. In time, Suzanne's estranged father married Alma but still pined for time with his daughter.

Suzanne later heard stories of how her father would park at the end of her grandparents' laneway at their farm in Saint-Eugène, Quebec, in hopes of catching a glimpse of Suzanne. Her grandfather kept a rifle close at hand and made it clear that there would be no safe drive up his laneway. "He said, 'You cannot see Suzanne because my daughter made that rule,'" Suzanne recalled. "'You went with Alma. You're out of the picture.'"

Her father died in 1954, never resolving the anger that split his family. "I never met him," Suzanne said.

In time, Suzanne's mother decided her girl should learn English, the language she associated with business and success. Hearing she could find a job at the General Motors plant in Oshawa, she and Suzanne packed up and left for English-speaking Ontario.

Around this time, Bernie's mother loaned him five hundred dollars to buy a dark blue 1949 MG convertible with a white cloth top. He would pay her back, bit by bit, and it didn't escape him that her loan was a grand gesture of love. "She had to work on her knees. Scraping floors and washing floors." Suzanne loved the convertible too and was thrilled when he took her to the movies and bowling. "I'll always be your protector," he told her. "You can call on me any time."

When Suzanne's mother was unable to land a job at GM, she took a job steaming sweaters in Toronto. Suzanne decided to drop out of school to help pay the bills. In May 1959, she called Guindon and asked if he would drive them to Toronto so they could look for an apartment.

"He helped us out with no hesitation, more than once," Suzanne said. "By this time, Bernie and I had become quite close, and I wanted to stay in Oshawa."

The teenagers planned to meet one evening in Toronto and go for dinner, but Bernie didn't show up. Suzanne got tired of waiting and went on to the restaurant herself. He didn't appear there either and she ate alone.

Bernie wrote her a letter, dated January 24, 1960, explaining that one of the MG's headlights had gone out and he had needed to get back to Oshawa before dark. He suggested that Suzanne take a bus out to Oshawa so they could get together, and that he could drop by her home in Toronto with his good friend Vince Barrese.

> *Dear Nicky how are you coming along. I received your letter while I was watching TV . . . So I decided to write my first letter to a girl. Vince and I went to see if you were home and your Mother told us to go to the Pacific. We went there and you were not there so we went back to your apt. and your mother wasn't there so we decided that we would take off home. It was getting dark out so we wanted to make it home fast. I'll try to get up there as soon as possible maybe within two-weeks or less . . . I hope you will give me something when I go up there. If you would like . . . come to Oshawa . . . I wouldn't mind at all. I would be very pleased. I hope you'll write me back as soon as possible and tell me if she wants Vince to come and if you made up your mind to come to Oshawa. I hope youl' forgive my writing. I know it's sloppy but I can't help it*

> *Boyfriend*
> *Bernie*

> *XXXXXXXXXXX I am waiting for some soon.*

Money was tight and Suzanne couldn't afford the trip to Oshawa. By the next time she saw Guindon, both of their lives had changed in large ways.

CHAPTER 3

Branching Out

Some guys fight to win and other guys just fight.

BERNIE GUINDON

Guindon trained under Grant O'Reilly at the Oshawa Boys Club, where boxers were expected to mind their manners. Cursing was forbidden. Guindon liked how O'Reilly could fight far above his weight division. O'Reilly boxed between 118 and 124 pounds while Guindon was between 132 and 135 pounds, but O'Reilly made up for the size deficit with a jab that he snapped at a speed unavailable to the bigger fighters. "Size doesn't mean shit," Guindon said. "I've seen big guys who are like mama's boys and little wee guys who've been picked on their whole life fight like a rattlesnake. Some guys fight to win and other guys just fight."

Plenty of fighters obsess about their hand speed, and Guindon did too, but he wanted something more. He studied other fighters' footwork, balance, punching power and reaction patterns. "There's quite a few different aspects to boxing. It's not just going in and clubbing each other." He paid particular attention to his footwork because he realized that the lower body is where real punching power begins. In order to improve his balance and lay a foundation for his punching, he practised dribbling a basketball. Years later, former world-ranked heavyweight

George Chuvalo said he was impressed with how Guindon channelled maximum power into his punches. "You hit harder when you twist your rear end," Chuvalo said. "You maximize your leverage."

Guindon developed as an amateur fighter, displaying a pronounced comfort level in the ring and a natural ability to take a punch. Violence felt like his natural element.

After the downtown Oshawa club folded, Bernie took to the road to find training and competition. In the Buffalo area, he connected with Monsignor Franklin M. Kelliher, a priest who had a strong amateur career and a past double life. In addition to wearing the robes of the clergy on Sunday, Father Kelliher had donned a pro wrestler's tights and mask on weekdays, rassling as the Red Devil and the original Masked Marvel. In 1932, someone tore off his mask and exposed his true identity, which to that point had been a secret to almost everyone but God. The local bishop wasn't crazy about having a priest who doubled as the Red Devil, and he body-slammed Kelliher's ring career.

From that point on, the fighting Father concentrated on developing young boxers. A man of few words, he impressed Guindon with his down-to-earth, no BS attitude. "He wouldn't swear and he wouldn't want you to either. He was a terrific guy. He was a more serious type of guy."

At six foot four and in the neighbourhood of 300 pounds, Kelliher was a physically imposing guy. He spoke in a soft voice and expected fighters to shut up and pay attention. "Boy, those kids did what they were told when Father K told them," Canadian fighter Walter Henry said. "We knew to keep our mouths shut when Monsignor Kelliher was around."

Back at home, Guindon found that trouble was coming now from an unexpected source: would-be altar boy Jack, who had left school at age fifteen with a Grade 6 education. Although Jack liked to needle Bernie, he felt a certain pride that his younger brother was the youngest member of the Golden Hawks. Jack thought about joining, to add some glamour to his life, but deep-sixed that notion after a brush with the law when he was seventeen.

As Jack tells the story, he was more of a curious passenger than a criminal the day he became a car thief. He and an Oshawa friend named Herman lifted a car from the lot of a dealership on Bond Street with a set of keys Herman managed to steal from the office. Herman wanted to visit some relatives north of Toronto, near Barrie. "We went back that evening and away we went," Jack said. "It was a fine car. He was the driver."

Oshawa police caught them on the return trip. For the theft, Jack was chained and sent by bus to the Ontario Reformatory in Guelph for three months. He was assigned to a dormitory for twenty youths, where he slept on a bed with no mattress, just a blanket on top and another blanket under him.

Some of his new companions immediately met to test him. "These guys told me, 'Jack, we want you to punch this guy out.' I went over and punched this guy. Then he grabbed me, had me down on the bed. Somebody was keeping six—watching for the guard."

For that, Jack spent some time in segregation. After that, he settled down and earned a job in the reformatory slaughter house. "It was good," Jack recalled. "I didn't mind it at all. The time went by fast."

He got in a few fights and also boxed one bout in the reformatory, against the father of a stripper Bernie had dated. "I won. Got a chocolate bar for it."

Once released, Jack felt he had spent enough time in a cage. Wearing a Golden Hawks' patch would only make him an obvious target for police. "After that, I said to myself, 'Never again do I want to go back.' I didn't want to join the clubs. I didn't want to go to jail."

Bernie knew that jail was a real possibility in his own future, if he stayed in biker clubs, but he charged ahead anyway.

CHAPTER 4

Supreme Commander

*I knocked out two of them. I started with the sergeant-at-arms and
knocked him out, and then Johnny Sombrero chased me down the field
with a log.*

BERNIE GUINDON

Canada's best-known biker in the early 1960s was a square-shaped man from Toronto named Harry Barnes, who demanded that people call him "Johnny Sombrero," "Chief," "Boss," "Supreme Commander" or, if they were in his inner circle, "Sombrero." He'd grown up in the Junction area of west Toronto. He recalled his childhood as "violent, very violent," even in preschool. "I nailed my first customer when I was four years old," Sombrero said. "I was in kindergarten, making a little castle with my blocks. He kept pushing them over. They were little maple blocks with ABCs on them. I picked one up and conked the kid over the head with it."

In the Barnes household, Harry's mother was the one to be feared. She was a member of the Italian Commisso clan. Many of their relatives were active in organized crime. Harry's father, an Englishman from the North Country, was more restrained. He was socially isolated after marrying into his wife's tightly knit family. She lived to be a hundred while his father didn't make it to retirement age before falling dead from asthma over his morning newspaper.

When Harry's kindergarten teacher called, his mother immediately took charge, lecturing the teacher on the proper way to handle her boy: "You can't touch his toys when he's playing with something. You leave him alone." Then she dealt with Harry. "My mother was very violent," Sombrero recalled. "She used to beat the shit out of me. She told me every day of my life she was going to kill me . . . She hit me with her hand and hurt her hand. Kicked me and hurt her foot. Then she went for the rolling pin."

Years later, a judge asked Sombrero, "Do you fear any man?"

"I fear no man and only one woman," he replied.

Sombrero was just entering puberty when the soldiers returned from World War II. The thought of men bonding over violence appealed to him. Highways were becoming a big thing and he wanted to be a part of that action too. He and a group of his teen buddies joined a bike club called the Humber Valley Riders, despite a serious age gap between Sombrero's friends and the club's leaders. "We were fourteen, fifteen, sixteen. They were forty-four, forty-five."

All of the Riders wore matching silk shirts while on public runs. In the right light, they looked a bit like cowboys riding together in the Rose Parade. In the wrong light, they looked like they got lost on their way to a square dance.

When the club set up a branch called the women's auxiliary to allow the wives of its middle-aged members to meet, Sombrero couldn't stomach it any longer. He led a splinter group of a dozen or so teens into a new club he called the Black Diamond Riders. Sombrero also took to calling himself the "Supreme Commander," a reference to Dwight D. Eisenhower and his role as supreme commander of Allied forces at the end of World War II. As it was in the military, Sombrero had no desire to make his club democratic. "I don't care what you say," he told members. "It's done my way or it's not done."

Powerfully built, Sombrero stood around five foot ten and carried 245 pounds on a barrel-shaped frame ("I've got muscles bulging out of me everywhere"). He rode a Harley chopper with squared-off, galvanized sheet metal mufflers that obviously didn't come from a dealership.

When he wasn't riding his chopper, Sombrero cruised behind the wheel of a Cadillac. Sometimes he could be found living in a hotel, like a celebrity on tour. He brawled like a petulant star, too. He fought hard and dirty and often, but he prided himself on fighting only other bikers.

Some fights were so ferocious that Queen Street in Toronto had to be blocked off to accommodate the young thugs. When police intervened, Sombrero and his gang jumped on their bikes and barrelled away. Outrunning cops was exhilarating but no great challenge. The Toronto area was home to thirteen separate police forces who generally didn't cross into each other's jurisdictions. "The police forces couldn't follow us. They had no power in those days . . . We used to outrun them."

In 1956, Sombrero took notice when a new club called the Satan's Choice Motorcycle Club appeared on Niagara Street in downtown Toronto. "The first time I invaded their clubhouse, I had to. They were invading our property." That's when the "beer bounties" began. Sombrero gave a case of brew to any member who could strip a Satan's Choice member of his club crest, the "colours" on the back of his vest. "The guys used to go hunt them down like animals."

In time, Sombrero forced the Satan's Choice off the road. Then Sombrero reconsidered and let them return, reasoning that they would distract the police and make life easier. "If the cops bother them, they are not bothering us."

Sombrero often travelled with a goon or two by his side. They sometimes carried violin and guitar cases, although these hadn't been recruited from any music conservatory. The cases, he said, held Thompson submachine guns from his private collection, since he was a licensed gunsmith with a legal stash of military firearms. As if the goons and violin cases weren't unsettling enough, Sombrero adopted an unlikely club mascot: a fluffy white bunny rabbit. The club's five-acre property at Steeles Avenue and Dufferin Street in north Toronto was complete with a swimming pool and groundhog burial site. "We had five acres of land. We had rabbits, foxes, pheasants by the dozens, groundhogs."

When Sombrero first met Guindon, he was freshly inducted into the Golden Hawks. Sombrero announced to the teenager that he expected to be called "Supreme Commander." Sombrero later admitted that this was a tad provocative. "The word 'supreme' is a little heavy," he allowed.

Guindon declined and told Sombrero to get fucked instead. Not surprisingly, things between them went immediately downhill.

Guindon had an uneasy feeling when Sombrero and his "BDR" arrived in force at a field day in 1961. Beside the Pebblestone Golf Course, in what is now the village of Courtice, east of Oshawa, the Golden Hawks had turned a barn into their clubhouse and invited a number of other clubs to the field day. Among them were the Para-Dice Riders from Toronto, the Canadian Lancers from Scarborough, the Vagabonds from Toronto, and local car clubs like the Spacemen and Nomads.

Sombrero recalled his club winning a lot of motorcycle skills events and expected to be rewarded accordingly. Then they realized what kind of prizes were up for grabs. "They didn't have a trophy for us. They wanted to give us a can of Castrol 50." The master of ceremonies wasn't helping. "Son of a bitch swung a chord at me with a microphone on it."

Guindon was already nursing two black eyes and a broken nose from a beating he took the previous week in Grand Bend when he tried to punch his way through three guys. As the Black Diamond Riders got angrier, Guindon pulled on his helmet, anticipating the worst. Then he warned the president of the Oshawa chapter of the Golden Hawks that things were going to get nasty. "Bill wouldn't listen to me," Guindon recalled. "He said they wouldn't do that in a field day." Guindon was astonished at the senior biker's naïveté. "They were out in the bush cutting trees and branches and whatever they could use to beat us with!"

Once they had gathered sufficient lumber, Sombrero's men attacked. "I knocked out two of them," Guindon said. "I started with the sergeant-at-arms and knocked him out, and then Johnny Sombrero chased me down the field with a log. I wasn't going to stand around waiting until he hit me. I ran."

Armed as they were with branches and tree trunks, the Black Diamond Riders were in the minority that day, while the Golden Hawks had plenty of Oshawa auto workers on their side. "There was about six-teen of us there plus a few Vagabonds, who were always on our side," Sombrero recalled. "We were fighting half of GM."

Sombrero remembered the enemy coming in waves. "They were up on a hill. They kept sending down fifteen at a time to fight us. We were polishing them all off." Then skinny, teenaged Guindon reappeared, carrying a massive pile of lumber he had torn off the barn. "This kid came up on me with half a barn," Sombrero said. The planks teetered and then fell onto the Black Diamond Riders. "He almost suffocated us all," Sombrero said. "He turned around and he ran like a deer . . . I thought, *That's good. I don't have to kill that little kid.*"

The melee became known in biker circles as the "Battle of Pebblestone." One of the Hawks suffered a broken arm while another was treated in hospital for a blow-induced blood clot on his brain. Sombrero followed up the beating by bashing the Golden Hawks' bikes and burning down the barn. They were all lucky no one was killed.

The victory made Sombrero even more arrogant and harder for his rivals to take. In 1962, he led the Black Diamond Riders down the west-ern end of Toronto's brand new Gardiner Expressway in formation, two abreast, heading the wrong way, which seemed wholly appropri-ate. The Gardiner hadn't opened yet, so there was no traffic to spoil the rough pageantry.

In the aftermath of the Battle of Pebblestone, the Golden Hawks, Canadian Lancers, Nomads and Para-Dice Riders struck an alliance. They grandly called it the Amalgamated Riders Association, and under the terms of their mutual defence pact, all of the clubs kept their old colours and structure but now also wore two-inch round patches over their hearts with the letters "AR."

Then Sombrero made what appeared to be a friendly overture to the local club with the coolest name, the Satan's Choice, whose mem-bers included characters like Black Peter and Spaceman. They were all invited by the Riders to a party in their honour. Instead of offering cake and beer, however, the Riders pulled out guns and stripped them of their patches. It was the second time Sombrero forced the Satan's Choice off the road in just a few years. "We took all their crests and told them they couldn't exist any longer," Sombrero said. "I wiped them out twice, the Choice."

When the other clubs heard the news, they hung back and cringed, thankful they weren't the ones suffering the humiliation. A surge of disgust cut through Guindon. He was eighteen and impatient for action. When none came, he quit the Golden Hawks and began calling them the "Chicken Hawks." He washed his hands of the whole scene, moving to Quebec for a short time, where he competed in motorcycle ice racing and stunt riding.

Quebec was fun but Guindon couldn't ignore a sense of responsibility toward his mother, who still couldn't read or write in English. Oshawa was inevitable. When he returned, he took up with an attractive, reli-gious teenager named Veronica, who lived in an area of the city where Guindon used to deliver newspapers. In short order, he got her preg-nant. In November 1961, true to the practice of the time, he married her and then continued to have sex with any woman who would accom-modate him. Their daughter was named Teresa.

Guindon's mother told Suzanne Blais about the marriage, and Bernie's old girlfriend saw it in a flattering light for him. "I wasn't surprised. She was pregnant. He wanted to honour it. A lot of guys wouldn't."

Suzanne had plenty of her own problems. She underwent back surgery in December 1962 at Toronto General Hospital. The eight-hour operation to fuse her spine went horribly wrong. She was later told that her heart had stopped and she had to be revived during the operation. "I could hear the priest giving me the prayers," she said. "My mom was crying."

Five months later, in April 1963, Suzanne got married in Toronto. She and Guindon hadn't seen each other since the previous year, just before he missed their date because of car trouble. If his car had stayed on the road that day, they might have married each other. Instead, they were each newly married to someone else. But Guindon was consumed not with thoughts of romance, but revenge.

CHAPTER 5

Fight Club

He only took his cane to me once. I hit him with a right and down he went. He never tried that again . . . You had to be careful with him. Those canes were thick.

BERNIE GUINDON on fighting a disabled biker

As a teenaged father, Guindon supported his young family by hoisting cattle hides on and off an assembly line in a tannery. He was seldom home, and when he was there, he was often impatient and abusive. That's what Teresa heard in retrospect, growing up, although she was just a baby at the time. "I confronted him years later," Teresa said. "He doesn't remember a lot of it. Some of it he does."

In 1963, Guindon scored the motherlode for a high school dropout in Oshawa: a union job at General Motors. Suddenly he was doing better financially than his father ever had. The couple and baby Teresa moved into a nice brick bungalow on tree-lined Browning Avenue, edging their way out of Oshawa's troubled south end.

Parenthood and life on an assembly line were helping move Guindon up in the world, but they were also leaving him supremely bored. He started up a new motorcycle club called the Phantom Riders and began obsessing about how to make it better. While the name had a certain coolness, the club's crest of a ghost riding a chopper looked like something a grade-school kid might draw. "We were saddled with the worst-looking crest in Ontario," he said.

Phantom Riders rode Japanese bikes, BSA Triumphs and Nortons, but many of their bikes were old police-issue, American-made Harleys. Guindon wasn't troubled by his gang riding Harley Panheads that were once used by police to chase criminals, including some of his club members. "If you painted it, who would know it was a cop bike?"

Guindon began work on a custom chrome fantasy bike, built out of a 1953 Harley-Davidson Panhead. He salvaged some of the parts from old army bikes and lovingly coaxed them back into service. The twin front lights were from the local GM plant and had originally been intended for a Pontiac Grande Parisienne. He did much of the work on the bike inside the GM machine shop. "It took me all winter to do it," Bernie said. "I had to go everywhere to find parts and get them chromed. The chrome shop was in Toronto." His friend Vince Carducci from the Para-Dice Riders in Toronto painted Guindon's new ride a metallic tangerine colour, offset by gold plate and chrome everywhere else.

Guindon enjoyed the attention and feeling of power that his fantasy-come-true brought him. He had come a long way since he and Jack were scared kids hiding out from their father in a junkyard. Now he was front and centre on the street where he used to live, atop a one-of-a-kind, badass, otherworldly creation that was unmistakably his own. The fact that his father hated motorcycles made the feeling all the better. "People would say, 'Geez, that looks like a wild thing.'" Guindon agreed and named his ride "The Wild Thing." (This was before The Troggs' hit song "Wild Thing.") Guindon cut an impressive figure as he looked out between its high-rise handlebars and over its ridiculously extended front forks. "I used to love riding that thing," he said. "Going around corners, it was like a transport truck. On a straight line, it was great. The seat was cozy. I was king of the road."

When not on the road, the Phantom Riders honed their fighting skills in a "fight club" Guindon ran out of the basement of his new home. The basement often hosted fellow workers from GM, as Guindon tested them to see if they were club-worthy. There was a heavy bag, a speed bag, and a ring for fighting with a concrete floor to fall on, if you took a hard shot to the chin. The first rule of Guindon's basement biker fight club was to always be on guard, for there was no medical care and little sympathy for anyone starched with a hard punch.

Canadian anthropologist Daniel R. Wolf described outlaw bikers as an urban, industrial, bohemian subculture generally drawn from the lower middle class. "If the labourer is a young man in search of himself, he will find nothing in his self-image at work that will excite him; he had best look elsewhere," Wolf wrote in *The Rebels: A Brotherhood of Outlaw Bikers*. "Men who are chained to these circumstances share a compelling desire to escape."

That certainly described Guindon's basement fight-club regulars, who included Carmen Neal, the club's Oshawa vice-president, whose temper often got the better of him. "I had to put him in his place," Guindon said. "He was okay. He settled down."

There was also Reginald Robert (Reg) Hawke, an alcoholic with a massive upper body and stumps for legs, who walked with canes and drove a customized tricycle. His short temper was made worse whenever someone called him "Shorty." Hawke fought by his own rules, which included his personal brand of kendo. "He only took his cane to me once," Guindon recalled. "I hit him with a right and down he went. He never tried that again . . . You had to be careful with him. Those canes were thick."

Hawke served as the club's first secretary treasurer, which meant he was in charge of picky things, like remembering anniversaries and communications. It was an important job—bikers are particularly sensitive about anniversaries. Many had had birthdays and other key dates repeatedly spoiled when they were children and still craved a little recognition.

Guindon's wife, Veronica, hated conflict. She even had trouble returning defective goods to the store. But even she had her limits, and she felt she had to do something to protect her young family from the men who were consuming her husband's time. "My mother loved him to pieces, regardless of what he did to her," Teresa said. "My mom gave him an ultimatum: you pick the family or the club. He picked the club."

Veronica moved to her parents' home, where Teresa was raised in a

God-fearing, sheltered environment. "You've got to play it a day at a time and hope the next day is better," Guindon said, thinking of the lost time with his daughter and the dissolution of his young marriage. At the time, however, he was more a biker than a husband or father. He didn't dwell on the loss.

CHAPTER 6

Expansion

It wasn't organized crime, as it became. But I don't think you wanted to cross them.

Filmmaker DON SHEBIB on early bikers

Twenty-seven-year-old filmmaker Don Shebib read an article about new bike clubs in Toronto in 1965 and immediately wanted to know more. He was trained as a sociologist and fringe groups fascinated him. His first professional documentary was about surfers in California, and something about these hometown bikers seemed like a natural follow-up. Neither surfers nor bikers trusted the media, which made them all the more authentic and interesting. "The bikers were just a little rougher around the edges," Shebib said in an interview. "They were very similar to surfers. Talking of how free they felt on a bike or on a board. They're classic rebels."

Shebib went to a hamburger joint on the Danforth near Warden Avenue in Scarborough where the Canadian Lancers hung out. In those early days, bikers had hangouts more than real clubhouses. Most of them were greasy spoons, like the Army Navy Club on Spadina Avenue in Toronto for the early Satan's Choice, before they shifted over to Aida's Restaurant at St. Clair Avenue and Kingston Road. Shebib kept going back, trying to get to know the club members. The Lancers appreciated the respect and began opening up to him. He learned that most of the Lancers were in their late teens and early twenties but their ranks also included an ex-con in his thirties who had served time for theft, and a forty-four-year-old veteran of World War II named Ken. The military connection made sense. The bike clubs forming in California at the time were established by veterans of bomber squadrons who had been issued motorcycles to get around air bases and conserve gasoline during the war.

As a trust developed, Shebib began meeting members from neighbouring clubs. One, Edjo, lived west of Toronto, by the lakeshore, and ran the Vagabonds. Edjo, aka Captain Ed, was a savvy man who could sometimes be found behind the wheel of a red Cadillac convertible or Italian sports car. He ran a charter boat company and a motorcycle shop. His Vagabonds met on Britain Street, near Moss Park at Queen and Sherbourne Streets, and in a downtown laneway near the Art Gallery of Ontario. "I thought he was a riot," Shebib said of Edjo.

The bikers had attitude and were tough. They liked their beer, booze and marijuana. A couple of them pimped out their stripper girlfriends. Several were middle-class kids who bridled when their parents pushed them toward university and the professional life. Many didn't see belonging to a motorcycle club as a permanent thing, but more of a temporary state of mind. "It was a lot of booze, broads and bikes," Shebib said. "It wasn't organized crime, as it became. But I don't think you wanted to cross them."

As Shebib began to work on his documentary with cinematographer Martin Duckworth, Guindon shook up the biker community with a sudden move that startled police and bikers alike. He merged his Phantom Riders with the Canadian Lancers, the Wild Ones from Port Credit and the Throttle Twisters from Preston (near Kitchener, an hour west of Toronto). There were now 110 members in his club, which suddenly made them the largest motorcycle club in the country. As a final, provocative jab, they took the name and patch of a club that Sombrero had driven off the road twice: Satan's Choice. It was an intimidating name that would make outsiders think twice about giving its members a hard time. Those who knew its history would be even more impressed.

Guindon imagined how it would enrage Sombrero to see more than a hundred of the grinning devil patches roaring past him on the highway. As an added bonus, they could finally lay to rest the lame patch of the ghost riding a motorcycle that had haunted the Phantom Riders.

Shebib recorded their thoughts on film, like how they grandly said they rejected materialism and valued no possessions beyond their bikes. They boasted about how they were rejecting conformity, even though they were conforming to a newly invented culture of their own in a tight-knit group. The bikers expressed something between pity and contempt for members of mainstream society and the importance they placed on security, money and haircuts. "They let other people rule their lives," one member said on camera. "We just laugh at them."

There was a summer camp or hootenanny feel to the bikers Shebib filmed, especially when they sang "Satan's Choice We Roll Along" to the tune of "Merrily We Roll Along." Club meetings were held in an apartment above a store—a far cry from the metal doors, security cameras and barbed wire that would one day become common features of biker bunkers. Shebib also followed them with a movie camera to the Heidelberg hill climb near Kitchener, where they showed off their riding skills.

The opening chords in the soundtrack of Shebib's documentary were performed by John Kay, who sang for a band called The Sparrow. Within a few years, The Sparrow evolved into Steppenwolf and those opening chords were developed into "Born to Be Wild," which was used in the soundtrack to the Hollywood blockbuster movie *Easy Rider*.

Shebib's documentary featured a rotund biker called "Tiny," one of a countless number of Tinys in the biker world. Guindon also made a fleeting appearance. He didn't object when Shebib called his documentary *Satan's Choice*. While Guindon didn't like the way many in the club came off as scruffy whiners, he liked the attention.

Not long before, a club named Satan's Choice had been forced off the road by a braggart in a fancy shirt. Now Guindon's club had laid claim to that fearsome name as their own and become known, and even feared, from coast to coast.

CHAPTER 7

National President

They fired me and then they said they'd give me back my job, if I quit riding my bike to work.

BERNIE GUINDON

ormalizing a status that had never been in doubt, Guindon was voted national president of the Satan's Choice at age twenty-two. The title placed him squarely on the radar of ambitious police officers. His club members also made themselves hard to miss. They travelled in a pack that included—aside from the bikes and the snazzy, plastic, glow-in-the-dark grinning devil patches on their backs—a green 1948 Packard hearse, complete with a coffin in the back. For a time, a dummy took up residence in the coffin. It never doubled as a beer cooler, as some suspected. "It just blew people's minds," Guindon recalled.

He was a commanding presence, despite standing no more than five foot nine and weighing about 150 pounds. Sometimes he travelled in a black 1956 Cadillac stretch limo with his 350-pound, wildly bearded second-in-command, Big Jack Olliffe, also known to members as "Bear." Though he was no fitness enthusiast, he knew how to fight, which helped in meting out discipline. Despite Big Jack's considerable girth, he'd had enough martial arts training to boot a tall man in the chin.

The Choice might look unkempt and out of control, but they did have some rules. "You could buy hot [bike] parts but you couldn't steal them," Guindon said. "There were a lot of bike thefts. Parts were expensive and they weren't plentiful. You used to have to order them right from Harley-Davidson."

Another rule was more an attempt to stop fights than legislate morality. "You couldn't come on to another guy's old lady." That rule wasn't carved in stone, however. In one extreme case, a biker contracted a social disease from the old lady of another biker. The bikers' friendship carried on, and the woman departed the scene.

Guindon was strongly anti-drug at this point. He beat and expelled members for any illegal substance use. Eventually, the rules were relaxed and only needles were prohibited, unless they were medically prescribed. Membership was closed to any current or former police officers or prison guards. Rules also forbade homosexuality and repeated excessive drunkenness.

Members also had to have a motorcycle on the road by the Victoria Day weekend, the third week of May. In most of Canada that marked the start of riding season, which continued until Labour Day. The mileage would be noted on both dates, and a club member who hadn't racked up serious travel could expect to lose his patch. "If he didn't put any miles on his bike, he's out," Guindon said. "You're not a biker. You're a wannabe."

For Satan's Choice members, those bikes had to be Harley-Davidsons, except for first-year strikers, who were allowed to ride British Nortons, Triumphs and BSAs. Under no circumstances was anyone connected to the club allowed to be seen atop a Japanese motorcycle. They might be good bikes, but they were alternately associated with the Japanese attack on Pearl Harbor, the establishment and the cringe-worthy "Nice Guys Ride Hondas" ad campaign.

One rule mattered more than all others: members couldn't be rats. Nothing was simpler or more important than that. They couldn't cooperate with police to deprive someone of his or her freedom, even if that person was an enemy. Members could beat or even kill someone and not violate club rules, but they couldn't rat on anyone under any circumstances. Even associating with a rat was trouble. Sponsoring someone for membership who turned out to be a rat meant the sponsor would be lucky to escape with a one-month suspension and a ban from holding club offices.

The thrill of roaring about in a pack while wearing a big devil's head patch proved to be too much adrenalin for some new members. Guindon found himself pressured to enter skirmishes created by new Satan's Choice members whose shiny new patches made them feel ten feet tall and invincible. "We tried to stop those guys from fighting the small clubs, but we couldn't."

The club didn't have a clubhouse yet, so they met in the basement of a home on Colborne Street in Oshawa. It was hard for neighbours to miss members as they rode in. Hawke sported a six-inch beard cut like a Pharaoh's. Vice-president Carmen Neal had a nasty scar across his nose that made the violence in his past impossible to ignore. A member named Puff wore his devil patch on the back of a fur coat.

The Choice strived for attention but bristled when they got too much. Guindon felt that an Oshawa cop named Forgette was watching them all too closely and going out of his way to make life miserable. The constable was stopping Choice vehicles for making too much noise or not having working signals or other violations the Choice president considered petty. One day, Forgette hit Guindon with both a traffic ticket and a challenge. "If you want to get even for this, we can duke it out in the ring at the [boxing] club," the cop offered.

When Guindon agreed to the bout, Forgette added, "I think it's only fair to warn you that I was a pretty good boxer in the navy." Guindon didn't know anything about Forgette being some kind of navy boxing champion. He did know that he badly wanted to give him a righteous beating. "He was a bully. He'd beat the kids up with the billy [club]."

They met at the Cedardale community centre in Oshawa. Guindon handled him easily and, sensing that victory was imminent, began to have fun and prolong the bout. "I just played with him." After that, Guindon didn't miss an opportunity to taunt the officer. "I'd meet him downtown. I'd say, 'For-shit, isn't it?'

"He'd say, 'You know it's Forgette.' I'd say, 'That's what I said. For-shit.' He'd get fucking mad."

One summer afternoon, Forgette showed up in a cruiser outside Guindon's Browning Avenue bungalow. According to Guindon, Forgette sucker-punched him and in response he immediately shifted into a fighting stance, popping him with three straight shots and then dropping to the ground on top of him. Forgette's partner came to his rescue, pulling Guindon to his feet and handcuffing him. He spent the next three months in the Guelph jail that had once held Jack, serving an assault sentence. Upon his release, Guindon returned to work at GM, but the mood had soured considerably. Company executives didn't like the way he rode his Harley to work instead of a GM car or how he wore his Satan's Choice crest into the plant. They particularly didn't like how some GM workers were finding their way into his club. Had they known that a Grande Parisienne headlamp lit the road for Guindon's Wild Thing, they wouldn't have liked that either. "They fired me and then they said they'd give me back my job, if I quit riding my bike to work. It was my only way of getting to work. I told them to stuff the job up their ass."

Contrary to the popular image of boozing bikers, Guindon defied his father's example and remained a strict teetotaller. "When we were kids, we used to steal booze from my dad. I was a bad drunk. I knew at a very early age that booze and I don't mix. I got drunk and stupid. Fighting. I always felt bad the next day," he said, then hinted at the discipline that allowed him to stay on top of his unruly club: "If you want to get respect from people, you've got to respect yourself."

Boxing was another rebellion of sorts against his father, who kicked his way through many fights. Bernie never used his feet in a fight. His fists were enough, and he continued to get better with them. He rode the Wild Thing to gyms where greats like George Chuvalo, Clyde Gray and Muhammad Ali trained, such as the Lansdowne Boxing Club in west-end Toronto and Sully's Boxing Gym at Dupont and Dufferin Streets, downtown.

At Sully's, visitors could expand their nostrils with the sweat of the greats and the not-so-greats, as the club didn't have air conditioning or showers. The air at the Lansdowne Boxing Club wasn't so pungent, thanks to several live-in cleaners. "There were a lot of old guys staying there overnight," Guindon said. "They cleaned up." A sign posted by the pay phone warned that police might be listening in on calls.

Middleweight boxer Spider Jones had served a two-year stint for robbery at the Millbrook provincial jail, near Peterborough. While inside, he'd heard of Guindon's tough reputation as a street fighter. "Bernie was a legend in the joint," he said.

Jones had an unsettling feeling the first time he saw Guindon ride up to Sully's on the Wild Thing. He had had some nasty clashes with racist bikers while growing up in Windsor and East Detroit. "There was a lot of shit going on then, back in the 60s, racial stuff," said Jones, who is black. "I used to fight bikers a lot." Since getting out of jail, Jones had been living upstairs at the club. "I remember him coming in on his big chopper," Jones said. "I didn't know what to expect."

Jones was pleasantly surprised. "When I first met Bernie, we just hit it right off," he said. "Bernie didn't give a shit about your colour. He was a gentleman. I know he was a biker, but he was a gentleman." Guindon didn't fit with the bikers' beer-swilling image, which Jones also appreciated. "I was a teetotaller too."

Sully's was a pure boxing gym, not a fitness centre with a few punching bags, and Guindon loved it. "You knew you were in a club. It smelled like sweat. You knew there were guys working out in that club."

Guindon wanted tough, high-level sparring partners, and Jones was able to fill that role. He showed Guindon a different style of fighting that was becoming popular at the time. "He was totally different, like Muhammad Ali," Guindon said. "Moved around."

Jones outweighed him by twenty pounds and was good enough to win three Golden Glove championships and eventually turn pro. Even with his size advantage, he felt he had to bring his A game into the ring with Guindon or suffer the consequences. "He was a tough guy, a helluva fighter," Jones said. "He was very serious." Most of the time, Guindon got the better of him, Jones said. "He was a natural fighter."

Jones considered him "a stone warrior" whose power belied his smallish stature. "He had a lot of power and he could wear you down. He liked to hit to the body. He would keep coming at you. He knew how to slip and slide and counter . . . Boy, he could bring it. He'd get in your kitchen big time. He'd make you feel like you had eaten some bad food."

Guindon also spent time in the ring with Clyde Gray, who was moving toward boxing's top level. "When we used to spar, I hit him with some good shots," Guindon said. "I didn't hold my punches. He didn't like that. He thought he should be the only guy to do the hitting. A lot of pros are like that . . . He was a jabber. Right hand. An all-round good fighter as far as I was concerned."

Long-time Canadian heavyweight champion George Chuvalo was considerably bigger than Guindon, so they didn't get into the ring together. Still, Chuvalo liked what he saw when Guindon rode in to train. He called Guindon a "good stiff banger," whose big punch was his left hook. Chuvalo already knew plenty about left hooks, since he possessed a tenderizing one of his own. They both also shared a no-nonsense, in-your-face style. "I don't remember him going all over the ring like Muhammad Ali," said Chuvalo, who fought Ali in two epic losses that went the full distance.

Instead of dancing about, Guindon pressured forward with a non-stop, old-school attack. He was happy to trade punches, with the hope of finding chin space for his left hook. His right hand also had stopping power, but it was the left hook—showcasing a Satan's Choice tattoo on the bicep—that routinely rendered opponents horizontal. Chuvalo recalled that Guindon sometimes livened things up with a leaping left hook. That punch seemed to come out of nowhere. "Sometimes you'd get lucky with it," Guindon said. "Usually the other fighter isn't looking at a left hook to be thrown at him from that distance. He's sort of relaxed." Chuvalo remembered the leaping left hook as being a genuine threat, since boxers are conditioned to expect their opponent to lead with a jab. "He landed it with some accuracy," Chuvalo said. "It's a rare punch."

Like Jones, Chuvalo was impressed that Guindon could be a ferocious competitor and then show genuine respect for his opponent once the punches stopped. Chuvalo maintained that was in the best tradition of his sport. "I think it's the most dangerous sport," he said. "There's a very healthy respect for an opponent."

The heavyweight wasn't impressed only with Guindon's manner in the ring. "He was a decent guy," he continued. "He wasn't a wise guy." Jones agreed: "He was a good mentor. He helped a lot of people."

Sometimes Guindon drove in from Oshawa with Jack, whose later memories were of the hits he took, rather than any he meted out. One particular blow to the midsection from his brother remained sharp in his mind decades later. "He hit me so hard I stood there in shock," Jack said. "It was like putting your hand in an electrical socket. A shock went down your whole body."

When his workouts were over, Guindon often hung around with members of the Satan's Choice at Webster's all-night diner at 131 Avenue Road, on the fringes of the Yorkville hippie district. There was cheap food and edgy music like Bob Dylan's "Gates of Eden" on the tabletop jukeboxes. "They [hippies] were well behaved. You never saw hippies looking for trouble." On any given night, there was a good chance you'd find bikers from the Vagabonds, Para-Dice Riders and Black Diamond Riders. Often, some of the club leaders would be on hand. "You'd talk to the presidents and try to solve problems," Guindon said. "If one of our guys was having a problem, you try to settle it before it gets out of hand."

Jones sometimes dropped by Webster's too and said he didn't have any trouble from the all-white motorcycle club members. "I stayed out of their business. Who am I to judge them?" Guindon, he observed, took a live and let live attitude in public. "He [Guindon] didn't go around intimidating people. As long as you didn't mess with him."

One night, Jones was at a Yorkville hangout near Webster's when half a dozen whites started giving him a rough time. Jones went over to Webster's, where Guindon was talking with some club members. "I told him what was happening. Bernie came over with some of the guys." Once they saw Guindon and his friends, the mood dramatically changed and the racist slurs suddenly stopped. "Bernie backed me up that time," Jones said. "Those guys didn't want to fight anymore."

"He didn't go with the N-word shit," Jones said. "Nigger calling. He didn't like that shit . . . Bernie wasn't no racist."

Despite his serious training, Guindon continued to smoke two packs of cigarettes a day. He had smoked from the time he was a kid, back when he could steal them from his father's bootlegging customers. His father tried to force Bernie to stop by making him inhale until he threw up. Bernie refused to be bullied and his smoking continued.

When smoking caused his fitness to lapse, he could often gut his way through his three- to five-round amateur bouts. If his left hook connected, as it often did, bouts were considerably shorter.

He blamed a lack of sparring partners and not cigarettes for conditioning problems. "I never was in good shape. I didn't have nobody to spar with." Dragging his brother into the ring as a sparring partner was frustrating. "Jack would say, 'Fuck you, I'm not going to go with you. Don't hit me.' [I would say,] 'Jesus Christ, Jack, what do you think I'm here for? You're in the ring.' All I'd do is speed punches at him and he'd still get mad because I hit him."

On one trip into Toronto, Jack forgot his athletic cup and he warned Bernie about it before they stepped into the ring. The sparring set went well for a while, until Bernie lost himself in the action. "He came up with an uppercut and caught me square in the balls," Jack recalled. "I must have laid there for twenty minutes before they took me to the dressing room. Bernie kept on sparring." Jack was taken to a doctor in Oshawa, where he was given pills and a courtesy athletic supporter. He couldn't recall his brother ever saying he was sorry but didn't really expect it anyway. "I was kinda pissed off, but what can I do?"

Guindon was still training with Monsignor Kelliher in Buffalo as well. One night, he and the priest were in Salt Lake City for a boxing tournament. Guindon was in his club colours and the priest was in his robes.

"Come on, Bernie," the priest said. "You're wearing your colours. Don't be wearing your colours."

"You wear your colours and I'll wear my colours and we'll get along just great," Guindon replied.

CHAPTER 8

Pigpen

I remember my mother saying, "Get under the bed. Dad's got the shotgun again."

HOWARD DOYLE (PIGPEN) BERRY

n the summer of 1967, Canada's celebratory centennial year, a biker named Rod MacLeod rode north to Wasaga Beach and announced himself to the Ontario biker world. The resort town on Georgian Bay, a two-hour ride north of Toronto, was a favourite summer spot. Another was Grand Bend on Lake Huron, less than an hour northwest of London. Married bikers tended to keep their wives away from both locales. "A lot of the girls would be there for summer holidays, weekend holidays," Guindon said. "You'd pick up all the girls and take them riding on your bike."

MacLeod impressed Guindon immediately for several reasons. There was his aura of leadership, easy sense of humour and willingness to scrap, even though he wasn't much bigger than Guindon. His motorcycle chain wrapped around the front forks of his bike in a way that made it easy to detach and call into service—a biker had to be prepared to mix it up in MacLeod's native Quebec, then home to some 350 clubs. The newcomer struck Guindon as the kind of guy he wanted beside him in a brawl. "He was solid," Guindon said. "Didn't take shit from nobody."

However, the qualities that Guindon admired in MacLeod weren't what most bikers first noticed about him. "He was the only black guy I ever saw riding a bike in those days," Guindon said. "He rode a motorcycle and he liked the idea of a motorcycle club. There were clubs in Montreal, but they wouldn't let him go because he was black." MacLeod had clearly been riding for a while and knew what he was doing atop a Harley. "He liked pulling wheelies. He rode a Sportster. Rod was a good rider."

MacLeod had a black friend from Montreal called "Jono." Jono was a bank robber and an enthusiastic one at that. He once robbed two neighbouring banks on the same day. As investigators were checking out the first bank, Jono was just down the street, sticking up the second one.

Guindon was amused when MacLeod would tear into Jono verbally. "He would say, 'Shut up, you fucking nigger!' He wasn't joking."

MacLeod told Guindon that he wanted to start a Satan's Choice chapter in Montreal, and Guindon thought he would be a good addition to the club. MacLeod brought with him twenty-five members who were black and white, French and English. Most of them were in their late teens and early twenties, and a few had jobs as electricians or truck drivers. Some of their girlfriends worked in factories or offices. For his part, MacLeod was an unemployed mechanic who lived in a garage with his dog, Satan.

Up to that point, all outlaw biker gang members in Canada had been white, and several clubs had specific policies that barred anyone of colour. Guindon sensed an opportunity to scoop up some overlooked talent.

Like other outlaw bike clubs, members of the Satan's Choice often tattooed swastikas onto their flesh and wore Nazi helmets and Third Reich memorabilia like Iron Crosses. It wasn't meant as a political comment. "We just wore that to blow peoples' minds," Guindon said. Some people, however, read a little more into the rude fashion statement. One was Martin Weiche, head of Canada's National Socialist Party—or Nazis.

Weiche was a wealthy London, Ontario, real estate developer, white supremacist and friend of the Ku Klux Klan, and he liked to burn crosses with like-minded friends. During his youth in Germany, he belonged to the National Socialist Power Drivers Corps, a Nazi bike gang. After fighting for Germany in World War II as a pilot and a soldier, he immigrated to Canada in 1951 and amassed a small fortune in real estate. That gave him the funds to offer Guindon's Satan's Choice ten acres of land in an undisclosed location, in exchange for acting as the Canadian Nazi party's bodyguards.

Guindon quickly squashed that idea. His Choice members might wear Nazi gear for shock value, but they still considered themselves Canadian patriots.

On Labour Day weekend in September 1967, Guindon decided to hold what he grandly billed as the first annual Satan's Choice national convention. The event site was a ramshackle farmhouse in Markham, north of Toronto, and more than three hundred delegates rode in from the club's chapters in Windsor, Montreal, Preston, Kingston, Ottawa, Peterborough, Hamilton, St. Catharines, Guelph and Oshawa. Guindon's mother attended and danced with members along to the music of the Beatles, the Rolling Stones, Elvis and whatever else was filling the airwaves on popular radio.

On the Saturday night of the convention, the Vagabonds rode in as guests of honour. The clubs had made plans for a football game to take place the next day in Toronto's Riverdale Park. Then, shortly before midnight, a couple dozen Markham police officers stormed the farmhouse. Officers were punched, kicked, spat upon and hit with flying beer bottles. After a "tactical withdrawal," Markham deputy police chief Robert Hood called on the Ontario Provincial Police (OPP) for reinforcements. Officers from Stouffville, Markham Village, Whitchurch, Vaughan, East Gwillimbury, Richmond Hill and Metro Toronto hastily assembled at the local police office in Buttonville. Then they drove down darkened country roads, with their lights out, to the farmhouse. Once assembled outside, Hood turned on his loudspeaker.

"This is the police," he announced. "You are surrounded. Come out with your hands in the air."

No one came out.

Then officers smashed through the farmhouse's front and rear doors. Bikers leapt through windows to escape. One punched a cop hard and fled across a field. Others crawled on their bellies to freedom. Another curled up in an unlit basement furnace and waited for three hours until police left. Four bikers piled into a Cadillac before realizing that none of them had the keys. A cop coaxed them out by brandishing a tear gas grenade next to a cracked window and announcing, "Come out, or I'll pull the pin and this comes in." Other cops took billy clubs to bike lights and deliberately scraped custom paint jobs.

The evening could have gone far worse for the Choice. Fewer than a hundred delegates were at the farmhouse when police arrived. "Most had driven to Yorkville to get something to eat and pick up some fresh girls," a biker later told the *Toronto Daily Star*.

Police confiscated marijuana, two hundred dollars and a hundred cases of beer, a sawed-off shotgun, baseball bats, spike-studded belts, bicycle and saw chains, axe handles, knives, brass knuckles, a whip, switchblades and a .32 revolver, which was found hidden inside a television console. They also scooped up a price list that stated potato chips and pop were fifteen cents, while beer and condoms cost twenty-five cents.

Among those arrested were Guindon, then twenty-five, and his nineteen-year-old second wife, Barbara Ann. Also arrested were Reg Hawke, thirty-four, of Oshawa (he of the dangerous canes), and Howard Doyle Berry, twenty-six, of Peterborough. Berry would later become infamous under his biker name of "Pigpen." In a world that celebrated uniqueness and living life on its own terms, Pigpen was already something of a legend.

Few bikers knew that Pigpen had once been a successful Buddy Holly impersonator or that he had worked as a chef at Toronto's posh Royal York hotel. Fewer still knew of his horrific upbringing. "I remember my mother saying, 'Get under the bed. Dad's got the shotgun again,'" he later said.

Pigpen's dad never did blow off anyone's head, but his parents inflicted emotional damage on him that psychologists and psychiatrists would struggle to repair in later years. By the time he was five years old, his father had moved out of their Peterborough-area home, and for several years, Pigpen was the only boy in a family of girls and women with plenty of grudges against men. He was often confined to the basement, where he spent his nights in fear of demons that might discover and torture him. Real-life people weren't much better. "I lived half the time in the basement on a dirt floor and a rubber sheet. I got scared that the bogeyman would get me. She [my mother] used to make me go to church all of the time. I used to piss the bed scared."

Pigpen became quick with his fists, and refined his fighting style by boxing as an amateur at the Peterborough Boxing Club and East City Bowl Boxing Club. He grew to be solidly built, carrying about 245 pounds on a six-foot frame. His most memorable organized fights were settled far from referees, including one that spilled onto a major Toronto street against George Clark of the Vagabonds. The punches and bloodshed weren't necessarily started in anger but they weren't meaningless either, and spectators could sense they were witnessing something truly epic. "They blocked off Avenue Road—the cops—for an hour," Pigpen said. "They didn't want to stop it. They had bets on it. I wore him down." Neither man was knocked out, but Clark later said he had never been hit so hard in his life.

A six-foot-seven Vagabond named Igor provided Berry with a much easier test than Clark. "I knocked him out," Pigpen recalled. There was also a dust-up with the formidable Howard (Baldy) Chard, "King of the Bouncers," a five-foot-eight, barrel-chested 280 pounds. Chard fought with professional cool, as befitted someone who collected debts for the likes of mob boss John (Pops) Papalia of Hamilton. "He never lost a street fight, a fight in reform school, in reformatory or in the pen," Paul Rimstead of the *Toronto Sun* wrote of Chard (though he wasn't counting a less-successful tussle in which Chard was pitted against seven men).

Pigpen's self-defence tactics went far beyond weathering and throwing punches. Bikers liked to reminisce about a time when Pigpen was arrested with a pack of outlaw bikers. One by one, the bikers were led outside by police, who put a hurt on them to teach them a lesson. "He shit his underwear and covered his face in shit," former Choice member Cecil Kirby recalled. "It worked. Better than getting a phone book against your head." Police wouldn't touch Pigpen in that condition.

"There are guys who would start fights and then they'd say, 'Come and help me.' I can't stand people like that. Be a stand-up guy," Kirby said, with Pigpen in mind. "He was a stand-up guy. That's what I liked about him."

The Markham police raid made the front page of the *Toronto Daily Star*. "If they don't get a fair shake in court, we'll tear that place apart and then come into Toronto," a biker vowed to the newspaper's Eddy Roworth. The bikers were indignant at having to spend a night in the Don Jail, as well as at their mangled bikes. None of their rides was in worse shape than the Wild Thing, whose three-foot-long front forks had been ruined by the tires of a police cruiser. "Just horseshit," Guindon later said. "It was worth good money. It was a show bike."

"We'll get even," a biker said at the time. "When the guys that own these machines get out, you're going to see a lot of cops with scars. We know who they are. We've got names and addresses." Someone called Scarborough police to say, "Let the guys out or we'll blow up that hellhole."

Some of the bikers sounded surprised and even a little offended that police had crashed their party. They had already retreated from the city after police had made them feel unwelcome. "We got out of the plazas because of them," one told the newspaper. "Now they follow us out here. We don't want trouble. We moved out here so we could have our blowouts without bothering anyone. And we're going to blow, man, no matter what. Maybe they'd like it if we went back to the plazas."

From a police van outside the courthouse, Guindon called out to reporters that police had deliberately ruined their bikes. "The bikes were right underneath a light," Guindon shouted. "The police car ran right over them on purpose. Thirty guys lost their jobs over this. They wouldn't let us make phone calls." Another biker who had attended the party with his wife shouted about not being allowed to phone their babysitter.

"Hey, Bernie," one biker piped in. "Tell them how they made us take a shower."

"Yeah, that's police brutality," Guindon said, warming up to the press attention. "We're only supposed to do that once a year."

Markham deputy police chief Robert Hood said some bikes were damaged but much of it was "the doing of the motorcycle gang members themselves." Hood added that he couldn't understand the accusation that his men ruined the farmhouse, since it was "a pigsty to begin with."

In the end, Guindon and the other bikers got off with a series of one-hundred-dollar fines. They didn't have to follow through on their threat to ride three hundred bikes into the heart of Toronto on a rampage, which was just as well since they didn't have anything close to that number of roadworthy bikes to rampage with. That weekend, Guindon said goodbye to the Wild Thing. He swapped its mangled remains for a 1947 Knucklehead. Guindon could measure phases of his life by the bikes he had ridden. After the Matchless G80, he had owned a Triumph Bonneville, then a Norton 750 twin and then a series of Harleys, the official ride of true outlaw bikers. He had ridden them all hard, sometimes with painful consequences. The worst mishaps were when he scraped off skin during a slide. "Road rashes, they're the worst," he said. "I'd rather have a broken leg than a road rash."

Guindon lost some heavy-duty support in December 1967, when his right-hand man, Big Jack Olliffe, was packed off to prison. The charges came from a beating that Big Jack and a biker named "Tank" had laid upon a junior member from Kitchener named Arnold Bilitz at a party the previous year. Bilitz had come on to another guy's old lady. A member named Terry Siblock had thrown in a kick for good measure.

They'd meant the beating to be a harsh lesson, but Bilitz died and Big Jack and Tank ended up with prison time. Siblock was allowed to walk free as he had only struck one blow, which wasn't likely the fatal one.

Wondering at Siblock's freedom, Big Jack couldn't resist calling him a stool pigeon, even though Siblock was a solid member and no police informant. For a biker like Siblock, whose dad was an ex-con and had raised his son to hate stool pigeons, Big Jack's insult was the type that festers, threatening to one day explode.

CHAPTER 9

Yorkville

If anyone gave one of my dealers a hard time, I was swift to use my type of justice on them.

Satan's Choice member FRANK (HIPPY) HOBSON on life in Yorkville

The Satan's Choice had seventy or so members in Toronto by early 1968, which put them on a par locally with the Wild Ones, well ahead of the Para-Dice Riders, which had thirty members, and far ahead of the once mighty Black Diamond Riders, which had dwindled to fifteen mainly older bikers. The Vagabonds remained the city's dominant club, with a hundred members, many of whom could be found hanging around in Yorkville.

In the late 1960s, Yorkville was close to bursting on weekends with middle-class kids wearing granny glasses, love beads, paisley shirts, sandals and bell bottoms. Many were "commuter hippies"—in from the suburbs to buy marijuana and LSD and feel groovy until classes or work started up again on Monday.

At The Purple Onion coffee house, they listened to Buffy Sainte-Marie, who wrote "Universal Soldier" in the basement there. At The Mynah Bird there were go-go dancers in a glass booth, a pet bird that once appeared on The Johnny Carson Show, X-rated film screenings, and Neil Young and Rick James playing in the house band. For a limited time, a cook did his basting and frying wearing nothing but a chef's hat. At the Riverboat, hippies fawned over Young, Joni Mitchell, Gordon Lightfoot, the Staple Singers and Phil Ochs. Sometimes Bob Dylan, Jack Nicholson and Eric Clapton were in the audience.

For the most part, the bikers and hippies happily co-existed, since the hippies wanted to buy drugs and the bikers wanted to sell them, as well as have sex with hippie girls. For Guindon, trips to Yorkville were a bit like visits to the zoo. It was interesting but not threatening, and he didn't feel the urge to partake in any poetry readings or play the bongo drums. "I wore my big boots, my leathers, my patch. They did their thing and we did our thing."

Flying the Satan's Choice flag regulary in Yorkville was a biker fittingly nicknamed "Hippy," who was originally from Kingston, Ontario, and whose real name was Frank Hobson. Later in life, he wrote down his thoughts on the road that led him to the Choice and Yorkville. Like many bikers, his childhood included a violent father: "My father was an alcoholic who was not afraid to slap me around. I remember some of those beatings when I was very young. Some of those were for very minor things and some were for things I had never done."

Hippy's father had a warm side too, and he sometimes took his son fishing. He was an army veteran and, like many a biker father, wanted his boy to grow up tough:

> One day when I was about nine years old, a classmate was bullying me outside of our home. I was scared and did not want to fight back. My father saw what was going on and shouted out from the window, "You either fight him or I will tan your ass." I punched the kid in the face and he started crying and ran home. From that time, I never backed down from a fight. That was both a blessing and a curse.

Like Guindon, Hippy found himself protecting his mother from his father at home:

> My father's abusive behaviour toward my mother and I came to an end when I was around seventeen years old. He would often come home

drunk and push my mother around. On one occasion, I went into the kitchen and grabbed a pair of scissors and stood up to him. He cursed at me, saying, "I'll kick your face in with my boots!" He had big, double-soled army boots and I was not looking forward to having them in my face. I was lucky; he backed down and went upstairs to sleep. From that day, my father left my mother alone. We never talked about it.

Hippy often wondered about the roots of his father's rage, and one day he felt he found the answer. "My grandfather was gassed in World War I and he was never the same when he returned home." The pain kept getting worse, and when Hippy's father was five years old, he watched his father cut his throat on the kitchen floor. "My father never told me about his father committing suicide and I never brought it up."

Hippy travelled to Windsor in 1968 in the hopes of landing a production line job at Chrysler. He succeeded and bought a customized BSA. It wasn't a Harley but it was the next best thing: chopped, awash in chrome and painted candy apple red and tangerine orange with "Hippy" written on the gas tank. "I did this so that it would be easier for me to pick up girls. The hippie girls back then were totally freaked out with bikers."

He became a striker for the Choice in Windsor, who had patched over from a local club called the Heathens in 1967. Its two dozen members were a tightly knit group. Strikers were gofers for full members, on call twenty-four hours a day to do menial jobs like scrub the clubhouse and fetch cigarettes and hamburgers. "Striking was likely the most difficult thing I have gone through. The problem with striking is that it demoralizes you. It breaks you down. There is really no 'you' anymore. It was like the basic training I took in the air force but worse."

The Windsor Satan's Choice was very close to the Outlaws in Detroit, which allowed the Detroit Outlaws free rein to treat Choice strikers any way they wanted. Once, Hippy was in Jackson Park in downtown Windsor with his girlfriend when he was spotted by a Detroit Outlaw. "He told me to get on his bike and said he was following a Queensman. The Queensmen in Windsor were rivals of the Choice in Windsor. He turned around and handed me a gun, telling me to shoot the Queensman when we caught up to him. It was my lucky day because we never did catch up to him."

Three of the Detroit Outlaws—Yankee Tom, Scotty and Walter—actually lived on the Canadian side of the Detroit River in 1968, and often hung out in the Choice clubhouse. That led to Hippy planning a visit across the river with some Outlaws, including the Detroit president, who went by the unlikely name of "Harmony." But he received a word of caution before setting out. Hippy had long hair and constantly wore black bell-bottomed pants. "I remember my brothers telling me not to go to Detroit with the name 'Hippy' and dressed in those bell bottoms. I went anyway."

During that first trip to meet Detroit Outlaws, Hippy spoke with a Florida Outlaw nicknamed "Crazy," who was said by the press to have crucified his old lady. Crazy told Hippy that the whole crucifixion thing was a hoax and that the story of her being nailed to an orange tree had been staged for shock value. Exactly how a crucifixion could be faked was not explained. But Crazy proved to be as crazy as the trip would get, and despite his apparel Hippy's trip to Detroit was a success. "We really hit it off with those guys, and before leaving, they offered me a full patch."

Hippy decided to stay on with the Satan's Choice, eventually quitting his job at Chrysler and moving into an old billiards hall that had been converted into a clubhouse in Windsor's Westminster district. His bed was a mattress atop one of the clubhouse's many pool tables.

He was now a full-time drug dealer, driving to Detroit to buy kilos of marijuana and thousands of hits of LSD for sale in Yorkville. Sometimes Hippy brought the drugs into Toronto himself. Other times, he had them flown in from Detroit. "If it was weed, I would clean it up and bag it. I would distribute it to my people on the street, who were all hippies. I gave them a good commission for selling my stuff and I protected them. I would go around the next day and collect my money and give them more product. They were happy and so was I."

Hippy had a girlfriend who used to turn tricks for him in Detroit. Tired of that scene, he took her to Toronto to try their luck, where she caught the eye of a Black Diamond Rider. He offered Hippy a bike and some cash for her. The bike was flush with chrome and metal flake, radiating drug dealer success. Hippy jumped at the offer. "I left Toronto with an amazing custom-built Panhead, five hundred cash and no girlfriend. Best deal I ever made."

CHAPTER 10

Darwinism

You've got to be on top to survive.

BERNIE GUINDON

The Choice weren't yet dominant, but they knew what it took to survive, a skill sometimes exercised in small cruelties. Motorcycle clubs kept testing each other in a two-wheeled version of Darwinism in which the weakest clubs became extinct. At a Thanksgiving weekend hill climb attended by six thousand people in the village of Heidelberg, nine miles west of Kitchener, four Toronto Choice members used a jackknife to trim off the patch of a member of the London Road Runners Motorcycle Club. The Road Runners soon lost respect and were no more. One less rival who couldn't stand up or get in their way.

Sometimes Guindon's club was tested by its rivals too, like when someone in May 1968 torched the rundown Scarborough barn on Finch Avenue East that the Choice had most recently adopted as a clubhouse. There was also what police called a "no-holds-barred rumble" between more than two dozen men from the Satan's Choice, Chainsmen, Henchmen and Fourth Reich in a downtown Kitchener garage.

As the Choice ascended the biker food chain, a potential rival in the Cross Breeds of Niagara Falls posed unique challenges. The Cross Breeds looked like a throwback to the early biker club days, wearing black and white shirts rather than leather jackets or vests. More importantly, their clubhouse was an easy stone's throw from the Niagara Falls police station, making it virtually impossible to attack them and not be seen by police.

Perhaps most significantly, some members of the Cross Breeds felt they had the local mob on their side. While the club had only one chapter with no more than fifteen members, they appeared to be well connected with the local underworld. Some members stood guard in the parking lot outside the high-stakes gambling game of Louis Iannuzzelli, whose family owned a hotel and the House of Frankenstein on Clifton Hill in Niagara Falls' touristy downtown. Iannuzzelli also had mob money on the street as a loan shark.

The Cross Breeds didn't want to expand or be absorbed into a larger club like the Satan's Choice, Outlaws or Red Devils. "They didn't want to cross over to anything," said Mark DeMarco, a long-time Niagara Falls resident who did custom painting on club members' bikes as well as stock cars. "They figured Niagara Falls, the border town, they were in with the Italians. They didn't want anybody to interfere with their Italian association."

That made the Satan's Choice attack on the Cross Breeds on Sunday, June 1, 1968, all the more audacious and satisfying for Guindon and his club. They trashed bikes and beat Breeds members, then jumped on their own bikes and raced away. "They never thought we'd be there," Guindon said. The Cross Breeds' black and white club shirts soon went the way of the dodo and the passenger pigeon. "I think we told them to either take [the club shirts] off or else," Guindon said.

Guindon didn't quote Charles Darwin exactly, but he alluded to his theory of evolution when explaining the necessity of such violence, even if it looked wild from the outside. "You've got to be on top to survive."

In Toronto, high-spirited Choice members managed to rile up both the Vagabonds and the Black Diamond Riders, and they expected their Choice brothers from other chapters to rally behind them. That was a problem. The Vagabonds had plenty of friends in the Choice outside Toronto, and a solid reputation in the biker world. Choice in Oshawa, Kingston, Ottawa, Kitchener and Brampton scoffed at the idea of a war with the Vagabonds. Meanwhile, the Choice from Hamilton, Montreal and Brantford were spoiling to jump into the tensions, just for the sake of a good fight, while St. Catharines, Niagara Falls, Peterborough and Richmond Hill didn't know what to do. Guindon enjoyed a rumble as much as anyone, but he had no beef with the Vagabonds and realized that an escalation of hostilities with them could irreparably split his own club.

The Vagabonds invited Guindon to a meeting on Hamilton Mountain. He didn't want a war, but he couldn't appear soft. More than a hundred Choice members accompanied him. They were still outnumbered. Guindon approached the Vagabonds' leader, Edjo, to tell him: "Let's you and I get it on and we'll solve the problem."

The Vagabond leader declined and, for the time being, the threat of war was averted.

A year after joining the Satan's Choice, the former Canadian Lancers and Wild Ones decided to quit and resume riding under their old colours. The split was friendly enough—it was against Guindon's nature to beg anyone to keep his company. Besides, life was getting more hardcore in the outlaw biker world and not everyone liked it.

Others in his circle were feeling pressure to trade on their associations with him. Mark DeMarco was building a thriving business, painting bikes and race cars, and he was always welcome at field days in Oshawa, Kitchener, Niagara and Kingston. One day, two police officers visited him at his shop in St. Catharines. He recalled the conversation going like this: "You paint motorcycles, right?"

"We paint everything. What are you here for?"

DeMarco remembered being quite hot-tempered and impatient in those days.

The officers showed a series of photos of bikers and their wives and girlfriends. DeMarco knew all of them.

"What did they say to you?"

"They said thank you after I painted their motorcycles."

At this point, DeMarco recalled, the officers became testy. One of them commented, "You're either part of the problem or part of the solution. If you're part of the problem, we'll dog you every day and visit you every day."

"That ain't going to work."

"That means you're not going to co-operate."

"I'm not going to do your work for you."

Over the next few weeks, DeMarco said, he was pulled over almost twenty times by officers. There was also a police visit to his house, which rattled his wife. He said officers pointed out that his uncle Hap had connections to mobster Johnny (Pops) Papalia of Hamilton. This came as no shock to DeMarco, who had a Johnny Pops association of his own. DeMarco used to bring old jukeboxes and slot machines over to Monarch Vending on Railway Street in downtown Hamilton, where Papalia spent much of his time. Papalia fixed the machines gratis, but asked DeMarco to keep an eye out for interesting clocks for him. The mobster had a fascination with timepieces. "Mark, if you ever get any old clocks . . . ," Papalia would say.

DeMarco didn't rat, and the police continued to dog him: "You're either part of the problem or part of the solution. To this point, we think you're not part of the solution."

"You've got the wrong guy. I'm not going to do your work for you."

Things were heating up around Guindon. Just being his friend was enough to put someone on the police radar.

Fire trucks were back at the Satan's Choice Scarborough clubhouse on Thursday, August 1, 1968. This time, firefighters couldn't contain a blaze that consumed the farmhouse on the same property where the barn had burned to the ground earlier in the year.

"I'm glad," a middle-aged woman near the scene told Don Dutton of the *Toronto Daily Star*. "They used to come here, hundreds of them—dirty bears and those stinking motorcycles—just about every weekend. They called them conventions and they came from Ottawa and Hamilton and all over with their girls, and the parties went on all night."

As she spoke, a couple of teenaged girls picked up broken glass from an abandoned hearse with a crudely labelled sign on it reading "Danger—Keep Out." They took the glass away as a souvenir.

The first weekend of August 1968 was a big one on the social calendar for the Choice. There was a field day in a pasture near Nestleton, north of Oshawa. *Toronto Daily Star* readers were mortified as they read of bikers "lightly whipping" a teenaged girl who had reportedly got out of hand. One biker told a reporter that she was punished "as an example" to others. The reporter also noted that the girl resumed socializing with the bikers that evening.

Shocking as the public found the bikers' treatment of the young woman, the biggest outrage was reserved for the chicken race. As grand marshal of the weekend, Guindon threw a live chicken into the air so that bikers could race to it and fight for it. Whoever emerged with the biggest chunk of chicken was declared the winner. "I bet the Humane Society doesn't like it, but it was a lot of fun," Guindon told a reporter.

As the party pushed on into the weekend, police had to block off two highways as fifteen chapters of the Choice and their friends showed up on some five hundred motorcycles. There were the obligatory stare downs between the bikers and police. Some of the OPP even drew batons.

Canada's national newspaper, *The Globe and Mail*, published some serious tut-tutting about the chicken incident and mocked a Satan's Choice member who wore war medals that were not his own:

> *Obviously, he was an admirer of gallantry in the field. Let no one accuse the Satan's Choice members of running away from danger, however. Why, only the other day, 60 of them stood their ground against a savage attack by a single chicken. In a breathtaking display of fearlessness, they rode it down and tore it apart before the ferocious fowl could harm anyone.*

The Humane Society offered a reward to any member of the public who could bring the bikers to justice for the chicken race, but no one obliged. "They had a thousand-dollar reward for anybody who'd put me away regarding the chicken," Guindon recalled. "A thousand dollars for anybody that would squeal on me. That was a lot of money in those days."

Guindon hadn't expected anything like the reaction the chicken story brought, and he remained absolutely unapologetic decades later. "I didn't give a shit," he said. "Farmers kill chickens any time they want. Thousands of chickens get killed every day to feed people. How are they killed? We don't know."

The unwelcome attention Guindon was drawing extended beyond his associates in the biker world.

Teresa Guindon was thrilled to become the proud owner of a bicycle with high handlebars and a banana seat. She was just six or seven years old and thrilled when her uncle Jack painted it a metallic purple. "It looked like there were diamonds in the paint," Teresa said.

Then one day, it was gone and little Teresa was distraught. Veronica still lived in Oshawa but had cut off any contact with Bernie. She took the problem to the local police, and officers took her daughter into a station room alone, ostensibly to identify bicycles. Once she was separated from her mother, the conversation quickly became about her father, not bicycles, Teresa later said. "They're scaring the crap out of me. Telling me how evil my dad is. That they're going to rub him out. They're trying to get information out of me. I'm a little girl. I don't know."

Teresa was in tears when she returned to her mother. Naturally, Veronica wanted to know why her little girl was crying. Teresa recalled an officer replying, "She's just upset we couldn't get her bike."

Just sharing Bernie Guindon's last name was now a liability.

CHAPTER 11

Shock Value

Whatever you do, don't eat a frog and a toad. Gross.

HOWARD (PIGPEN) BERRY

Within six months of joining the Satan's Choice, Pigpen Berry was a man transformed. Long gone was his clean-shaven, campus hootenanny look, although he still wore his dark-rimmed Buddy Holly glasses. He had grabbed onto the image of a boorish outlaw biker and ridden it to dizzying, stomach-turning, eye-watering extremes.

While some bikers sought out women at parties, Pigpen craved shock and disgust. In biker terminology, to truly unnerve someone by grossing them out was called "showing class" or giving a "high one," and no one did it better than Pigpen.

At one biker get-together, he put a live starling in a hot dog bun and bit through it, then offered a nibble to visiting members of the Outlaws. They passed. There are worse snacks, Pigpen later said. "I've ate mouse lots of times. A bird. Doo-doo. Heavy on the doo-doo. Whatever you do, don't eat a frog and a toad. Gross."

The Vagabonds routinely brought Pigpen food, marijuana and beer at parties, on the condition that he consume them at a distance. "They'd say, 'Have this and stay away from us,'" Pigpen recalled. Rather than be offended, he took this as a well-earned compliment.

Pigpen viewed his vomiting on new members' vests as a rite of passage. He managed to be creative as well as revolting. On one particularly memorable day, Pigpen saw a dead skunk in the middle of a road and pulled over to pick it up. He pinned it onto his Choice vest, wearing it like he once wore a boutonniere on his suit jacket back when he sang Buddy Holly songs. "I went from a corsage to a skunk in a couple of years," he said.

"I walked in the clubhouse," he later recalled. "Cleared it out. They sent in some strikers. I cleared them out. They hung me up off the tree upside down." When he was finally lowered to the ground, he dispatched a striker to retrieve the skunk carcass, and then Pigpen pinned it back on his vest as if nothing had happened. "What did it smell like wearing a skunk? Stunk. It makes your eyes tear. It's really hard on your eyes."

Pigpen appeared impervious to physical pain or pleas to be less disgusting. Revulsion was like oxygen for him, but it also seemed to unleash his rampant paranoia. The more disgustingly he behaved, the more paranoid he became. He yanked his own teeth to be sure there weren't hearing devices inserted in them. He smeared himself with his own feces while in a police holding cell to avoid being brought into court. Other bikers debated whether he was truly nuts. Pigpen thought his behaviour was more a product of discipline than craziness. "It was just a gross-out thing," Pigpen later said. "I just put my mind into space. It's mind over matter. If you don't mind, it don't matter."

The longer Guindon knew Pigpen, the more the gross-out artist amused and confused him. "A couple of times, I had to turn around because I had to get away from him. I remember it [vomit] coming up to my throat twice." Pigpen gave him plenty to think about, if he wanted to let his mind go in that direction. Here was a trained chef who would drink a glass full of chewing tobacco spit or publicly eat his own feces; a sometimes painfully shy man who could be a revolting exhibitionist or yank out a strange woman's earrings. "I always liked Howard. The first time, I couldn't believe it. A college guy coming around? Glasses. Straitlaced," Guindon said. He chalked up a lot of Berry's Pigpen act to competitiveness. "He always wanted to be number one. He couldn't be number one as the head of the club, but he was number one as entertainment. He blew a lot of minds, that fucking guy."

Guindon also considered Pigpen's repulsive behaviour to be a defence mechanism, like a porcupine's quills or a skunk's terrible smell. "He'd do things just to blow your lights and get a reputation so people would leave him alone . . . He wasn't crazy. He was just acting crazy."

For those who truly knew Pigpen, he was at his most horrifying not when he was munching on a bird or a mouse or feces, but when he was dressing up in a jacket and tie and combing his hair perfectly into place, just like in his Buddy Holly impersonator days. He looked like a husky choirmaster, not an outlaw biker. If you didn't know him, he would look quite normal. Those were the days he was planning something truly fearsome.

"Nobody would recognize me," Pigpen later said. "Then I went to the dark side of town."

CHAPTER 12

Big Apple

From a distance, I thought he was a chick.

BERNIE GUINDON on the young Bob Dylan

For all the politics of club life, Guindon was a biker at heart and enjoyed nothing more than the freedom of the open road. One day in the late 1960s, he decided to ride to the Maritimes on his Harley Panhead, which was a definite step up from the old Knuckleheads. "The Knuckleheads used to leak like a sonofabitch." Whatever the model, he was a Harley man, and Harley men need to be on the road, moving, listening to the motor rumble and watching the scenery blow by. "There's just something about them. The old ones at least. When you're growing up with them."

Hydraulics hadn't advanced to the point that riding a Harley was anywhere near comfortable. "You hit a bump, you can just feel your back going crunch." But that wasn't the point. There was something both primal and soothing about the sound of a Harley's short-stroke V-twin engine between your legs that made up for the jarring ride. All it took was a flip of the wrists and a working-class kid from Oshawa could feel like a snob, a modern-day knight atop the best, loudest bike money could buy. So distinctive was the Harley sound that the company would actually try decades later to patent it.

On Guindon's way to the East Coast, the romance of Harley and high-way didn't hold up. His Panhead sputtered to a stop in Montreal, where he was told it would take a couple days to get the parts to fix it. While passing time at the Montreal clubhouse, he heard that Rod MacLeod and a few Choice members were headed for New York City to check out the hippie scene in Greenwich Village.

"Can I come?" Guindon asked.

They obliged and Guindon hopped a ride on the back of the 1959 Decker of the club's road captain, a suburban Italian named Tony. Also along for the ride were the Kitchener chapter president and vice-president and MacLeod's friend Jono, the serial bank robber. Across the border, they tried camping on a rocky ridge by the side of the highway but were rousted by highway cops and told that no one camps by the side of the road in New York.

When Guindon saw the police, he wondered if his little crew had brought hashish with them. Chances were good that they had. It was fairly easy to hide it in a bike's handlebars or under the seat. Borders didn't really scare them then, in the more relaxed days before 9/11. "That's life," Guindon said. "You take your chance. You win or you lose." On that night, they won and kept riding.

When they got to New York City, MacLeod took the lead, even though Tony was officially road captain. "It's my territory," MacLeod explained. "They're all black here."

That sounded good to Guindon. "I got to see parts of New York that I didn't see before," he reflected.

At 42nd and Broadway, in the heart of Manhattan, the throttle stuck on Tony's bike and it crashed onto a crowded sidewalk. Tent poles on the bike smashed a shop window, and soon police were on the scene. Tony escaped with a warning and an order to immediately pay for the window.

After covering the cost of the damage, the bikers slipped from poor to broke and headed off to a blood bank to raise money for food and gas. Guindon was proud that his Rh-negative blood was relatively rare and fetched seven dollars—two dollars more than the blood of each of the others. That meant he was able to buy a hot dog for fifty cents and gas up the tank.

That night, they pitched their tents in Central Park but kept getting moved on by the police. Through the darkness, they could see a woman who recognized MacLeod and Jono from a visit a few months earlier. She was hard to miss since she was stoned, topless and running hard toward them. Her Hells Angel boyfriend was chasing her down, and he caught her before there could be any reunion with the Canadian bikers.

After pitching their tents, Guindon and his friends went to Greenwich Village to see an outdoor concert. Guindon found the curly-haired singer alluring in an unconventional way. He considered making an approach but was uncharacteristically shy. Later, he discovered that this was just as well. The guitar-playing folk singer was actually a man and a famous one at that: Bob Dylan. "He sounded like a female in those days. I wasn't into the folk art in those days. I was into the country and the rock. From a distance, I thought he was a chick." Guindon was more partial to the music of Johnny Cash, Buddy Holly and Merle Haggard.

That wasn't the only time Guindon experienced a gender-related surprise. Hippy recalled a time in Toronto when they were in a second-floor nightclub at Avenue and Webster Avenues, across from Webster's diner: "There were about ten of us there getting drunk and having a great time. Bernie had his eye on one gal there that looked super sexy. We all kept bugging him to go and have a dance with her . . . Bernie started dancing with her. He was really into her and they were dancing up close in a slow dance, kind of grinding away if you know what I mean."

Guindon's buddies realized his dance partner was a man, although Hippy considered him the "best damn good-looking man I ever saw!" Guindon, however, didn't notice.

"We were laughing hysterically, but nobody was man enough to tell Bernie. Bernie was a tough guy and could knock you out with one punch. It took a long time for us to tell him. I don't think I have ever laughed like that in my life. In the end, Bernie was okay with it."

CHAPTER 13

Ring Wars

He knew what he had to do to be a good fighter. He had the stuff.

GEORGE CHUVALO on Bernie Guindon

G uindon was so caught up in club business that he wasn't in good enough shape to make the Canadian boxing team for the 1968 Summer Olympics in Mexico City. He did fight in qualifying matches but wasn't at his best. "You'd get so involved. I never used to train. I'd be doing club stuff and then I'd go out and box. It shows in your boxing."

His friend Walter Henry made the Canadian Olympic team again as a flyweight, after representing Canada in the 1964 Olympic Games in Tokyo. He thought Guindon could have made the Mexico City team, despite his substandard conditioning, but some judges of his bouts had other ideas. "There were some very bad decisions that went against him," Henry said.

It didn't help that Guindon drew large, vocal crowds of Satan's Choice to his matches, which rankled officials worried about the sport's image. "I would think that was working against him," Henry said. "They knew who he was and they probably leaned the other way not to let him go to the Olympics."

Still, there were offers for Guindon to turn pro, but he worried that it could be used against him in court after one of his many street brawls.

He suspected that a simple assault could become assault with a weapon if an ambitious Crown attorney argued that the fists of a professional fighter should be considered weapons. He also didn't trust the boxing business in general. There were fixed fights, managers who didn't care about their athletes, and not much money for most fighters. "There are a lot of crooks who are managers. Fucking crooks take all of your money."

"He could have done well as a pro," Canadian heavyweight champion George Chuvalo said. "He was ready to turn pro. He could take a punch. He could deliver a punch. You weren't going to go in there quickly and knock him out, that's for sure. He knew what he had to do to be a good fighter. He had the stuff."

Henry said there was always a special buzz whenever Guindon appeared on a fight card. "Everyone would go just to see him because he was in Satan's Choice."

"He was intimidating," Henry recalled. "Stick his chin out. Go, 'Come on, hit me again.' One of those types of people. A lot of them were afraid of him . . . He was just a tough fighter. A good boxer but mostly looked to fight. Looked to get in and slug it out."

Coming from Belfast, Henry didn't know a thing about the Satan's Choice, beyond the club's obviously tough reputation and cryptic things Guindon would tell him. "People would say, 'You're friends with Bernie?' I'd say, 'All I see about Bernie is good stuff. I've never seen him do any bad.'

"All I ever knew about Bernie was that he was such a nice person. A gentleman . . . We were very close friends. We got along very well. He never spoke about it."

Henry was impressed that Guindon helped out other boxers with money when he could. He also sometimes covered for them, taking the blame for things he didn't actually do. "He'd take the rap for a lot of things that he wasn't the instigator of," Henry said. "He was loyal to a fault. He just feels that's the way the leader should be."

On June 3, 1968, Guindon was doing well enough in the ring to be one of the local sports celebrities honoured at the Oshawa Sports Celebrity Dinner at the Oshawa Civic Auditorium, despite his growing notoriety as an outlaw biker. Guests of honour that night included

Montreal Canadiens' captain Jean Béliveau, former world boxing champion Rocky Marciano and Oshawa mayor Ernie Marks. Guindon was suitably impressed by Marciano but didn't approach him. "He was busy. I just don't like bugging guys. You see the man. You know who he is. You respect him for what he has done. What else can you do? He wasn't going to be able to help you."

Sometimes Guindon wondered if Sister Dirty Gertie at Holy Cross Catholic Elementary knew who he had become. He certainly hoped she did. He still considered her a bully. "She lived long enough to know who the hell I was. I was so fucking happy when she died."

Guindon still made training trips to Buffalo. Monsignor Kelliher didn't talk much about Bernie's biker club with the ungodly name. "I'd go and see him on a one-on-one basis. Me being a Satan's Choice, he knew that. I just said it was a motorcycle club."

Once when Guindon was fighting in Buffalo, a vocal contingent of Satan's Choice members showed up, and one filled in as his corner man. Guindon was handily winning the three-round bout when the clubmate in his corner ran out of water just after round two. He grabbed another member's Coke, drained it and then dropped the ice cubes into Guindon's trunks, just in time for the third round to begin. Guindon managed to hang on to win the fight, although he was shivering visibly.

No one questioned his durability in the ring. He possessed the rare ability to stay on his feet even when temporarily detached from his senses. "The only time I ever got knocked out was at the beginning of the third round of one fight," Guindon said. "I don't remember anything else. My corner man was cutting off my hand bandages at the end of the fight. I said, 'Grant, who won the fight?' He goes, 'You did.' I said, 'I don't remember anything after the third round.' He said, 'Oh, you fought better in the last few rounds.'"

CHAPTER 14

Eye on Montreal

He'd be in the far corner. Staying away from everybody. Make sure his back was to the wall.

BERNIE GUINDON on Montreal hitman Yves (Apache) Trudeau

G uindon wasn't much concerned about his club's local rivals as the 1970s approached. His focus was on Montreal. The Satan's Choice had more than outgrown its Toronto peers, it had grown into the second-largest outlaw biker club in the world—behind only the Hells Angels. Now Guindon wanted to expand coast to coast. To do so, he needed to build on his toehold in Montreal, which at that time was Canada's largest city.

Rod MacLeod's Montreal chapter was tough but threadbare. They didn't have the money for a clubhouse and often hung out at Joe's Snack Bar in the Saint-Henri district. They met every Tuesday night, paying weekly membership dues of two bucks. The dues buttressed an emergency fund, from which members could borrow for repairs to their bikes or for bail.

When in Montreal, Guindon stayed with MacLeod and noted that he didn't live lavishly by any stretch, but that he also didn't seem to need work. "He had a bunch of guys working for him. He had something going. I don't remember him having a job." It was all quite modest stuff, especially since MacLeod's bunch was playing in a very rough league.

Montreal's geography ordained it would be a hot spot for Canadian organized crime. The long St. Lawrence River shoreline and access to the Atlantic Ocean made it a natural for drug smuggling. It was also less than four hundred miles by highway to New York City, the continent's richest drug market. The violence in Montreal intensified as drug use inside and outside the city's many clubs increased.

MacLeod gave Guindon a guided tour of various rival clubhouses in Montreal. Guindon still wasn't comfortable with guns, which made him stand out in Montreal's underworld like a vegetarian at a pig roast, even within his own club. "There were a few guys in the Montreal chapter you had to be careful with. They were notorious. You knew they would shoot you." The more Guindon saw of Montreal, the more he realized how competitive its streets were. "They did a lot of killing there in Montreal. Montreal is a rough, tough town."

He found one slender, smallish Montreal biker particularly chilling. Even his fellow members in the Popeyes were creeped out by Yves (Apache) Trudeau's habit of just staring into space as they partied. Perhaps he had horrific things on his mind, or maybe his head was as empty as his stare—or his soul. Nicknamed "The Mad Bomber" and "The Mad Bumper," Trudeau once worked for Canadian Industries Limited, which manufactured dynamite and detonator caps. That early training proved useful in his current job: making people disappear.

When Guindon met him, Trudeau was on his way to becoming one of the most prolific killers in Canadian history, responsible for an estimated forty-three murders. "He'd be in the far corner. Staying away from everybody. Make sure his back was to the wall. He only paid attention to his own close friends. He tried to stay away from everybody." Trudeau's Popeyes were a particularly dangerous club, despite their cartoonish name. "When they had wars, they really had wars," Guindon said. "No hesitation to bring out the shotguns and the machine guns."

Among the frequent visitors to the Choice's Montreal chapter was Pigpen Berry, who was affectionately known in some rough Montreal circles as "Piggy." Pigpen also did enforcement work for the West End

Gang, or Irish mob. This involved spending time in Pointe-Saint-Charles, a community along the St. Lawrence River southwest of the downtown, built by a broad range of European immigrants in the mid-nineteenth century, when it became one of Canada's first industrial slums.

The Pointe had been home to an early incarnation of the West End Gang since the early 1900s. By the 1960s, they worked mostly in truck hijackings, home invasions, kidnapping, protection rackets, drug trafficking, extortion and armed robbery. They moved heavily into hashish and cocaine importation in the 1970s, developing links to the Mafia, Hells Angels and Colombian cartels.

"I had the Irish mafia behind me," Pigpen recalled.

The Irish mob wanted Pigpen to help in their war against the Dubois, a clan of nine brothers with interests in prostitution, loan sharking, extortion and dealing cocaine and a host of other narcotics. That said, members of the Irish mob weren't always amused by Pigpen's eccentric nature: "On one hand, they wanted to kill me. On the other, they wanted to keep me on," Pigpen later said. Some of Pigpen's Quebec time was spent in the Bordeaux jail, where he was sent to the hole and taunted: "Hey English, when you come out in the yard, we'll fuck you in the ass."

By this time, Pigpen had befriended Armand (In the Trunk) Sanguigni of the Toronto Choice chapter. Sanguigni was a smallish man with the empty eyes of a heroin user and a reputation as someone who handled murder contracts for the Montreal mob. "He was a good guy," Pigpen later said of Sanguigni. "I got along with him good . . . I don't agree with the homicide part."

Guindon also found Sanguigni to be okay, although he added that he didn't know him or his side business well. Even if he had, the club didn't have rules against killing for money or to eliminate witnesses. "I didn't have much to do with those guys," Guindon said. "I was from Oshawa. They were trying to make a living as well."

It was hard to stay on the sidelines in Montreal, and Guindon's Choice was drawn into the Devil's Disciples' conflict with the Dubois. Pigpen was particularly in demand, and Cecil Kirby, the former biker and mob enforcer, explained why: "If there was trouble somewhere, they'd send Howard Berry out to take care of it. He was the Choice hitman and everybody knew it." Pigpen said that wasn't exactly correct; he shot people but never killed anyone.

Kirby said he was in Montreal when Pigpen opened fire on the Popeyes' clubhouse with a sawed-off .303 with a ten-round clip. "It was like a cannon going off," Kirby said.

Closer to home, the Satan's Choice clashed with the Chosen Few, Saddletramps, Chairmen, Fourth Reich, Devil's Law, Coffin Wheelers, Plague, Wild Breed, Los Santos, Outlawed Morticians and, most notably, the Henchmen Motorcycle Clubs. The Henchmen even outnumbered the Choice in the Kitchener-Waterloo area, but the Choice had more members throughout the province. Any rival could pose a threat, but none of the smaller clubs could take Guindon's down.

The violence was escalating, though, and it took very little to incite it. On one occasion, a Choice member attended a party with the Cross Breeds in Niagara Falls. He and a member of the Para-Dice Riders were thrown out for bad behaviour. They returned with a bomb and blew up part of the house. That understandably angered everyone still inside, including members of the Wild Ones and Vagabonds. A wave of violent retribution hit the Choice, which hit back even harder, blowing up other clubhouses. A Wild One was shot in front of his house in Hamilton. Shooting and bombing continued, but somehow no one was killed. Even the tiny Fourth Reich and Chainmen joined in against the Choice.

But for all this heat in Ontario, nowhere was hotter than Montreal. The city's underworld was expanding as demand for drugs increased. The bigger business got, the closer the turf was to exploding. "You used to see Montreal guys disappear just like that," Guindon said. "You wonder, 'When is my trip up?'"

Ultimately, it wasn't another motorcycle club that struck the hardest blow against Guindon and his Satan's Choice.

CHAPTER 15

Skin Beef

I knew that a skin beef made a guy undesirable in the general population.

BERNIE GUINDON talks of prison

Guindon, not to be slowed down by the fact that he was a young father with three daughters from two marriages, hooked up routinely with random women. He wasn't sure why some of the women were attracted to him, and he didn't waste much time trying to figure it out. Certainly, many of them seemed drawn to anyone wearing a biker patch, and it didn't hurt that Guindon ran the club. "Maybe they like the wild side. He's not straight up and down like her father was. Who knows?" Certainly, Guindon didn't have any illusions that he was a great lover, but he was happy to oblige them. "They called me needle dick, the big flea fucker. Hung like a stud field mouse."

Guindon was at the Choice's Ottawa clubhouse in October 1968 when he met a fifteen-year-old girl who was hanging around with members. That day, she went to the house of a man who hung around the Choice. At one point Guindon joined them. There was group sex and then things got particularly ugly when the man's wife showed up unexpectedly and phoned the police. "The concocted story was that they saved her from being raped and beaten at the Satan's Choice clubhouse," Guindon said.

Using the call and accusation of rape against a minor as a reason, police raided the Ottawa clubhouse.

Transcripts of the case don't exist and accounts are widely divergent. There was violence as well as group sex, although Guindon was not himself accused of hitting anyone.

As the indecent assault trial began, the girl described being confined for three days and forced to have sex with five men. Guindon's mother wanted to attend the trial but he didn't want her to see her boy in court facing such sordid charges. He assured her he wasn't guilty, but he also knew that that didn't really matter. "You know you're getting fucked, no matter how you look at it . . . You look at the jury. You can't blame them for judging you the way they judge you. I had a good idea we were going to get it."

In May 1969, the bottom fell out of Guindon's world. He was twenty-five and in his athletic prime when he was sentenced to five years in prison—what criminals call a "solid nickel." Four other club members were also sent to prison, while a woman who associated with the club was sentenced to two years in reformatory for assault after she admitted she kicked the girl with steel-tipped cowboy boots. Their one small relief came when the judge denied a Crown submission that Guindon's punishment should also include lashing.

Criminals locked up for "skin beefs" are considered the dregs of prison society and fair game for anyone with a shank, a nasty attitude and an urge to make a name for himself. In the Ottawa jail, Guindon got into a fight with a prisoner whom he considered mouthy, and cut him with his fists for eleven stitches. But he knew far worse lay ahead when he got to Kingston Penitentiary, the place his father had once told him he was going to end up.

The Choice at that point had chapters in Hamilton, Oshawa, Guelph, St. Catharines, Preston, Peterborough, Ottawa, Kingston, Windsor, Montreal and Vancouver and about three hundred members. All of that muscle on the streets would do Guindon no good as he headed alone behind the infamous prison's thick limestone walls.

"When they closed those gates, it was just *boom*," Guindon recalled. "Big steel gates closing. You just have shivers going down your spine.

You sure knew you're in jail when those fucking gates closed." Long-time inmate Paul Gravelle has been locked inside plenty of prisons and jails and said there was an especially harsh feeling when he heard himself locked inside Kingston. "It was like going into a dungeon," Gravelle said. "It was something else. You knew your place."

New prisoners at the Kingston Penitentiary were marched through a shower, like a car wash for humans. Staff then covered the newcomers with a disinfectant powder and hosed them down again.

Guindon arrived at Kingston at a time when conversations among inmates were forbidden. So were radios and televisions in their cells. Guindon found the penitentiary oddly silent. "We weren't supposed to talk to anybody," he said. "We used to send messages to the guys who were doing the cleaning." Prisoners would whisper messages to the cleaners to pass on to other prisoners, also in whispers. There was great power in controlling the flow of information in the prison ranges. "I used to try to get out on the cleaning job quite a bit," Guindon said.

None of the other Satan's Choice members who were convicted with Guindon went to Kingston. Their club president was isolated and vulnerable. "It's scary . . . A lot of them don't like bikers. You have problems, you don't know who the hell is going to back you up."

One of the first prisoners Guindon befriended cautioned him that he should tell fellow prisoners he was locked up for armed robbery rather than indecent assault. Armed robbery is a socially acceptable, suitably tough crime among inmates. Guindon argued that he was in custody on a bogus beef and he shouldn't have to hide anything or lie. The prisoner was just trying to be helpful and told him that there were a lot of prisoners who would rather "off a skinner" than have to look at him every day.

"You just give them the number of my house [prison cell], okay?" Guindon answered back.

He had the chilling feeling that he was being set up for attack, but he refused to go into the special protective unit. That area was known as the "skinner range," and Guindon would rather risk death on the main range than set foot there. That would look like an admission of guilt. "I knew that a skin beef made a guy undesirable in the general population."

There was no mercy in the pen for undesirables. "When I got in there, they gave me the room of the guy who got thrown off the tier. And that was the third floor at Kingston. He was right beside me when he got thrown off." Guindon kept his mouth shut about seeing the forced three-storey death dive and moved into the victim's six-by-ten-foot cell. "I was minding my own business. You don't ask questions. You save a lot of goddamn problems."

The railing outside his cell was a constant reminder of how quickly his life could end. Guindon later saw an inmate hanging on to that railing for dear life to prevent a fatal plunge onto the concrete below. "I was in the cell. I couldn't get out of the cell." It was after lockdown and Guindon could only watch as guards pulled the inmate to safety.

Fellow inmate Paul Gravelle said he once saw an inmate preparing to throw himself to his death when a guard rushed onto the scene. The incident cleared up any uncertainty about the value of an inmate's life. The guard's first instinct wasn't to halt the suicide. Instead, he tossed down a blanket so that the mess wouldn't be too difficult to clean. "The guy jumped on the blanket: 'Boom!'" Gravelle said.

Not long into his stay, Guindon also saw a prisoner stabbed repeatedly. He recognized the victim as the same guy who had mouthed off to him in the Ottawa jail cell. This time, the inmate was killed. Guindon was now in a world where sticking someone in the thigh or shoulder with a homemade knife—or shank or shiv—was a routine way of telling him to smarten up. In his new home, white wooden wheelbarrows with red crosses painted on them were at the ready for collecting the bodies of victims of stabbings and forced tumbles from the third floor.

Shanks were plentiful but seldom seen. To make one, yard workers and cleaners would gather little pieces of metal and quietly bring them inside. "You'd have to depend on a lot of guys," Guindon said. The deadliest shanks were fashioned from flattened pieces of metal that were easy to conceal. "You can hide that in your mattress with no problem," he said. They would be rolled tight, like straws, and inserted into a piece of wood, which acted as a handle. The shank would be driven hard into the heart of an enemy. "The handle comes off, so you've got no prints. You walk away with the handle, leave the blade there."

Shanks didn't have to be elaborate. "It wouldn't take much. Guys used to make shivs in the machine shops. Welding shops. Machine shop. It would have to be long enough to go in the heart."

Guards looked down constantly from towers when prisoners were outside. It was hard for them to see exactly what was happening when prisoners stood in close quarters in a line, waiting to be marched back to their cells. "A lot of guys get shanked going to your room," Guindon said. "In the yard, you'd have to line up. Sometimes that's where a guy gets stabbed. Smack! That's all you hear."

Inmate Richard Mallory said the shanks also often came out at Friday movie night. "When the show was over and you walked out, most of the time, there was one or two people who weren't moving. You'd hear uh, uh [a moaning sound]. You have to know what was going on. You didn't know nothing. It could happen right in front of you."

Gravelle also saw zip guns, which resemble ballpoint pens. "You can build them in the machine shop," he said. "All you need is the bullets . . . Sometimes it's kill or be killed." Guindon preferred to stay away from shanks and zip guns. "I used my hands. Much faster."

He soon learned the hard and fast rules to survive Kingston. "Keep your mouth shut," Guindon said. "You don't snitch and you don't steal off of inmates. For me, that's when you get a beating. That's when you get stabbed. If somebody finds out you're a rat, that's when you get a blade or a beating or thrown off the tier. And you mind your own goddamn business." That includes not asking a prisoner why he is serving time. If he wants to tell you, he'll tell you. "Mind your business and do your own time." Put another way, don't meddle. "Do your own time and try not to get involved in the politics. A lot of guys got involved with somebody. A guy's got a problem and they get you to solve their problem, then where are you? You're in shit. All of a sudden, you've got four or five guys on your case," Guindon said.

Words travel fast in a prison, and sometimes those words hang in the air like a toxic cloud until they are addressed. One inmate said he didn't like bikers and bragged that he was going to kill Guindon. When he heard about it, Guindon put a beating on him and the comments stopped.

Paul Henry was a young prison psychologist when Guindon arrived in Kingston, and he was quickly impressed with the boxer and how well he adapted to the prison culture. "He was a man's man," Henry said. "There's nothing I didn't like about him." He said the other prisoners didn't see Guindon as a skinner, once they got to know him. "He never needed a psychologist. He was too solid. Rock solid."

Henry noticed that Guindon quickly became friends with George Bradley, a smallish, intense man who looked like he had walked off the set of a 1940s George Raft gangster movie. Other prisoners treated Bradley like he was a somebody, in part because he was considered one of the youngest fugitives ever to be on the FBI's Ten Most Wanted list. "George was a wheel," Henry said.

"George was a smart guy," Guindon recalled. "He wasn't very big. I think he was trying to be one of those big bad bandits . . . He was serious. I don't think he was a tough guy. His mind was always rolling. He was a very likeable person. George was all right . . . He was smart. He was always wheeling and dealing in his mind. Always used to come up with different things for me. I didn't want nothing to do with it . . . Otherwise, I'd be doing life. Either that or dead."

In July 1969, Bradley was just twenty-one when he was sentenced to nineteen years for a near-fatal shooting during a bank holdup in Toronto. He was also convicted of two other armed robberies and a break-in and was said to have spent much of his total take, estimated at fifty thousand dollars. But for all of his criminally industrious ways, Bradley still exaggerated his accomplishments.

Bradley's appearance on the FBI's most-wanted list was a notable achievement in Guindon's prison circles, akin to the Dean's Honour List in straight society. In truth, the bank-robbing George Bradley on the FBI's most-wanted list wasn't the George Bradley that Guindon knew. George Bradley had started robbing banks in the 1950s, when the Kingston Penitentiary George Bradley was still in diapers.

It was an easy enough lie to tell, though, and Bradley lapped up the enhanced status. Hanging around with Guindon also helped his image. "Nobody ever had any issue with Bernie," Henry said. "He was A1 in the hierarchy.

"He just had leadership oozing out of him—and good leadership, not bad ideas," Henry continued. "He used his time properly . . . He was a strongly positive influence on many, many experienced people. He wanted fairness." Henry appreciated Guindon's straightforward nature. "When you work with these guys, you can tell who's straight and who's not."

Despite all of the bravado and respect, Guindon's mind found plenty of depressing things to think about. There was the future of his club without him to guide it, and the fact that he had already burned through two marriages. There was the ever present threat of the lash from guards or a shiv from inmates. His body bloated up and he had to begin taking medication to still his nerves.

Further, he felt abandoned. Within weeks of Guindon going to prison, his second wife, Barbara Ann, left for the West Coast with their two daughters and a former clubmate called Two-Stroke. Guindon suspected Two-Stroke got out of the province fast to avoid retribution from Guindon's friends. If he did harbour any bad feelings, they didn't linger. "He probably did me a favour."

Guindon hadn't exactly been faithful himself. While behind bars, he got the news that his daughter Debbie was born on November 28, 1969, to Marlene Anne Donovan, a friend since his early teens. Marlene had grown up near his old boxing club. Her mother was an Oshawa bootlegger.

Prisoners often received sexually explicit letters from women who wanted their very own captive bad boy. Typically, they would describe how many tattoos and children they had, as well as their dreams of finding a strong, protective man. "I think we all got a lot of crazy fucking letters," Guindon said. But one such letter arrived that was several cuts above the usual missive.

The woman wrote to introduce herself and then followed with more letters. She clearly had options but her attraction for Guindon was undeniable. Soon Jack was driving her to Kingston for visits, which were precious, since his brother was allowed visitors only once a month, for an hour. "I used to take all of his friends down there," Jack said. "If it wasn't for me, there wouldn't have been any visitors."

Prisoners have been known to hurt themselves, just to get a change of scenery through a few nights in the infirmary. They've also switched religions so they can add more fish or fruit to their diets. And they've gotten married just for the prospect of a wedding night. Guindon insisted he cared for this woman enough to make her his third wife. At the ceremony, inside the limestone prison walls, there was only the bride, groom, best man and minister present. At the end of the ceremony, she was allowed to stay overnight. Their visits continued, and she soon gave birth to twins. One died in infancy on Christmas Eve, the other on Christmas Day.

A year after their wedding, the marriage was annulled, at her request. That gave Guindon a divorce, an annulment and three new children while behind bars on his indecent assault stint. The last he heard of his third ex-wife, she had achieved a university degree of some sort. Guindon seldom spoke of her. In the 1970s, a woman's reputation could be tarred forever by an association with a convicted felon and biker like Guindon, and he exercised the utmost of discretion, keeping a respectful silence about her. "I was fond of her," he said.

Eventually, Guindon was transferred to nearby Joyceville, a minimum and medium security institution. There, he spent time with Gravelle, who said Guindon's reputation as a boxer meant more to fellow inmates than the fact he ran a biker gang. "A lot of people don't like [biker] club guys," Gravelle said. They also didn't consider him a real sex offender. He didn't fit the mould, to their minds. "He was surrounded by a whole bunch of people. He had a very good reputation."

Gravelle was an authority of sorts about prison life. He was in just his early twenties when he met Guindon, but he already had a considerable criminal resumé. He was glib about his frequent trips into custody, saying they reminded him of homecomings. "It's just like going to a summer camp, when you meet all of your old buddies."

When he met Guindon in Joyceville, Gravelle was doing time for bank robbery and running a seven-step program for rehabilitation. It was aimed at hardened criminals. Sex offenders and stool pigeons need not apply. In the program, inmates were supposed to tell the truth about themselves, and Gravelle would generally talk tough and advise them to pursue an honest trade. This often led to what Lorne Campbell of the

Choice called "snotting and bawling." Campbell did plenty of time of his own, and he witnessed several prisoners cry until they could cry no more and then vow to do far better with their lives in the future.

For those inmates with no remorse or desire to change, Gravelle provided other options. They were the prisoners he really wanted. He counselled them to become better criminals. That included helping a Hamilton man who killed a gay man learn to become a safecracker. "He said, 'I wish I was in here for bank robbery like you,'" Gravelle said. "I taught him the trade."

Certainly, the seven-step program had no cleansing effect on Gravelle himself. "It never straightened me out," he said. "I'm a criminal at heart. I think it's not as boring as the other way around. There's never a dull moment."

Guindon, on the other hand, struck Gravelle more as a criminal of consequence than intent. He had a reputation as basically an honest person who did the best he could for his friends, even when he knew it might come back to bite him. "He's always trying to help people, and those are the guys that go to jail," Gravelle said. "He'd give you the shirt off of his back. He wasn't a heavy-duty criminal. They [the police] tried to just get him because he was the leader of the gang. He's a trophy fish."

Inside Joyceville, Guindon worked in the kitchen and occasionally snuck out to go fishing for trout. He adopted a baby raccoon as a pet and kept him in a yard shack. His furry new friend would sometimes sit on his shoulder and nibble on his ear. "We'd be playing around and he'd bite me and I'd bite him back on his paw. He'd squeal and he'd quit biting me." After a few months, he heard some guards had plans to kill the pet, and so he gave him away to a friendly guard, who said he'd turn him over to a family.

Of all the marriages and girlfriends that Guindon had burned through, one of the first women in his life never disappeared for long, even if she had long been just a friend. Suzanne Blais was still married, but she and Guindon often thought of each other fondly. Guindon wrote her from Joyceville:

Dear Suznn:

Hi Beautiful so how's life treating you of late? Sure hope this letter finds yourself & family in the very best of health & in fine spirits. Finally got some good news this afternoon & like I promise you're the first one I let know. Yes, the Parole Board finally sent me the other votes I needed. It looks like I'll be out on my pass (3 days) the second week in Sept if all goes well. My C.D. [case director] also asked me if I wanted to see my father for Xmas & he'd give me an extra day or two for travelling as long as I pay for the whole trip. He's also going to put me in for Bath Farm annex & hopefully they'll get me out by the end of Sept. Also Teresa finally wrote yesterday & she even let my youngest sign the card. I've asked her to attend Family Day on Sept 6 . . . she said "let bygones be bygones." Real busy of late & getting way behind. Maybe this will put me in a much better mood. Give my very best to your mom & as always I'm thinking of you. Sorry if I don't answer all your notes.

Love & Respect Bernie No #1 Frog
XXXXXOOOOOSWAELKAHF.

"SWAELKAHF" stands for "Sealed with an Everlasting Kiss and Hug Forever."

Guindon's mind also often drifted to memories of the open road. When he was in the yard, he could hear motorcycles passing by, gearing up and down, and he would try to determine which ones were Japanese or Triumphs or Harleys. "You'd hear the bikes go by when you were in the yard, or the guards would ride them in."

There was some peace in knowing that someday his time would be served, and he would be free and back on his Harley too.

CHAPTER 16

Proud Riders

You can beat my brains in. I don't care. But don't touch my bike.

DOUG (CHICKLET) MACDONALD of Satan's Choice

ig Jack Olliffe was fresh out of custody and serving as interim president of the Choice in Guindon's absence when Canadian moviemakers approached the club with a plan. Producer George Fras and his team wanted to make a truly authentic biker movie using Oshawa as the backdrop. Their low-budget movie *The Proud Rider* featured twenty-five-year-old former model Arthur Hindle, but they wanted to use members of the Oshawa and Toronto chapters of the Satan's Choice as extras and saturate the film with their grubby realism. The plan was to use the Satan's Choice name, and the tag line for their oeuvre was "Tough? You bet your . . ."

The *Toronto Daily Star* reported on Saturday, October 3, 1970, that on the first day of shooting, one of the Choice was arrested on an outstanding, unspecified warrant. Journalist Marci McDonald also described how a biker named Crow sported a glass eye diaper-pinned to the front of his jacket while another biker named Lovely Larry dangled an Iron Cross from his ear.

Co-director Walter Baczynsky explained to the reporter another advantage of employing real-life bikers. "Just think how we save on wardrobe and makeup." It sounded good in theory, but the robust eating habits of Big Jack and his biker brothers caused the film's budget to balloon by two thousand dollars. Big Jack alone could hoover down six burgers and still find room for a half-dozen doughnuts and a pint of milk. "Half the guys ain't workin'," Big Jack explained. "They don't get to eat too regularly."

Club members threatened to walk out after they were told they couldn't have real booze for a party scene, until Big Jack sorted them out. Apparently, he hadn't learned anything from his time behind bars for beating a man to death. "When they get outta line," he said, "sometimes I gotta take a swing at them with my helmet."

The movie was also the screen debut of Pigpen Berry, who was now thirty and sporting a beatnik-style goatee. He still had his Buddy Holly glasses, faraway look and sometimes crazy-shy manner. Big Jack couldn't keep Pigpen fully under control, but no one really could. Trouble started on set when Pigpen's clubmates dropped their pants to shock a script girl. True to character, Pigpen needed to top that, so he grabbed a nearby garter snake and bit off its head, then casually put the leftovers in his pocket for a later snack.

Scriptwriter and assistant director Chester Stocki described his mood to journalist Paul King of *The Canadian Magazine* as, "Scared, scared, scared. Just look at them." One member explained the club's leadership in terms that justified Stocki's mood. "When Bernie went down, Bear was the obvious choice," he said. "He's big enough to back up what he says."

Big Jack described himself to the journalist as a thirty-two-year-old father of sons aged two and nine. He had worked as a truck driver, welder and apprentice mechanic since dropping out of school in Grade 7, when he was fifteen years old. Big Jack sounded a little self-effacing and vulnerable as he explained that he grew his bushy red beard in a conscious attempt to cultivate an image. "I grew it to hide my chins and my baby face," he told King. "I could get a job tomorrow if I cleaned up a bit and shaved. But I wouldn't be happy." The article made no mention of Big Jack beating Kitchener biker Arnold Bilitz to death.

"Don't call us a gang," Big Jack continued. "That's a group with no organization. We're a club, with a full set of officers. We answer only to ourselves. The Canadian Nazi Party offered us a ten-acre farm in 1967 if we'd agree to protect their political rallies. We told them to shove it. Now I'm not calling us goody-goodies, far from it. We only want to be left alone. But the cops won't leave us alone. If we went around raping, and terrorizing towns, we'd deserve it. But we don't. The first night the boys came here for the picture, they all stayed at my house. And just after midnight, we got raided by sixty cops, both local and provincial. A kitchen window was broken, a girl got cut over her eyes, and six of our bikes were confiscated. We hadn't done a damn thing."

Also in the cast of extras was Choice clubmate Ted (Blue) Anderson, a twenty-six-year-old on his third marriage who had once run a health club. "I don't work. My wife doesn't work. But we get by, by hook or by crook." Anderson didn't apologize for the hook and crook part, telling King that he was facing charges of robbery with violence and assault causing bodily harm. "First my club," he said, explaining his personal values. "Second my bike, and then my wife and kids."

Then there was twenty-three-year-old David White, who looked a little like General George Custer, with his flowing hair and whiskers. White told King he had spent eight years in English boarding schools and nineteen months in reformatory for assault.

Also on set was twenty-two-year-old Doug (Chicklet) MacDonald, the Toronto chapter president. MacDonald said that he lived in the club-house and that nothing made him prouder than his nine-hundred-pound Harley Dresser. "You can beat my brains in. I don't care. But don't touch my bike."

King didn't interview Giovanni (John) Raso, who was also on set. Raso was impressed as a young teenager by Guindon and joined the club when he grew up. Raso would go on to lead the Loners Motorcycle Club based in York Region, north of Toronto. "I met Bernie in the early 1970s. I always looked up to him. I thought he was a cool guy, a very smart man. Bernie's Bernie. Bernie doesn't take shit from anybody." Guns were becoming a staple in the biker life, but Guindon still preferred to use his fists. "He didn't have to [carry a gun]. It was a different life back then," Raso said.

The movie features nice close-ups of Pigpen and Big Jack sans hel-mets. There are scenes showing bikes on a lawn, bikes running red lights and a bike wipeout. No one expected Ingmar Bergman and no one was disappointed.

The *Proud Rider* opened strongly in Toronto-area theatres, then crashed like a Harley with a faulty suicide clutch on a tight corner. Critic Clyde Gilmour of the *Toronto Daily Star* gave it a stomping, calling it a "ramshackle melodrama." He sniffed, "*The Proud Rider*, a Canadian movie topping the bill at the Capri, was filmed in Oshawa in the fall of 1970 but kept out of release until now, making it eligible for consideration as one of the worst of 1972."

On the West Coast, Choice member Ken Goobie was working behind the scenes to make connections with the Satan's Angels Motorcycle Club. "Goobie wanted to get a drug connection with them," clubmate Cecil Kirby said.

"Goobie was a kind of a different kind of guy," Guindon recalled. "He was smart, very smart. He wasn't really a biker. He was a street person. He'd rather ride in his car than ride on his bike. It wasn't in his heart. He just liked the association with the guys, what the guys could help him with and what he could help them with."

Pigpen stayed close to home, where he was needed as the Satan's Choice fought with the Wild Ones and Henchmen of Southern Ontario. Dynamite was ignited and crowbars were bloodied. The Henchmen's Kitchener clubhouse was torched. In a clever *coup de grâce*, Choice members kidnapped two Henchmen. In exchange for their release, the rest of the club had to hand over their colours. Then, as a parting shot, one of the Henchmen had his legs broken when a car drove into him.

"I shot a couple guys," Pigpen later said. "Never killed anyone. I was the general. Do this and do that." He said the Henchmen had tough members, though they didn't have a lot of them. "They were tough. They were not pushovers."

As she became a young woman, Guindon's eldest daughter, Teresa, didn't have many memories of her father. Even when he wasn't in prison, he was seldom in touch. "He wasn't very active in my life," she said. Still, she was a Guindon living in Oshawa, which made her different. One day, when she was fifteen years old and in Grade 10, she was summoned over the intercom to the principal's office. She could guess it had something to do with her father when she saw a Harley-Davidson parked in the hallway outside the office. She went in. "There's this big burly biker sitting there, and my principal is sitting there, scared to death."

The biker told her that her dad would like her to visit him in prison. She didn't go visit her father, but the clubmate's visit to her school did have an impact on her life. Already, she felt that boys were afraid to date her because of her family name. Now it seemed like everyone was talking about her. "I quit high school after that. You know what an embarrassment that was?"

CHAPTER 17

Thunder Bay I

He had the face of a boxer and his nose was a little bent.

VERG ERSLAVAS describing his first impression of Bernie Guindon

Guindon was finally paroled from Joyceville Institution in January 1971. His release conditions required him to join his father, who now ran a small diner and confectionary store on the Port Arthur side of Thunder Bay. He was also strictly prohibited from associating with outlaw bikers. Guindon later marvelled at the nerve of the parole board even considering placing such a restriction upon him. "That's like telling the pope not to hang out with Catholics."

Verg Erslavas was a twenty-year-old biker in Thunder Bay. He'd had a series of minor run-ins with the law for offences like shoplifting and other forms of theft. "In 1970, Port Arthur and Fort William had just amalgamated to form Canada's newest city," Erslavas said in an interview. "My buddies and I hung out in downtown PA [Port Arthur] and could usually be found in Fiero's Restaurant or the New Ontario Hotel. We'd heard some rumours about a Choice in town asking a few questions. The first thing we thought was it must be cops doing some clumsy undercover work, as they were known to do. A couple of days later, we were in Fiero's when a guy came in and came over to our booth and introduced himself as Bernie of the Satan's Choice. He had the face of a boxer and his nose was a little bent. I noticed that his gestures with his hands and body indicated he'd spent time in the ring."

Guindon hit it off immediately with the Thunder Bay guys. "We were Harley riders," Erslavas said. "We were no strangers to the cops or bike clubs. We were young but we were pretty badass. It was a natural fit when we met."

Erslavas had read the recent magazine articles about the Satan's Choice and had hoped they might one day meet their leader in person. "Needless to say, we were pretty impressed with Bernie. We knew all about the Choice, the biggest and baddest club in all Canada. Here was Bernie, national president, sitting with us small-town boys, chewing the fat just like one of the guys. There was nothing pretentious about him and he was friendly in every way."

Erslavas and his friends were all building Harley-Davidson Panhead choppers for the next riding season. Erslavas took Guindon to the basement of his parents' home and showed him his bike. "He rolled up his sleeves and turned a few wrenches and offered some helpful suggestions. He told us about his Knucklehead and how the first thing he wanted to do was get his bike up to T. Bay so he could go for a ride. Remember, this was still the middle of winter."

Erslavas could barely believe what was happening: "Here's Bernie Guindon, leader of the Choice, down in my parents' basement, checking out the bike. We were really impressed. We really never met anybody like Bernie."

Later that night, Guindon, Erslavas and a couple of others drove over to the Flamingo Club, a watering hole on the Fort William side of town. "Thunder Bay was just newly formed as one city, but before that, it was always one side against the other, from politics to barroom brawls," Erslavas said. "In 1970, things had changed in name only for the most part."

Just a few years earlier, the Flamingo had been a nice enough place that handled wedding receptions and featured live bands, including Neil Young and The Squires. By the time Guindon and his new friends drove up that Saturday night, it was well into a seedy, downward slide. Inside were members of a local motorcycle club called the Eagles, all of whom were from Fort William. "The Eagles were a poor excuse for a club," Erslavas said. "We called them 'the Beagles' and generally gave them little respect."

It wasn't long before a fight was on, spilling out to the parking lot. Erslavas saw Guindon reaching for a tire jack in the trunk of his car. "Not the handle, but the whole jack and he was going to use it on these guys. He said, 'I'm gonna kill these fuckers. I don't care if they send me back right now.'"

Erslavas jumped in, hoping Guindon would think twice about hitting someone with the jack. "You don't need that for these guys," he told him, hoping to calm him down a little. "Thankfully, he didn't use it, but I could see he was ready. I thought to myself, This guy is nobody to fuck with."

The brawl made for a full and memorable introductory evening for Erslavas and his friends. "We headed back over to our own side of town to talk it over and to have some laughs about the whole thing—the best part of bar fights. Stuff happens which later, thinking about it, is really comical. You have to remember the ground was frozen like a skating rink. Ask any hockey player, fighting on ice requires a special technique: hang on and punch the other guy's lights out."

They managed to get Guindon home in time for his parole curfew, and then discussed their new buddy amongst themselves. "He didn't try to be impressive. He just was. He was cool. Someone to emulate."

News that Guindon had arrived in town soon reached local tough guy Harold Dorlander, who showed up at their house where they had gathered, looking for him. "I guess he wanted to prove he was tougher than Bernie," Erslavas said. "He wanted to wait for Bernie."

As Dorlander waited, he began the trash talk. "I don't think that Guindon is so tough," he said.

"Okay, just hang on," Erslavas replied. "He said, 'There's nobody else worth fighting here.' He said, 'I could clean your clock. You're not worth fighting.' He probably was right."

Dorlander was bigger than Guindon and clearly confident with his fists. Eventually, Guindon snuck back to Erslavas's house and the fight was on. "They squared off in the living room," Erslavas said. "Bernie left-hooked him and dropped him. He got up. He left-hooked him again, knocked him down again. I think he got him with one more."

Erslavas was impressed at how Guindon kept bobbing and weaving, moving forward, slipping punches and connecting with shots of his own. "He didn't land a hand on Bernie. That was the first time I saw his boxing skills."

A little later that same winter, Erslavas, Guindon and a buddy named Pete took a trip "down east" to pick up Guindon's 1947 Harley Knucklehead chopper from a former girlfriend. "What a great time it was meeting a lot of the guys," Erslavas said. "Everyone we met treated us great, and it was hard to miss the respect accorded to Bernie everywhere we went. The more I saw, the more I liked."

They returned north with the Knucklehead and some parts loaded onto a truck. Soon, Guindon had the bike running. Unable to wait for spring, he took it for a couple of rides across Thunder Bay in minus thirty-five degrees Fahrenheit. After a prison stretch spent dreaming about bikes, he couldn't wait for the snow to thaw. "It was fucking cold . . . The front end went out hitting ice," he recalled.

Erslavas and his friends stayed close with Guindon throughout the winter, and things soon reached the point where they were ready to strike for the Satan's Choice. "Of course, we wanted to form our own chapter in T. Bay, but we didn't have enough guys. So the first step would be striking for Oshawa chapter. SCMC [Satan's Choice Motorcycle Club] wasn't for everyone, but it sure seemed like the right move for me. We were all for it. I proudly put on my Oshawa striker patch."

Erslavas and his friends were the sons and daughters of the Italians, Poles, Finns, Ukrainians, Lithuanians and others from across Europe who changed the face of Thunder Bay after World War II. His Lithuanian father crossed the ocean to Canada in 1948, and his Polish mother landed in Canada the next year. Erslavas was born a year later in Pickle Lake in Northern Ontario, where his father worked in a gold mine. "I can recall as a child being taunted as a 'fuckin' DP.' I didn't know until much later what the DP meant [displaced person] or to have the sense to say, 'Fuck you, I was born in Canada.'"

Thunder Bay was isolated and had its own particular brand of roughness. "Northern Ontario winters were long and cold, and you had to travel 420 miles in either direction to the nearest city of any size," Erslavas said. "Saturday nights were for drinking and fighting. There were a lot of bars and clubs and they were generally full of rounders and local toughs. Everyone had a 'rep' to build or protect. Often we had to assert ourselves because we would get called out. We had a lot to prove, and backing down was not an option."

By the time he met Guindon, Erslavas was a regular at Cook Street (a police station, court and jail) and the "DJ" (the district jail), and "the Mountain" (Stony Mountain penitentiary) was a logical next step. "Looking back, I think after I met Bernie, he had a positive influence on me," Erslavas said. "Being older and just out of the pen, he was a mentor in many ways. It's not so much what he said but just the way he did things."

Guindon gave Erslavas and his buddies some advice about joining a one percenter club. He didn't want them getting drunk on any perceived power that might come from wearing a grinning devil patch on their backs. "He said to be yourself. That was something I stuck by."

Erslavas saw that Guindon took being a motorcyclist seriously. "He could really handle a bike well and make it do things for which it was not intended." Once, at a motocross track, Guindon decided to take Erslavas's 1965 Panhead out for a spin. It was a former police bike with the dubious distinction of appearing in the movie *The Proud Rider* as a law enforcement vehicle. "You have to understand even though it was ex-police, it was still a police-type bagger with everything but the radio," Erslavas said. "So here goes Bernie laying it over in the turns with the front end crossed over, flat-track style, getting air off the jumps, standing on the floorboards, all in full control. You could see him smiling from ear to ear."

When Guindon brought the bike back, Erslavas saw that there was a big gap in his smile. "When he was sliding around, he snagged a wire attached to a fence picket, which had swung around and caught him flush in the teeth," Erslavas said. "He was laughing though, and I thought it was funny as hell too."

Motorcycles provided a connection between Guindon and Erslavas that didn't have to be spoken. It went beyond words. Erslavas had longed for that connection since he saw Steve McQueen atop a Triumph in the movie *The Great Escape* back when he was a teenager. "McQueen was so cool, and I knew I had to ride and it had to be a Triumph. It took a while, but before my eighteenth birthday, I finally got a Triumph. It was a beauty, a shiny red '69 Bonneville, not new but pretty close." Erslavas liked riding his Triumph so much, he quit his final year of school, to his parents' consternation. He didn't care. "Nobody was going to tell me different. I loved riding my 'Bonnie' and hanging out. I didn't have much money then, but the Triumph didn't take much gas and a siphon hose helped."

Erslavas found that Triumphs and other English bikes were cool but not particularly reliable. "If you rode them hard, which we did, they often wouldn't last the riding season." Harley-Davidsons seemed the way to go. "The Harleys were heavier, stronger and more robust in every way . . . They were also beautiful to look at."

For Erslavas, nothing topped the fun of club runs, which were usually planned around field days. There were plenty of preparations to make to ensure their bikes were ready for the 994 miles between Thunder Bay and "down east."

"It would be a real adventure, and no two runs were alike," Erslavas said. "We'd travel with a tent and camp gear, never using motels. Real life on the road. It was the greatest feeling motoring down the road with a bunch of like-minded guys. Sometimes it seemed like we never got off the road. We'd get home from a run and turn around and go again."

The only negative for Erslavas was law enforcement. "They'd be out there always on the lookout, and once seen, we'd inevitably be pulled over for the obligatory road checks and usually resulting in tickets."

That summer, Erslavas and his friends met the characters he had previously only read about in newspapers and magazines, including Big Jack Olliffe, Chicklet MacDonald and Pigpen Berry. Guindon warned Erslavas about Pigpen: "I said to the guys, 'He's going to blow your fucking lights. He's going to try to make you get sick. Just act normal, like it's not bothering you.' He only acted like that when he knew he could blow lights."

Erslavas had never met anyone like Pigpen. "Once, he came up behind me and quickly popped a tiny ball of shit, which had been formed into just the right size, up my nostril, where it jammed," Erslavas said. "Had I panicked, the result would have been disastrous, but I kept my cool and gently blew it out. I laughed along with him. To show fear would have been a mistake, because then he'd be on you relentlessly. I saw it happen to Mike, a guy in our chapter who had a weak stomach. Piggy worked the poor guy into such a state that he would only have to give Mike a certain look to make him start gagging and puking . . . [He'd shout,] 'Piggy, don't come near me! Please go away!'

"Did Pigpen really love it? I mean, we're talking about shit here. Or was he putting on the act just to show some class? With Pigpen, you never really knew. One thing certain about Pigpen was that if he succeeded freaking someone out, he would derive great pleasure from it. You could always tell by the completely demented look he would get on his face afterwards."

It was unnerving to attend a party with Pigpen, and a total test of character to wander out into the woods in the wintertime with him and a high-powered rifle to camp overnight. A handful of Choice members did just that after a club member who worked for CN was able to get them a train ride and the use of a line shack for a hunt.

"Our shack had some bunks and a wood stove and not much else," Erslavas said. "We made sure that we got Pigpen's promise that he would behave, as quarters were too tight in the small shack."

Woody, the most senior Thunder Bay member and an experienced hunter, who considered Pigpen practically a member of his family, was there, and so was John Raleigh, who had transferred from Southern Ontario, or "down east," to the small but proud chapter in Thunder Bay. "He was an all right guy," Guindon said. "I don't know why the hell he was up there. If it was something to do with a court case or just getting out of shit."

"One night, relaxing after the day's hunting, Pigpen burst into the shack and rushed out again after grabbing Woody's .308, a high-powered rifle," Erslavas said. "A moment later, we heard the loud discharge of the gun right outside the shack. We rushed out to see a large owl sitting in the snow, looking at us. He had only one wing because Howard [Pigpen] had blown the other one off. We were all pissed."

"What the fuck—why'd you do that?" a usually calm and collected Woody yelled at him.

"He wouldn't stop staring at me," Pigpen replied, looking both sorrowful and crazed.

"You don't shoot a fucking owl," Woody said, stressing each word.

The bikers quickly agreed that the owl should be put out of its misery. To do anything else would be simply cruel. Pigpen chambered a round, since no one else wanted the job. There was another rifle blast but . . .

"I couldn't believe it," Erslavas said. "The owl was still there, looking, and now he had no wings because Howard had shot the other one off! We looked at the owl aghast. Woody took the rifle and finished the job quickly."

Woody turned to Pigpen and asked, "Why didn't you finish him?"

"I couldn't look at him 'cause he was staring at me, so I closed my eyes when I pulled the trigger," Pigpen replied sheepishly.

"You couldn't help but laugh, but I can still see that owl's big eyes," Erslavas said. "Thankfully, we didn't see any moose or deer, but we did bag a couple of partridges, which we brought home and cooked at the clubhouse after soaking them in a brine overnight." As the crew sat around, savouring the last bites of an excellent meal, Pigpen made an announcement. He had pissed in the brine. True to form, Mike began to gag.

"Pigpen was happy. His face was beaming. You couldn't help but like the guy, but you had to be wary."

CHAPTER 18

Riot

If I can get into a good brawl, I'm happy.

BERNIE GUINDON

Guindon was on parole in April 1971 when things exploded inside Kingston Penitentiary. Prisoners gawked from the upper tiers as inmates dragged pedophiles and men who had done violence to children into the central dome and tied them to chairs.

"The fun is about to begin!" someone shouted.

"You've got a real nice nose there, but it's kind of twisted, so I think I'll reset it for you," a prisoner announced to one of the bound men.

He smashed the prisoner's face with an iron bar.

"Kill the child molesters!" prisoners screamed down from high above.

And so it went during four days of madness, as six guards were held hostage and two inmates were executed. Blaring rock music could do only so much to muffle the screams of the tortured child molesters. One of the doomed men was repeatedly burned with a lit cigarette before he was finally put out of his misery. Prisoners particularly hated the sex criminals because they couldn't protect their own wives and children from men like this while inside, so they took out their worst fears on the predators available to them. "Guys have got a wife at home, a mother, daughter, sisters," Paul Gravelle said.

The damage to the prison from the rioting was hard to fathom. "They bent the cell door right back, with their hands," said Gravelle. "It was something else. Incredible."

Among the prisoners charged with murder following the riot was twenty-three-year-old Brian Leslie Beaucage of London, Ontario, who eventually pleaded guilty to assault. Beaucage was a veteran of the prison system despite his young age and carried the emotional scars of sexual abuse from older inmates when he was a teenager. When he finally got out, he became a member of the Satan's Choice.

Guindon wasn't surprised when he heard of the murderous anger and sustained violence of the riot. "Nobody listens to you when you're a prisoner. Sometimes you've got to do what you've got to do."

Now that he was on the outside, Guindon decided to make up for lost time by rededicating himself to boxing. The clock was ticking if he wanted to make it as a big-time fighter. He was so close, but it would take a big push to get over the hump. It was tough to find fighters his size who could challenge him, so he sparred with light-heavyweights and heavyweights.

His hard work paid off. Between January and November 1971, Guindon won the Ontario Golden Gloves, Eastern Canadian Golden Gloves and Canadian Golden Gloves tournaments, and he was chosen to be part of the Canadian team in the Pan Am Games in Cali, Colombia. He was selected as a light-middleweight in the 156.5-pound weight class, even though he was naturally one weight division lighter than the welterweight class. Guindon was convinced he was put in the ring with the larger fighters because a key boxing official didn't want him to advance. "He didn't like me because I was a biker. He didn't like all that."

The tight security during the Colombia games jolted Guindon. "I've never seen so many guns. They even shot people down there while we were there. You'd say, 'Holy fuck, what kind of a country is this?' It's crazy down there."

Guindon brightened when a Cali cop let him try out his Harley in the downtown. Most of the time, coaches escorted them everywhere, but he did manage to slip away and spy on the Cuban team as they trained. He was impressed at the lengths they went to work their core areas, which meant plenty of sit-ups. He decided he would incorporate more of that into his own training. When the Cubans noticed him, "They told me to leave. 'Get out! Go!' I knew they were going to get pissed off. I was sort of hiding."

International amateur boxing is meant for technicians, not brawlers, which played away from Guindon's natural strengths. "That boxing is on points. How many times you hit a person, how you keep your hands, your balance. They watch that. How you move in. How you accept a punch. Sometimes it's a bitch. I like fighting. I like the toe-to-toe. If I can get into a good brawl, I'm happy."

The Games were a limited success. Guindon had always found south-paws tricky, and he drew Mexican left-hander Emetorio Villanueva in the semi-finals. He lost by a technical knockout and left the Games with a bronze medal. For this, he got his smiling image wearing a white shirt and string tie published in *The Daily Times-Journal* in Thunder Bay.

He kept up the hard training and was made captain of a Canadian boxing team that toured Europe, fighting five matches over twenty-one days in Stockholm, Helsinki and The Hague. Guindon won three of five fights against Olympic-level fighters, including Swedish light-middle-weight champion Christer Ottosson.

It felt special to wear a maple leaf on his chest, even though he had recently served hard time in Her Majesty's prisons. "It gives you a better feeling. It also shows that you've done something that's beneficial to you that you can always remember that at least you were on the team."

Along the way, he made a couple of connections with people overseas who were interested in setting up their own Choice chapters. It was exciting to think of expanding across the ocean but also daunting. "It's time-consuming. Nobody was paying me any fucking money. At the time, it was kinda hard, keeping it together."

The highlight of his first year back on the streets came when he was selected as Thunder Bay's Athlete of the Week and given a key to the city. Among those honouring him at a dinner was his old friend George Chuvalo, who famously was never knocked off his feet in bouts with top heavyweights like Floyd Patterson, Muhammad Ali, Joe Frazier and George Foreman. Chuvalo said he was happy to attend and honour

Guindon. "It was richly deserved, so it was easy to do," Chuvalo said.

"Everybody in town was there," Verg Erslavas said. That included Guindon's father, who was now off the bottle, bespectacled and looking smaller and frailer than when he had ruled the Simcoe Street South household by fear. "They went up on the stage together," Erslavas recalled. "Bernie introduced him. It was a great night all around."

But things got a little tense later in the evening, when Chuvalo asked Guindon when he was going to stop hanging around with the biker crowd, and Guindon replied that being a biker was better than being a punching bag for the whole world. At that point, they both jumped to their feet. Fortunately, others intervened and the celebration continued.

The magic of 1971 lasted until December, when Guindon was finally busted for breaching his parole by associating with bikers. It had been no secret that he was back with his old friends; the only question was why authorities waited so long. His fresh arrest meant spending Christmas 1971 behind bars in Thunder Bay. "Every Christmas was rough inside. Everybody sending you cards. You sat there and you looked at your Christmas cards and you think it would be nice to be out with your family and friends. You didn't do much in there."

Guindon's father dropped by the jail for a visit, but he didn't bring much warmth or good cheer and it felt a bit late for a stern fatherly lecture. "What are you going to do?" Guindon later said. "He can get mad at you but he can't do anything."

His father was a calmer man now. "He had seen the light, I guess." Lucienne Guindon's changed demeanour didn't do much to impress his oldest son, though, because he couldn't recall his father ever showing remorse. "I can't remember my old man saying he was sorry for kicking the shit out of me."

Guindon would have appreciated an apology, but he didn't kick his old man out of his life, either. Whether he suspected it at the time, he'd be grateful one day for that kind of unspoken forgiveness and the second chances it allows a father who wasn't often there.

CHAPTER 19

Olympic Contender

I have five bouts lined up. But when you're in maximum security,
it's tough getting away.

BERNIE GUINDON

Guindon was a favourite to qualify for Canada's boxing team at the 1972 Summer Olympics, right up until he heard the jail doors close behind him for violating his parole. As the Canadian team prepped to compete in Munich, Germany, Guindon settled into Stony Mountain Institution in Manitoba, a forbidding fortress on a slight hill on the plains. The prison didn't appear to have changed for the better since it housed Big Bear and other prisoners from the North-West Rebellion back in the 1880s. "You look outside and it's just fields. When guys got out of there [escaped], and they did, they'd always get them in a couple of days. They didn't know where to go."

Guindon tried to keep himself busy and not get sucked down into the historically proportioned morass of negativity permeating the building's stone walls. He felt awkward but appreciated the effort his mother made in venturing west on the train to visit him. "She came a long way. She didn't speak English. She couldn't read. That was hard. That was very hard for her to manage." Guindon got a day pass, borrowed a buddy's motorcycle and took his mother out for a spin that she would fondly remember for years. The ride was fun but there wasn't too much they could say. "What are you going to say to your mother when you're in jail, doing time? She's trying to get you to go the straight and narrow because you're a dirty biker."

Guindon did have a sharp message for his mother's boyfriend, who came along for the trip. He told him to treat his mother right, or "I'll come back and put you in a hole."

Back behind bars, Guindon seethed with aggression and the urge to work out, but there were no sparring partners of his own size and ability. There was also precious little in the way of equipment. For hand wraps, a prisoner stole bandages for him from the medical area. He also sometimes trained in leather work gloves. Guindon befriended a massive Native inmate who he knew as "Big Indian." His enormous new friend shadow-boxed with him and sacrificed his own body so that Guindon could get a proper workout. "Nice guy. He was an old pro. He used to let me use his body as a heavy bag. I would love to say thank you." Guindon never did learn why his new friend was in prison.

The spartan training paid off. Guindon won the Manitoba light-middleweight title on a pass and was eventually allowed night passes to train at a real gym, with real sparring partners. When his request for a transfer back to Ontario was granted, he was housed in the maximum-security prison Millhaven Institution ("The Haven") in Bath, Ontario, near Kingston. Millhaven had been built to replace the aging Kingston Penitentiary and had opened early because of the Kingston riot.

One of the workers preparing Millhaven was Frank Hobson. His employers didn't know that he had ridden with the Choice back in the 1960s and had sold drugs and pimped out his girlfriend in Yorkville under the name "Hippy." His biker days were behind him when he was hired to lay sod on the Millhaven grounds. He hatched the idea to plant a loaded Beretta 9 mm pistol somewhere inside the facility to help out bikers like Guindon and John Dunbar of the Lobos Motorcycle Club of Windsor. Perhaps the gun could be hidden under the sod of the new courtyard. "There was a park bench there, and I seriously considered wrapping a gun up and burying it there by the bench!" Hobson later said.

Or perhaps the best hiding spot would be somewhere in the prison's massive new heating system. It was a walk-in unit, big enough for Hobson to wander about in it, looking for a good spot to stash the Beretta. "I searched for a good place to put the gun I had brought in with me in my lunch box. Nobody was there! No guards! Nothing." He discovered a spot in the duct work that looked perfect, but he hesitated. "I had second thoughts. I thought about my wife and three children and the harm that could come to them. I put it back in my lunch box and . . . took it home." Hobson never told Guindon about his plan to stash a gun in the prison.

Guindon was housed on the fourth floor, which put him in danger of a thirty-foot drop over the railings if he angered the wrong inmate. He kept his eyes open around the "muscle guys," prisoners who would do the dirty work of other inmates for a fee. "I don't like muscle guys. Everybody's having a hard enough time doing their time." The muscle guys just amped up the tension, which was already considerable. Ten days could feel as bad as ten years if a prisoner wasn't mentally ready. There were so many nasty places for an inmate's mind to go if he let it. "Is somebody fucking my wife? Is somebody stealing this off me? Your mind is rotating, just rotating. Every person's time is different. They're all the same and all different."

Guindon quickly befriended Lauchlan (Lockey) MacDonald of the 13th Tribe Motorcycle Club in Nova Scotia. MacDonald and three others from the club were convicted of statutory rape of a sixteen-year-old in a highly publicized trial. Guindon didn't believe the news reports. "He was an okay guy. Didn't bother nobody. Just that he was in on that charge—sexual charge—and so was I. He was kind of quiet. Minded his own business. He could look after himself if he had to. He was nervous inside. That's why they shipped him out west, because he would have gotten killed out east."

MacDonald was stabbed inside Millhaven by a muscle guy he didn't know. He managed to drag his attacker into his cell, where he forced the assailant to admit that some mobsters from Hamilton had put him up to it.

Guindon stormed up to the Hamiltonians in the common room.

"Last time I seen you, Guindon, you was in PC in Kingston," one of them said.

That was exactly the wrong thing to say. Guindon had never agreed to protective custody, with the snitches and child molesters.

What happened next was the stuff of prison legend, and bikers talked about it with a touch of awe and gratitude decades later. It started with a crisp left hook to the jaw of the smart-mouthed mobster. Then the mobster's buddy stopped another punch and shared space on the floor. "He knocked two of them out," Satan's Choice member Lorne Campbell said. "Said, 'Anybody else got a problem with me and Lockey?'"

It was relatively easy work for Guindon to starch a non-boxer with a shot or two, and he certainly had enough practice doing it behind bars. "A lot of times, I didn't hit them in the chin. I hit them in the stomach first. Slow them down. Depends on my mood." In the case of the mobsters, it was their attitude that brought them in contact with Guindon's knuckles. "I remember they were just rapping away. I hooked a guy. I gave him a hooking and straightened 'em out. Usually, I gave a guy a left hook. Then if he mouths off, I gave him a right hand."

Guindon said the shots were meant as a clear message about MacDonald and himself. "Leave the guy alone. We don't bug you. Leave him alone."

Campbell went to prison himself a decade later for an assortment of assault and drug charges and said he and other bikers continued to benefit from Guindon's tough line. "That was what paved the way for every other biker who went to the pen after that," Campbell said. "I was glad I went in after Bernie."

Ottawa-area bouncer and armed robber Richard Mallory first met Guindon while crossing the Millhaven exercise yard and instantly knew this wasn't someone to be trifled with. "If you were smart, you didn't say anything about him," Mallory said. He had done time in Kingston in the late 1960s, when inmates still weren't allowed to talk to each other. He appreciated the reforms that followed the riot, like increased exercise and socializing time, but he was also cautious. When strangers tried to strike up a conversation, Mallory refused with a standard response: "Do I know you? No? Then go away."

Mallory described Guindon as a "little guy, pretty friendly. He wasn't ignorant." But Guindon hung around with bikers and Mallory spent his time with weightlifters, and the two groups generally kept a respectful distance. "You hung around with your own," Mallory said. "You don't get friendly with people you don't know right away. You don't know who's who."

Guindon was in charge of running the prison's sports shack, where equipment was stored. That made him visible to guys like Mallory. Like Guindon, Mallory was using his time behind bars to build himself up physically. "You've got nothing else to do in there," he said. "You've got proper nutrition, proper rest. I did it [weights] seven days a week."

He thrived physically while inside Millhaven, which had impressive new fitness facilities. He went into prison with a solid three-hundred-pound bench press but soon wanted better. "I seen a guy doing four hundred. I said, 'I want to beat that.'" Within a few years, he was able to push up a staggering 550 pounds. "I had a whole bunch of guys around me, cheering me on," he recalled of the day of his big lift. "The guys were all cheering me on. A lot of them were doing life. They had never seen that."

Mallory got up to twelve reps with a four-hundred-pound bench press. He could also dead-lift a thousand pounds, which is about the weight of a thoroughbred horse. Like Guindon, he was obsessed with planning his workouts. "You only had a couple hours in the yard. Two hours, seven days a week . . . Snow on the ground, I'd go out. Seven days a week. Parkas, mitts, I'd go out."

Guindon was allowed passes to compete in boxing and was a Canadian amateur champion again in 1972, but he wasn't surprised when the Canadian Olympic Association didn't send him to the Summer Olympic Games in Munich. He knew the association was against him representing the country, even when he'd been a free man. So at a time when he could have been heading overseas to fight in the Olympics, he was once almost killed during a high-spirited wrestling match on the second tier, when he nearly took a deadly tumble through the railing. "You do stupid things in stupid times."

The prison was now pushing more structured combative pursuits. A recreation officer occasionally brought in a former pro boxer to train with Guindon. He was also allowed out to Toronto to fight Bob Proulx, the former Canadian junior welterweight champion. Guindon had to drop ten pounds in two days to qualify. He lost the weight and took the decision against Proulx.

There were also matches in Kitchener, Guelph and Windsor. It didn't have the cachet of an international boxing tour or the Olympics, but it still felt good to rack up a win against an American Golden Gloves champion. Competition brought perks that went beyond the thrill of victory. Before starting the drive back from a bout in Windsor, Guindon persuaded his guards to stop over at the local Satan's Choice clubhouse. The guards were thanked with a party featuring plenty of booze and female companionship. Guindon passed on the liquor but indulged with the women. "We were there for three hours, then another clubhouse for another hour. We got lucky down there in Windsor." The guards were too hungover and exhausted to drive, so Guindon took the wheel himself and drove them all back to prison.

During a bout at the Cabbagetown Boxing Club in Toronto, Guindon caught the eye of *Toronto Daily Star* reporter Arlie Keller. "All I can do up there is hit the heavy bag, do lots of leg exercises, work with the weights and do exercises to strengthen my stomach," he told Keller. "There are no ropes which I can use to skip or mirrors to look into to check my style. Nothing resembling a weapon is allowed."

"I have five bouts lined up," Guindon continued. "But when you're in maximum security, it's tough getting away." He told the reporter that he refused to step away from his biker friends, even though he knew that would irritate the parole board. "I've been a biker since I was fifteen," he said. "They are the only friends I have. I'm not going to give them up."

It was while he was in Millhaven that he got a phone call from his brother, Jack, telling him that their father had died of lung cancer. The news didn't come as a shock and Guindon processed it coolly. "I knew he wasn't well. You gotta accept the fact that it's over."

There was a small ceremony in Thunder Bay, and then Guindon was allowed to ride with his father's body on the train to attend the funeral in Buckingham, Quebec. There weren't many people at either ceremony and there didn't seem to be much to say. Guindon's mother didn't show up at all. Few tears were shed and that seemed okay. His father hadn't been big on tears anyway, although Guindon could recall his father crying at the funerals of his own parents in the same town. Once the funeral was over, Guindon got on a plane and returned to his cell.

For all of its dangers, prison could be deadly boring. Many prisoners tried to find a hobby. "You're in a cell that's twelve by eight; you can't do much in there. You've got to think, What am I going to do to keep myself busy? Make myself some money?" Guindon said.

His mother and brother sent him some cash to buy a stash of supplies such as all-purpose cement, a cutting block and assorted dyes. He also stocked up on stamping tools, leather lace, screwdrivers, magic markers, hole punches, edge cutters, a utility knife, rawhide mallets, a book on Indian lore, and patterns for moccasins, purses and wallets. He used these to make clutch purses, wallets and a tan holster, for which he had no gun. He poured his energy into his projects, creating a petit point picture of a fist on a motorcycle throttle, in which the knuckles were a skull, snake, witch and devil. That project took three and a half months, with him sometimes working six hours a day. He made an estimated 88,000 stitches with single strands of thread to complete the image. "Many a time I had to cut the thread," he said. He also made a plaque with the Serenity Prayer adopted by Alcoholics Anonymous, a group he joined in prison to strengthen his resolve against drinking. The plaque read, "God, grant me the serenity to accept the things I cannot change, courage to change the things I can, and wisdom to know the difference."

He specialized in leather and copper. He created a series of decorative wallets and plaques of boxers, birds and sad clowns, which had the face of his mother's boyfriend. His mother liked the clowns, and she hung one on her wall.

Guindon hadn't done any artwork before he went to prison, and neither of his parents was particularly artistic. So he was surprised at how the work consumed him, how much pride he felt in his creations, and how closely he guarded his freedom to continue making them. As a serious hobbyist, he was allowed to use glue that was coveted by addicts, and X-Acto knives, which were valued by almost everyone. Guindon guarded his glue and his knives, not wanting to lose his crafting privileges. "That's what gets you in shit. Guys sell their glue to glue sniffers.

I would never loan my knives to anybody. My razors. I had little X-Acto knives. They can do a lot of damage."

He made a leather picture of a cougar in a tree for Suzanne Blais. She was still married, but her feelings for him hadn't died. When she received his gift, she cried.

CHAPTER 20

Expansion Troubles

He [mobster Frank Cotroni] should have gone into the club [where the bikers hung out], clients or no clients, lined everybody against the wall and rat-a-tat-tat.

Montreal Mafia boss PAOLO VIOLI

T he young man's body washed ashore at Curtis Point on Rice Lake, about eighteen miles south of Pigpen Berry's hometown, Peterborough, in the spring of 1973. He was wearing jeans and a denim jacket. In his left ear was a gold earring, and his mouth and hands were bound.

Forensic testing determined he had drowned. A Toronto Transit Commission subway transfer on his body indicated he had been in Toronto on March 9. Further testing revealed that the body was that of twenty-one-year-old William Lee Graham of Oakview Beach near Collingwood, several hours north of Toronto. During his final days alive, Graham had been a minor witness in a drug trial against the Satan's Choice.

What happened between the time of Graham's testimony and the discovery of his body in the water was later described by Cecil Kirby. After his court appearance, Graham had been spotted by bikers at a custom motorcycle shop in Toronto's west end and was taken to a Choice clubhouse at Woodbine Avenue and Highway 7, where he was beaten and bound. Among those who dumped his still breathing body into the lake was Armand (In the Trunk) Sanguigni. "I was told of it later by Armand himself," Kirby said.

If the weights had been properly applied to the body, he would never have surfaced.

On May 27, 1973, two badly decomposed bodies were found by a farmer in a ditch between two isolated fields about twenty-five miles east of Windsor. Dental records revealed that one of the bodies was eighteen-year-old Cathryn Hulko, wife of William (Wild Bill) Hulko, the president of the local Satan's Choice chapter. The other body was that of her fifteen-year-old friend Lynn Campeau. They had each been shot in the head at least four times.

The teenagers had vanished on January 31, 1972, the night Wild Bill and seven others with the Windsor Choice chapter were charged with the murder of twenty-three-year-old Leonard Craig, a fellow member of the local Choice. Craig was severely beaten inside the Windsor clubhouse during a party. He staggered outside, collapsed, then died in hospital.

Hulko was sentenced to eight years in prison for his role in the Craig killing. Kirby said it was rumoured that Hulko's wife and Campeau had co-operated with police to put him behind bars. As in the death of Graham, no charges were ever laid for their murders, which served as reminders that it was dangerous to stand up to the Choice in court.

The Satan's Choice was reaching out and trying to expand, even as Guindon was bunkered away in prison with his workouts and crafts. They had some success in Winnipeg, where the Spartans club decided to patchover to the Choice. Then came word that someone had torn the Choice patch off the back of one of the new members. This was taken as an attack on the honour of each and every member and it merited a group response. Fifteen Ontario members drove up to Winnipeg with their trunks full of guns. Pigpen was among them. Once there, they learned that they had been duped. The member had simply handed in his patch to a rival Los Bravo. "That guy got a helluva beating," Kirby said.

Things only got worse: the remaining members of the new Winnipeg Choice chapter decided they wanted to become Spartans again. Behind bars, there wasn't much Guindon could do but wonder about the often low quality of leadership in the club. "That's the way it goes. You wonder who's leading the pack. The club's only as good as its officers."

The expansion effort was also crumbling on the West Coast. Some of the Vancouver members were becoming an embarrassment with their out-of-control drug use. Ken Goobie, John Harvey and a member called "Rabbit" headed west with the hopes of cleaning up the chapter and establishing a viable drug pipeline. If that meant shutting down the existing Vancouver Satan's Choice chapter, then so be it.

Goobie was a different sort of biker. He was tall, lanky, and tough as beef jerky. He had boxed as an amateur and once fought bare-knuckles with former pro heavyweight boxer Joe (Ironman) Dinardo. That tussle ended in a draw. Certainly, that was impressive, but what set Goobie apart was his appearance, especially his fondness for business apparel. Goobie was the only club member known to wear his grinning devil patch on a three-piece suit.

The club's western front collapsed, as Goobie and his crew didn't have enough backing to take on existing clubs like the Satan's Slaves. That was the end of the coast-to-coast dream, at least for the time being. Hearing the news from behind bars, Guindon was disappointed but not heartbroken. "They've got so many clubs out there." It would have been too expensive for Vancouver members to make it over the Rocky Mountains for national meetings anyway. Keeping an eye on them would have been tough, and unsupervised chapters increased the chance of police infiltration. "The communication is too hard," Guindon added. "If we can't get everybody working together, you're never going to make it."

Toronto remained solid for the Choice. Despite his dust-up with Goobie, Dinardo was a friend and business partner with some of the members there. Dinardo offered them a sort of one-stop shopping. His criminal record included robbery, arson, theft, passing forged documents and counterfeit money, and weapons and parole violations. He provided Sanguigni and Kirby with targets for lucrative jobs. "Joe had all kinds of connections with people," Kirby said. "Break-and-enters. Armed robberies." While he was good with his fists, he always seemed to carry a gun. That came in handy when someone pulled a knife on him at Wasaga Beach. One wave of the handgun and the man ran away while Dinardo strolled along. "Joe just walked down the beach, buried the gun in the sand and kept on walking," Kirby said.

Toronto-area police could be forgiven in the early 1970s if they pined for the heyday of Johnny Sombrero and his street rumbles. Over the past decade, bikers had moved from being a rowdy nuisance to something much more menacing.

In 1970, the Ontario Police Commission started an intelligence unit that focused on bikers. In mid-June 1973, the Ministry of the Solicitor General of Ontario reported that motorcycle gangs were pushing to entrench themselves as the main suppliers of illegal narcotics in Ontario, with the primary street drug at the time being amphetamines, or speed. Police estimated at the time that there were six hundred outlaw bikers in Ontario, including two hundred members of the Satan's Choice. The Vagabonds and Para-Dice Riders remained important forces. Police didn't count the Black Diamond Riders among the six hundred because they were not believed to be in the drug trade.

Sombrero still lumbered about but he had become a quaint relic of another era, and the Battle of Pebblestone seemed like a Sunday school sack race compared to what Pigpen, Sanguigni and Kirby were doing. "So I broke a couple of arms and split some guy's skull from here to there," Sombrero told the *Globe and Mail*, running a finger down his head. As Sombrero held forth with the reporter, Black Diamond Riders splashed about in a pool at their clubhouse like kids on summer break.

Sombrero held on to delusions of grandeur and sipped champagne from his own personal silver goblet, which was refilled by members. "I'm a Liberal-monarchist. I feel like shooting some of those people the way they talk against the Queen."

He explained how one of his many brawls was handled by the courts, when he said he reached for a fence rail to dispense with a group he called "seven of the bastards."

"Judge was a great old guy. Said, 'Whatever happened to the old rules of one against one?' He convicted me of assault, but sentenced me to one day in jail and then told me to serve it in his chambers. Let me go about an hour later."

Sombrero was married now, with three children, but he still called his clubmates "my boys." He revelled in being a father figure of sorts. "I don't know what my boys do at home or someplace. You know, grass and stuff. Who knows? But nobody in this club's gonna get into the real drug thing."

"Look, this is going to sound corny, but I'm a nationalist, see," he told the *Globe and Mail*. "I believe in a strong Canada. You gonna have a strong country, you gotta have strong young men. And any guy gets on dope won't make it."

He spoke of his weariness of paying fines and court costs, like the time he was docked money for knocking someone's eye out of its socket. "When I go with one or two of my boys, to visit any other club, I let 'em know I'm coming. They clean the place out, tell their guys, 'Johnny Sombrero's coming,' and they get rid of any of that kind of stuff they have. They know me." He was proud that he hadn't changed with the times and that his members had a certain uniformity as well as club uniform shirts. Some bikers spoke of rugged individualism, but not Sombrero. "One guy leaves, another just exactly like him comes in."

While Sombrero didn't venture far from his Toronto home, in 1973, the Satan's Choice was pushing into Crescent Street in Montreal's downtown, home to a lively collection of bars and restaurants close to McGill University and the Sainte-Catherine Street tourist drag. Also trying to gain the upper hand on the Crescent Street drug trade was the Popeyes Motorcycle Club.

The police responded with a special squad of a dozen or so members to keep an eye on them. Leaders of the local Mafia favoured a more direct approach. After hearing that three members of the Cotroni crime family were killed by bikers in September 1973, Mafiosi Paolo Violi called for blood, according to a police bug planted at the ice cream shop on Jean-Talon East that doubled as his headquarters: "He [Frank Cotroni] should have gone into the club [where the bikers hung out], clients or no clients, lined everybody against the wall and rat-a-tat-tat."

It was around this time that a former Maritimer entered Guindon's world as quietly as a thief in the night. Garnet Douglas (Mother) McEwen was the hippie-ish proprietor of a head shop in St. Catharines, Ontario, having worked his way up from selling pencils on street corners. Mother hobbled about with the aid of an artificial leg after a nasty motorcycle accident. He sometimes altered tattoos, but he was not a tattoo artist by any stretch. Lorne Campbell of the Choice covered his arms with tattoos and felt the worst of the bunch were the ones inked by Mother. "He was just a fat, stinky guy," Campbell said. "That's all he was. He was just a dirty guy who looked like a 1950s biker. He was filthy." No doubt Mother was not amused when Campbell quipped that he didn't have a leg to stand on. Campbell threatened to tear off Mother's wooden leg so that he could beat him with it.

Niagara region motorcycle painter Mark DeMarco didn't like McEwen either, and he also didn't trust him. Mother borrowed DeMarco's dark blue Cadillac DeVille when he was getting married, saying it would be a great car for the occasion. In return, he loaned DeMarco his custom Harley. DeMarco found it odd that the pearl-white Super Glide had "SCMC" (Satan's Choice Motorcycle Club) on the sissy bar. Only club members could have club gear or markings like that. McEwen was late returning the Cadillac, and DeMarco was troubled by what he discovered when he finally got it back: three hidden recording devices. Two were on the inside and another was on the outside mirror, to catch conversations on the street. "That was my first giveaway that he was a rat," DeMarco said.

By 1974, McEwen was frequently associating with members of the Outlaws on the American side of the border, around Niagara Falls. McEwen, Kirby and a Kitchener member named Drago flew to Florida to visit with the Outlaws for two weeks. That trip was the start of a chain of events that would dramatically remake Guindon's world, with no shortage of blood spilled in the process.

The Outlaws were extremely territorial. Florida had become a cash cow and a rough playground for them since their South Florida chapter was founded in 1967. The state offered all-year bike riding, as well as proximity to South American drug routes and several military bases, which were prime spots for recruiting members. The Hells Angels held a firm grip on the West Coast and the Bandidos controlled Texas, but Florida belonged to the Outlaws.

Perhaps it was inevitable that the Outlaws and Hells Angels would butt up against each other in Florida. When an Outlaw raped the wife of a Hells Angel in 1969, it set off a chain of attacks and counterattacks that echoed for years. The woman's husband and other Hells Angels beat the rapist to death. In retaliation, three visiting Massachusetts Hells Angels were kidnapped in April 1974 and shot execution-style with shotguns. Their bodies were tied to cinder blocks and dumped off a cliff into a quarry in southwest Broward County. Violence bred more violence with no end in sight.

Upon their arrival in Florida, McEwen and Drago were grilled by airport security officers, but Kirby, a gym rat who was more clean-cut-looking, passed through unhassled.

Many of the Outlaws Kirby encountered in Fort Lauderdale were ex-servicemen, numb from the carnage of Vietnam, and their headquarters was a bungalow with gun ports instead of windows. "Their clubhouse was like a fortress," he said. "They put a chill in my spine."

McEwen had made several trips south already, and he owned a couple of body-rub parlours in the area. During the visit, one of them caught fire and a woman inside died. Kirby wondered if she had been murdered. McEwen's grief over her death seemed real to his clubmate.

Wherever McEwen went in the years to come, whoever's lives he touched, pain would follow, for them and the biker with the bugs in his car. But few would feel it as keenly as Guindon.

CHAPTER 21

Thunder Bay II

That time he ate the bird! He vomited that thing. You could hear the feathers cracking, the bones. Him chewing it down. The guts were on his chin, his chest, and then he barfed.

BERNIE GUINDON on Pigpen Berry

I n the summer of 1974, Guindon walked free from prison for the second time. He was sent on his way with a train ticket to Thunder Bay in his pocket. "That was about the only fucking place I'd call home."

Shortly afterwards, the good citizens and police of Thunder Bay braced themselves as 150 beer-swilling members of the Satan's Choice and their bike-loving buddies prepared to descend on their community. Guindon had served his entire sentence and he was free without conditions. He could socialize with whoever he wished.

The bikers planned to gather on a property that was owned by a prominent lawyer on Spruce River Road for what was improbably billed a "convention." Thoughts of two-wheeled terror brought a collective shiver to the land of the Sleeping Giant. Since poop-eating Pigpen was among the arriving delegates, concerns of an impending assault on the senses were justified. For Guindon, it was a chance to jump back into his old world with both boots.

At the top of the bikers' agenda that weekend was a memorial service at St. Andrew's Cemetery for John Raleigh. The club's vice-president had been killed in August 1972. It was a particularly poignant day for Verg Erslavas. "I first met John when we were riding back home from a field day," Erslavas said. "It was fall and we were on the Lake Superior stretch. The weather was brutal with freezing rain and wind blowing off the lake. Of course, we had no rain gear. No one wore it in those days. We met John and Jungle, a couple of Toronto guys coming up to Thunder Bay for a visit. They took a turn on the bikes, as we were cold and wet, and we jumped in the car to warm up. After becoming acquainted for a while, we became inseparable."

In 1972, Raleigh had been atop Toronto president Larry McIlroy's Harley on the last ride of his life. Raleigh took a curve at too high a speed, hit a bump and was thrown from the bike. "It hit me hard," Erslavas said. "I really loved the guy. We gave him a great send-off and a headstone inscribed with 'Satan's Choice M.C.' To this day, whenever I'm in T. Bay, I place a red rose on his grave and shed a tear or two." Erslavas even named his son John after his late clubmate.

To bolster the forces of decency in Thunder Bay that August, police chief Onni Harty cancelled all leave for Thunder Bay police officers and brought in twenty-five reinforcements from the South Porcupine detachment of the OPP. Even the four-dog unit of the local OPP, which was in town for training, was put on call for active duty.

Branch 5 of the Royal Canadian Legion indefinitely postponed its annual men's picnic, which had originally been planned for the same Sunday as the "convention," at the adjacent picnic site, no less. Some three hundred dollars in meat was put into deep freeze as the former servicemen braced for the worst that Guindon's hordes could offer. Restaurants and even a gas station announced their precautionary closures.

The abundance of caution made many locals only more curious. People ventured out to watch the procession of Harleys growl down Hodder Avenue to the cemetery.

"When we had that run, it was like the Choice's big parade," Erslavas said. "People were lined up three deep on the bike route . . . We were kinda proud of it . . . A lot of the girls wanted to meet the guys . . . Thunder Bay had some pretty friendly girls."

After that, there was an explosion of . . . nothing. No chickens were beheaded, no businesses were trashed and no police were attacked. Pigpen stayed amongst his fellow bikers and, in the end, it was the motorcyclists and not the locals who suffered his antics most. "That time he ate the bird!" Guindon later said. "He vomited that thing. You could hear the feathers cracking, the bones. Him chewing it down. The guts were on his chin, his chest, and then he barfed."

CHAPTER 22

Pigpen Goes South

*They capture them up. The girls. They send them to Saudi Arabia and
are slaves for the rest of their lives.*

PIGPEN BERRY on Florida Outlaws

Pigpen's digestive system had barely settled from its encounter with
the bird feathers in Thunder Bay when he hightailed it south to
Florida, his new home. Pigpen was an unlikely snowbird, migrat-
ing south before he could be arrested on pending charges for attempted
murder and wounding.

The Outlaws had agreed to hide Pigpen as part of a new fugitive
exchange program between the two clubs. His legal name was changed
to "Peter Ray Johnson" and his street name was changed to "Garbage."
"They said I was supposed to get ID and be looked after," Pigpen
recalled.

In Florida, Pigpen soon witnessed things so disgusting that even he
wouldn't do them. One was kidnapping young girls for sale in the overseas sex trade. "They capture them up," he said. "The girls. They send
them to Saudi Arabia and are slaves for the rest of their lives. Kids are
captured up. I said, 'I don't want to get into that.'"

Outlaws who met inside the fortified walls of the Hollywood, Florida,
clubhouse also made money from body rubs, topless dancers, hookers

and drugs. Problem workers were sometimes beaten and murdered. Hardcore bikers from Canada were not strangers to lethal violence, but the intensity of Southern business left Pigpen numb and suspicious. "Down there, they played the game for keeps," Pigpen said.

It wasn't just a sense of brotherhood that inspired the Outlaws to welcome Pigpen into their ranks. In 1974, tensions between the Outlaws and Hells Angels in the United States escalated into open street warfare. As the Hells Angels tried to push into Florida, Outlaws began wearing patches that read "ADIOS" for "Angels Die in Outlaw States."

It was common for Pigpen to ride around with a machine gun across the front of his Harley, a .44 strapped to his chest, and two more pistols behind his back. That was just prudent in Pigpen's new world. "Down there, everybody's got guns," he said.

When Pigpen's Canadian friends Larry Hurren and Sweet Kid came down for a visit, they were struck by how bikers there seemed to all ride in packs, and how, when a strange car went by, bikers naturally reached for a firearm.

During one ride through Hollywood, a van pulled alongside Pigpen and its doors swung open. As the guns came out, Pigpen recognized a biker named Swampy and some of his associates. Pigpen took two bullets in his chest, near his heart, but managed to return fire.

As the war escalated, Pigpen found himself making more rides into North Carolina, home of the Fort Bragg army base, Pope air force base and Camp Lejeune marine base. Pigpen noted that seven members of the Lexington, North Carolina, chapter of the Outlaws were members of the elite Special Forces unit, known as the Green Berets. Their skills included guerilla warfare, a useful background given the Southern biker climate.

While hiding out, Pigpen supported himself by stealing cars and yachts on their trailers. Other Outlaws were heavily into running prostitution rings and selling cocaine, designer drugs, marijuana and methamphetamines. For many of the bikers, selling drugs was vastly preferable to running women. It wasn't so much an ethical issue as a practical one. Drugs paid more, took up less space and they didn't talk back or squeal to authorities. They also didn't need to eat. As slovenly as Pigpen's new companions were, they did have a crude business sense. "They're well organized," he said. "They made money big-time."

Guindon, curious, decided to visit the Florida Outlaws around this time. "I just wanted to see what the other side looked like. And it didn't impress me. They think their shit doesn't smell." He considered many of the Florida Outlaws to be anti-Canadian and spoiling for some kind of a fight, just for the sake of fighting. "You had to be careful," he said.

He made a point of not losing himself to the partying. "I don't party in a sense. I don't drink. I definitely wouldn't do drugs down there. You don't know what kind of shit you'd get. They might give you the wrong fucking dosage. Better to be careful than sorry later. If you can keep your faculties, you're okay."

Despite his aspirations to expand Satan's Choice, maybe even into the United States, the gun culture there gave him pause. He also wondered about police informants within the American biker ranks. He thought it would be hard to pick them out, since so many American bikers were ex-servicemen and acted like yes-sir, no-sir cops or soldiers to begin with. "Most guys are military. You don't know where they're coming from."

During his visit to Florida, Guindon met up with Big Jim Nolan, a talkative, charming and cold-blooded Outlaws leader. Big Jim was a pretty good guitar player and had been his school's valedictorian. More importantly, he said that he would rather be an Outlaw in prison than just some jerk on the streets. That statement pretty much captured his life view.

Guindon respected the power of Outlaws like Nolan, but he didn't want his Canadian club to fall under their thumb. He and his members had built a viable, powerful all-Canadian club, and they weren't about to be swallowed up in some gigantic American enterprise. Guindon was willing, however, to lend limited support to the Outlaws' fight with the Hells Angels and the Warlocks, a southern U.S. club founded by ex–U.S. Navy servicemen, whose mottos include, "Our business is none of your fucking business."

The Outlaws were curious about what was going on up in Canada, in the land of Pigpen. During one Florida meeting, a member remarked, "They have niggers in the club up there." Big Jim smacked him in the head, but it wasn't to promote civil rights or political correctness. He was simply placating the Canadians and keeping business options open.

Stairway Harry Henderson, an Outlaws president from Dayton, Ohio, had already tried to pull the Satan's Choice en masse over to his club. Henderson offered to let the Satan's Choice into the Outlaws without probation in a patch-for-patch deal. While some others might consider the offer an honour, Guindon turned it down flat.

Meanwhile, the Outlaws supplied the Choice with weapons, which were always useful considering the club's challenging push into Quebec. For Kirby, guns were also a business opportunity. "They were all carrying guns, those guys down there," Kirby said. "That was my business, selling guns."

If business kept the Outlaws friendly toward their northern peers, Pigpen's crude antics were having the opposite effect. His moralistic stance on the sex trade didn't help either. "They didn't like him at all," Guindon said. "He was getting away with it up here. Down there, I don't think they took much to him." It wasn't long until a few of the Outlaws wanted to kill Pigpen. "They couldn't stand his fucking bullshit," Guindon said. "They thought he was totally crazy."

As Pigpen rankled his American hosts, the Choice reciprocated by hiding Big Jim Nolan in Ontario as he fled from American authorities, who were investigating him on firearms offences. Big Jim ended up near Kitchener, where the Choice had a strong presence. He didn't join a local club because he didn't want to attract police attention, and only a couple Choice members knew his new identity and whereabouts.

Bodies kept falling in Montreal, and those American guns were proving more and more useful. One Choice member didn't bother to check the peephole before answering a knock at his front door. He was shot dead with a .45. Another member was found hanging dead in a motel. The bloody evidence of torture made it clear his death wasn't a suicide.

The Popeyes and Satan's Choice were feuding, and peace was nowhere on the horizon.

CHAPTER 23

Last Olympic Hope

Everybody heard it. He broke three ribs. Man, it was a beautiful punch.

LORNE CAMPBELL describing a Bernie Guindon punch

Guindon hadn't given up on boxing when he got out of prison in 1974. Thirty-two was an advanced age for an amateur athlete in a sport that rewards reflexes, but he still had a puncher's shot at the Olympics in 1976. His strengths in the ring were power and brains and toughness, and they hadn't gone anywhere.

He trained now mostly with professional fighters. "I used to spar a lot with the pros, good top pros. I enjoyed that more." He fit right in when he tested himself at the sport's top levels. There was a loss by decision to Clyde Gray, a slick boxer with a crisp jab who would go on to become a world-ranked fighter and the British Commonwealth champion. "He gave Clyde a good fight," Spider Jones said.

There was also a win by decision over Gray's brother Stu, a solid professional. "He [Guindon] fought a lot of good, good guys who were more than his weight, and he beat most of them," Chuvalo said. "His record speaks for itself."

While Guindon was spending a lot of time with the pros, he still had no plans to turn pro himself, but it wasn't for lack of confidence or opportunities. He didn't go pro because he still feared it would have legal ramifications, giving authorities the excuse to ramp up any charges against him after a brawl. "When you're a pro, you're not allowed to hit anybody on the street. Your hands are weapons."

Outside the ring, Guindon remained a fearsome street fighter but not a particularly dirty one. He didn't go for the stomp circles, which was when some bikers would circle, kick and stomp a fallen enemy. Once, after dropping an Ottawa-area club president, he waved off other Choice members who wanted to give him what bikers call a boot-fucking. Guindon was matter-of-fact about the encounter. He'd asserted his dominance in the club and didn't want the dust-up to become something worse. He felt that his punches spoke loudly enough. "I said something. He said a smart remark. So I gave him a left hook, knocked him out." The club president wound up in hospital from the one-punch fight. When he got out, he sought out Guindon but not for revenge. "He said, 'Thanks for stopping those guys from kicking,'" Guindon recalled.

He still wasn't impressed by much of what he saw of the pro game, including how the handlers of Eddie (Hurricane) Melo of west Toronto matched him with top pros when Melo was still a teenager. Melo, who was a Canadian pro middleweight champ and an enforcer for mobster Frank Cotroni of Montreal, would likely have gone further with better management. "He was young and they just didn't care," Guindon said. "They threw him in with top fighters."

Once back in boxing circles, Guindon also renewed acquaintances with former pro Baldy Chard, who still supplemented his bouncer's income by collecting debts for the mob. "He was friendly. I didn't find him to be a belligerent person or rude. He just did his job."

The fights and the criminal underworld overlapped frequently, but few straddled the line between them more than Guindon. Needing work, he drifted onto Toronto's seedy Yonge Street strip, finding employment as a doorman and manager at the Venus Spa, a second-floor walk-up with peeling paint. "At the time, my girlfriend was a stripper/dancer. That's how I ended up in the area." A walk down Yonge Street in the mid-1970s wasn't too much different than a trip to the tenderloin district of Bangkok, except for the language on the sex club signs and the ethnicity of the hookers. Grainy skin flicks played at the Loews Theatre just north of Queen, where moviegoers had once watched silent pictures and vaudeville acts, and then the works of Joan Fontaine and Clark Gable. There were a hundred places like the Venus Spa around Yonge and Dundas, where for twenty or thirty bucks, a man could have a body rub with masturbation, oral sex or naked dancing. A little more cash bought full intercourse.

Guindon's job was to sort out customers who were mouthy or mistreating the women. It wasn't much of a job, but there was no heavy lifting and it left him time to train. One day, his teenaged daughter Teresa noticed he was sporting an expensive-looking suit and a Rolex watch.

"Well, you look like you're doing well," Teresa said.

"Of course I am," Guindon replied.

"What are you doing?"

"Well, I've got girls working for me."

Although she generally found her father charming, Teresa wasn't impressed with this particular boast. "He was laughing and thought it was funny."

One day around this time, Suzanne Blais's mother called her daughter to tell her that Bernie was going to be boxing at the Sheridan Mall in Mississauga. "I had moved into a new home in Erin Mills, and had two kids, but dropped everything and went out with my mom to see the fight," Suzanne recalled. "Bernie won and I was so proud. This was the first time I'd seen him since 1960."

Later that year, he fought on a card at the Burnhamthorpe Community Centre that included Nicky Furlano of the Cabbagetown Boxing Club in Toronto against Thomas Hearns of the Kronk boxing club in Detroit. Hearns would later become a world champion, but he left town that day a loser. Guindon was impressed by Furlano's potential and personality. "I used to give him a lot of pointers. He wasn't a smart aleck."

Guindon was paired against Wilson Bell of Detroit. They stayed close for all three rounds, but Bell won the decision with a series of left hooks. That said, Choice members appreciated the fury of Guindon's punching and cheered loudly. Among them was Ken Goobie, playing the role of his manager.

Jack Guindon still flirted with boxing but never displayed the primal rage or natural gifts that made his brother such a force in the ring. Jack had a boxing match of his own planned for the UAW union hall in Oshawa. While he didn't pretend to be a great fighter, Jack was good enough to have a solid shot at winning the regional Golden Gloves. He was looking forward to a little hometown glory. But Jack's opponent didn't show up, and a replacement was needed fast. Bernie was in the crowd and was hauled in as a last-minute opponent for the five-round main event. It was Jack's chance to finally beat his younger brother, since Bernie hadn't been training for it, while Jack had been working out hard.

Lorne Campbell considered both of the Guindon brothers friends, but that day he was in Jack's corner, taping his hands. He heard Jack warn Bernie that he meant business. He would be coming after him when the bell sounded. "I'm not going to fool around, Bernie," Jack said.

Despite the warning, Bernie started off like a joker. "He just dropped his hands and let Jack hit him," Campbell recalled. Then Bernie settled down to business, torquing a left hook that began at the soles of his feet and exploded somewhere deep in Jack's midsection. "You could hear the wind go right out of Jack," Campbell said. "Everybody heard it. He broke three ribs. Man, it was a beautiful punch."

Years later, Jack remembered that left hook just as vividly. "It just lifted me off of my feet and down I went on my back. I was in pain. Guess what? I was off work the next day. Sore. I could hardly walk. Everything seized up on me."

Guindon offered no apologies. Boxers are supposed to punch hard, and he felt he honoured the sport when he competed seriously. "He folded over like an accordion," Guindon said, adding, "He beat me up when I was a real young kid."

Guindon was a far gentler man when he thought of his young daughter Debbie Donovan, who was born in 1969. Guindon loved her company and shielded her from the club during their times together. "He never brought me around any of them," she recalled. "Any time I saw him was family time. He always picked me up on the bike. He would take me to the CN Tower, to breakfast."

Guindon would appear and then disappear from her life, and she never really understood what was going on when he was out of sight. "He was in and out of jail so much. I didn't really know where he was. I know he loved his mother. He was just a normal guy to me. Never drank. I've never seen him smoke. Never heard him swear. He was always soft-spoken."

Even during the occasional bike rides, he didn't present himself as a dangerous boxer or biker. "I never saw any bad side of him. I'd see him . . . He was always happy. I never seen him angry, yell. Nothing."

Years later, she would realize that her father was protecting her, in his own way. He was her dad, and dads are supposed to protect their little girls, even if Dad runs an outlaw biker gang.

CHAPTER 24

Strange Clubmate

You could feel he was just a little strange.

CECIL KIRBY on Satan's Choice member Gerald Michael Vaughan

For all of the Satan's Choice members' motorcycle thefts, break-and-enters, prostitution rings, drug and gambling rip-offs and production of "Canadian Blue" methamphetamines for export to U.S.-based Outlaws, several members weren't criminals at all. They held down regular jobs as labourers, electricians, plumbers and truck drivers. One member was a stock market executive. Members weren't required to commit crimes, and criminals in the club weren't obligated to share their scores with fellow members. Everyone, however, had to know how to keep his mouth shut.

Among the more active criminals in the Satan's Choice during the mid-1970s was Gerald Michael Vaughan of the Richmond Hill chapter. He was an odd candidate to join a biker club, since he didn't really like being around people much and he didn't even look like a biker, with his short hair and tattoo-less physique. What Vaughan did like was to steal cars, guns and pretty much anything else that wasn't nailed down and could fetch a price.

Membership in the Choice gave Vaughan a ready pool of potential partners in crime. Armand Sanguigni was a frequent one, joining

Vaughan for break-and-enters, clothing store robberies and jewellery store smash-and-grabs.

Kirby was another, and estimated he took part in more than a hundred break-and-enters, as well as auto insurance frauds. Vaughan particularly liked to steal 1962 Pontiacs, with their easy-to-change serial number tags. When the opportunity presented itself, he also got into weapons trafficking. He and Kirby once broke into the home of a Mississauga gun collector and made off with about a dozen pistols, including a .450 Webley, World War II Luger, .38 Special and 9mm Czech Star that Kirby kept for himself. Guns sold for about two hundred dollars each and were a profitable sideline for Kirby. "I used to buy a lot of guns off people who did break-and-enters. I didn't have to go out. They were coming to me with them."

Kirby helped Vaughan break into safes, at all manner of stores and offices. During one heist at a Food City grocery store, they had to improvise when the safe proved too hard to crack. "You can't open a steel cast safe, too hard," Kirby said. Instead, they'd tip them over and peel off their backs with firefighter axes.

Vaughan and Kirby went together on a drive-by shooting of the Black Diamond Riders' clubhouse on Steeles Avenue in Toronto one night, but that was more fun than business. They fired some lead into the clubhouse wall, just to piss off Johnny Sombrero. "I thought, *I don't like this guy*," Kirby said. "*He's got a really bad mouth* . . . I put about twelve shots into the house. I was aiming high . . . I just wanted to throw a scare into them."

While they were together, Kirby got an odd vibe from Vaughan, although it was nothing he could really put a finger on. "You could feel he was just a little strange," Kirby said. "He seemed to be a bit of a loner. He'd walk around talking to himself."

Once, as Vaughan was muttering unintelligibly in the Richmond Hill clubhouse, Kirby asked him what was wrong.

"He said, 'I'm just having a bad day.'"

Vaughan didn't talk about his personal issues during his time as a club member, between 1972 and 1974. He had a few. Born on December 11, 1950, he was the youngest of thirteen children in a family in which he was emotionally starved for positive attention or guidance. After his mother died of cancer when he was eight, he spent time in foster care before he was returned to his alcoholic father. His father tried to support his kids by driving a truck, then died of cirrhosis of the liver when Vaughan was fifteen.

Vaughan quit school at age sixteen, midway through Grade 9. He worked as a labourer and spent three months in the army, followed by a lot of time spent doing very little. He was unemployed when he joined the Satan's Choice at age twenty-one. He liked motorcycles and smoking and selling pot, and he'd piled up convictions for theft, assault causing bodily harm and break-and-enter, but nothing in his past suggested that he was particularly dangerous.

Still, Kirby got a hinky feeling about Vaughan, in part because Vaughan also hung around with a club member nicknamed "Duke," and Kirby had no doubts about Duke. "He's a rape hound."

There was money to be made working with Duke. He was about five-foot-four and wiry, and he was an exceptional climber who often broke into houses and robbed them while residents were sleeping. "He was a second-storey man," Kirby said. "He'd climb up balconies and apartments . . . I know that Michael Vaughan was hanging around with him . . . They went out and did some B and Es together."

Duke seemed to have frightening ideas about women. "He was always following women around Weston and Lawrence," Kirby said. "You couldn't trust him around women alone. I never wanted to leave him alone with any girlfriend I had." One shouldn't presume that all—or even most—bikers have a penchant for sexual assault. Though Sanguigni often partnered with Vaughan in criminal activities, Kirby said that Vaughan wouldn't have raped anyone in the mob killer's company. Even the hitman drew the line somewhere. "Armand Sanguigni was not the type of person to be raping women," Kirby said.

There was one club party where Kirby was certain that Duke took a woman into a bedroom and raped her. "He just walked out of the bedroom and shut the door . . . I was ready to fucking kill him for that. Another member intervened and said, 'We'll kick the shit out of him later.'"

The activities of Kirby, Vaughan, Duke and many others in the club were unknown to president Guindon. Choice membership changed often and many members were spread out, making it next to impossible to keep tabs on everyone. "We had all kinds in the club," Guindon said. "You never went to the club meetings because they're private, and if you did, it was after all of the business was closed. It was just, 'Hi, how are you, go fuck yourself.'"

Members with complaints against another member were required to make them at the chapter level first. The next level was the officers—the presidents, vice-presidents and secretaries—who met once a month. It was much more complicated than in the early days, when Guindon could turf a member on the spot. He didn't even know who they all were. "In those days, you were lucky to see the guys two times a year," Guindon said. "Maybe three times . . . Them days, you didn't get to meet a lot of the guys. If you're on a club run, everybody kind of kept to themselves, to their own chapters."

Despite the sometimes reserved welcome he received at his own club's gatherings, Guindon took pride in seeing clubhouse walls covered in patches torn from the backs of other clubs, including big ones like the Para-Dice Riders, Red Devils and Vagabonds. These displays made it clear to visitors that trying to set up shop in a Satan's Choice neighbourhood was a bad idea.

There was one patch Guindon hadn't seen on any Choice clubhouse wall, but he'd like to. The Hells Angels were rumoured to be preparing to use an underworld rounder—a sort of free agent in criminal circles—to help them establish their first chapters in Canada. When he heard the talk, Guindon threatened he would personally rip off the patch of Hells Angels' leader Ralph (Sonny) Barger if he ever showed his face in Toronto.

War was always brewing in Quebec, and the province sucked up much of Guindon's time and energy. Whenever police busted a meth lab, it created an opening for rival labs and renewed fighting for turf. There were twenty-three biker-related killings in 1974 and 1975 as bodies appeared in trailer parks, cafés, brasseries, rural fields, cottages, country roads and the St. Lawrence River. Most of the victims were bikers, but there was also a woman who knew too much and an innocent bystander. If the Popeyes had had their way, the number would have been twenty-four, with Guindon himself being one of the casualties.

Guindon was hardly surprised to hear that his club's Quebec rivals had a murder contract on his life. An Ontario biker cop told Guindon when and where the Popeyes were meeting. "He didn't give a shit," Guindon said of the cop. Guindon arrived at the meeting unannounced, wearing his Choice colours, and interrupted to say, "Let's talk."

The Popeyes didn't offer him a chair or a drink, but they didn't shoot him either. Around this time, a Popeye was found hanging by a rope in his home. Perhaps it was suicide or perhaps it was murder craftily packaged. Whatever the case, a ceasefire followed.

The Devil's Disciples had been rare and valued allies for Guindon in Montreal. But in 1975, they were finally bled dry. After fifteen members were killed in their war with the Dubois family over speed, the club disbanded. That left Guindon's Quebec chapter isolated and vulnerable.

In the mid-1970s, a massive biker wiped out his Harley during a local run with members of the Queensmen, a Windsor-area club close to the Satan's Choice. The rider wasn't badly hurt, and the incident wouldn't have been noteworthy if some of his possessions hadn't spilled across the roadway. The other bikers thought they saw police identification lying on the pavement.

The Queensman's sergeant-at-arms and another member went to check out the biker's apartment. There, they found police files on bikers and realized the guy was a cop. He was given a severe beating and lost several of his teeth to the toe of a Queensman's boot. That was the end of the undercover career of Terry Hall of the OPP. He had been trying to get his patch with the Queensmen, which would have given him the credibility to work his way into Guindon's larger, more powerful Satan's Choice.

"He was pretty smart," Guindon said of Hall, who would become all outlaw bikers' nemesis in Ontario. "I'm positive there was other [undercover] guys in all the clubs." Guindon also believed that the police had developed a fairly strong network of stool pigeons, insiders who were willing to trade information for favours. There were too many times when police knew precisely where bikers would be going on runs, even though members themselves only learned what their destination was at the last minute. "They definitely had our phones bugged," Guindon said.

The Choice now had enemies on the streets and in their clubhouses, wearing their patches. Even a calm man could be forgiven if he acted a little paranoid.

CHAPTER 25

Mountie Radar

*We didn't normally work the bikers. We happened to do this because
we wanted to get out of the office.*

Retired organized crime cop MARK MURPHY

n January 1975 two Royal Canadian Mounted Police (RCMP) officers
in Toronto went out for a cup of coffee. Mark Murphy and his partner Don (Pots) Pospeich of the national Criminal Intelligence Service
needed a break from the internecine bickering that often contaminates
police departments, just as it does biker clubhouses. The two Mounties
were anxious for a big project to get them out of the office for a while.
Maybe something involving drugs would do the trick. An investigation
into cocaine trafficking in Toronto could turn up big results if they started
pulling on strands.

Mother McEwen was caught up in some intense office politics of his
own. McEwen had invited some Chicago Outlaws up to Oshawa to
meet with Guindon and others in the Choice. McEwen wanted to forge
a more formal alliance between the two clubs. Not long after that, as a
sign they were making progress, they made up a mini-patch for both
clubs to wear: a piston overlapped with a devil's trident, under "1 %" and
the word "brotherhood."

The alliance wasn't just about the warm and fuzzy possibility of calling more hairy men "bro." It served a couple of practical purposes. The first was to block the Hells Angels from establishing chapters in Canada. The second was business. Tighter ties between the Choice and the Outlaws opened a ready southern market for Canadian-made speed.

It was around this time that McEwen introduced Guindon to Allan George Templain, who he said was from the Choice's Kitchener chapter. Templain appeared to have money and also boasted a black belt in karate. He lived in a custom-built, waterfront home in Guindon's old hometown of Sault Ste. Marie and flew a private aircraft with pontoons, so he could land it on water or land.

During his frequent runs over Lake Superior in the months that followed, Guindon stopped by a few times to see Templain at home. Something about those visits left Guindon with an uneasy feeling. "I said to myself, 'Stay the fuck away from him.' Every time I went to Thunder Bay, I'd stop there for something to do. I'd kick my ass. On the surface, he was a good guy."

Sometimes Templain and Guindon sparred, matching karate against boxing, although it never ended well for Templain. "He never liked it when I jabbed at him," Guindon said. "When I hit him, he stopped."

Templain also owned a secluded hunting lodge. Located on an island in the middle of Oba Lake, one hundred miles north of Wawa, it was surrounded by rugged bushland as far as the eye could see. Close to the lodge, hidden in the woods, was a lab he used to make phencyclidine, known on the street as PCP, angel dust, peace pills and hog. The animal tranquilizer and hallucinogen was originally developed as an anaesthetic but was withdrawn for human use because it caused convulsions.

Getting involved in the drug trade was an abrupt change of course for Guindon, who had beaten up club members for using drugs less than a decade before. But the times had changed, and he could use the money.

Bikers like Guindon, McEwen and Templain weren't yet on Murphy and Pospeich's radar. Their mandate within the RCMP was to fight organized crime, and they didn't consider the likes of Satan's Choice to be real organized crime. Bikers were rough and dangerous, but police still equated organized crime with the Mafia. If the bikers were involved in narcotics trafficking, two officers reasoned, that was an issue for the drug enforcement units.

One day, Murphy and Pospeich sat down with Sergeant Lou Nave of the RCMP drug section. Nave had a lead about someone on Danforth Avenue in Toronto's Greek neighbourhood who was suspected of delivering a weekly shipment of speed to Oshawa. He knew little about the suspect except that he drove an old white Chrysler.

Nave's lead held interesting possibilities for Murphy and Pospeich. If the man at the wheel of the old white Chrysler was indeed moving speed, then he most likely was getting his supply from a local lab. In an elevator back at their office, the two Mounties shook hands and agreed to investigate until they found that lab so that they could take out the whole organization. If they only arrested the delivery man, it would be like cutting off the head of a dandelion and then finding the pesky plants sprouting up all over your lawn the next day. They needed to bore right down to the roots and extract the entire weed.

Murphy and Pospeich cruised up and down the Danforth, looking for the Chrysler. They found a 1965 model parked in an alley behind the 2800 block of Danforth Avenue. A licence plate check showed it was owned by a man named Malcolm Raymond Bould. That name meant nothing to them. They arranged for eyeball surveillance on Bould, and also got wiretaps going. They followed him to hockey rinks and shopping centres, observing a few interactions that were clearly drug deals. At one point, the surveillance cops found themselves within a few feet of what appeared to be a drug buy. It wasn't a problem for Pospeich, in particular, whose resemblance to Hollywood tough guy Charles Bronson made him look more authentic than most bad guys. The cops seemed to go undetected as they followed their targets around Toronto, once even holding a door for one of them. They watched Bould drop packages off beside garbage pails and telephone poles.

One day, they intercepted a call Bould made to a man named Joe Prince. Exactly what they were talking about wasn't clear, but Prince certainly seemed important. On March 12, Prince led Murphy and Pospeich to the Cambridge Motor Hotel on Dixon Road, where they saw a man who became yet another target, James Mulryan. He wasn't a member of the Satan's Choice but he was connected to a few men who were. Both Mounties were surprised to suddenly see bikers entering their investigation.

With their bosses losing patience after months of surveillance and no arrests, Murphy and Pospeich tailed Mulryan to an address on Dundas Street West in Toronto. There, he met with Templain, who was accompanied by a boy who looked about ten and two other males. Mulryan drove them up Dundas Street to the Venus Spa in the downtown tenderloin district. They weren't there long before they headed to an apartment building in the far north end of the city, at 5949 Yonge Street. Neither of the Mounties knew enough about bikers yet to know they had just seen the downtown rub-and-tug where Guindon worked and the uptown apartment building where he lived.

The next day, the officers watched Templain and a second man leave the apartment building in a silver vehicle. They felt a rush when they recognized the second man as Bernie Guindon, head of the Satan's Choice and an international amateur boxer. As little as they knew about biker clubs, they knew Guindon to see him. Suddenly, their little probe had big game in its sites, and the OPP biker squad wanted in.

Including the provincial police force in their investigation offered an obvious political advantage for the two Mounties, whose bosses were constantly reminding them of the expense of their operation. If the OPP were involved, it would be a joint forces project and would be in less danger of being shut down due to lack of funds. The OPP volunteered as many as eight officers to help. Guindon was the trophy arrest they craved. Murphy and Pospeich said they only needed two additional officers for the time being. By now, they had wiretaps running on the phones of their key suspects, Guindon included.

Over the next several weeks, surveillance officers followed their targets to meetings in Toronto-area hotels and restaurants. In late March, Templain and the young boy appeared again in Toronto. The surveillance team enjoyed a pleasant night, tagging behind as they went to Maple Leaf Gardens and watched a Toronto Maple Leafs hockey game. After the game, the job became less enjoyable as they parked outside a restaurant on Yonge Street in the bitter cold, watching Templain dine inside on steak and wine.

The OPP felt it was time to arrest Mulryan, but the two Mounties still wanted to find that meth lab, as they had promised each other when the operation began.

Even while working security at a body-rub parlour to pay his bills, Guindon was pursuing his amateur boxing career with a vengeance. In April 1975, he won the all-Ontario championships at 147 pounds with a decision over Larry Llewellyn of Hamilton. He had also resumed contact with Suzanne Blais, even though they both had other partners yet again. That month, Suzanne was in hospital when she got a surprise visit from Guindon with "the largest flower arrangement I've ever received in my life." Later that month, he paid her another visit at home.

On May 6, 1975, surveillance officers at Toronto's Pearson International Airport watched discreetly as Templain disembarked Air Canada flight 429 from Montreal at 10:05 p.m. He was greeted at the airport by a man police didn't recognize. The stranger was in his mid-twenties and wore red high-top running shoes and jeans. He was carrying a yellow plastic bag and a brown tote bag.

Police identified the man as twenty-five-year-old Chuck Jones. Officers outside took a quick look in his Dodge van and found twenty thousand dollars in the glove compartment. Surveillance officers followed the van across the north end of town to Highway 404, and north to 130 Don Park Road, an inconsequential-looking industrial mall with several small businesses, including a chemical importation enterprise. The officers felt their pulses quicken. They wondered if this was the lab.

They had barely started sipping their coffee before the two targets were back in the van, this time returning west along Highway 401 to Dixon Road. There was little traffic and the police had only three surveillance cars, making it a challenge not to be noticed. At one point, Murphy pulled directly alongside the van at a red light on Dixon Road. Templain stared down at the officers from the van's passenger seat. Sensing he had to do something to lose his quarry's interest, Murphy enthusiastically picked his nose and then looked disgusted as he surveyed his findings on the tip of his finger. That was enough to get

Templain to look away until the light finally changed. The officers followed the van all the way to Niagara Street in St. Catharines, nearly an hour away, where Guindon joined their targets.

The next day, at three in the afternoon, surveillance latched on to Templain and Jones at a Yonge Street restaurant not far from Guindon's apartment building. Soon, the targets collected Guindon and returned with him to the restaurant. The mood was clearly upbeat as others joined in, with plenty of laughter. The officers marvelled that they still hadn't been spotted.

Guindon's group now included a man with pumped-up arms who held the door as the others left the restaurant. Police didn't recognize him, but the gym rat was Satan's Choice member Cecil Kirby, who was working as a speed courier then. Also present were Ken Goobie, a Para-Dice Rider named John the Hat and a man named Patty LeBlanc, whose body ended up in the trunk of a car in Vancouver years later. There was also a Montreal mobster involved in the pornography business. They were moving ten to twenty-eight pounds of yellow speed a week through the restaurant.

Guindon sometimes wondered if they were being watched, but he often felt that way. "Sometimes you get the feeling that your hair stands up on the back of your neck.

"There's something happening here. I had a funny feeling. You're always paranoid. Because you've been inside so much. You always think there's something wrong."

In May 1975, Guindon scored a technical knockout over Terry Boyd of Montreal and won the Eastern Canadian championship. If all went well, he might soon be fighting again with a Maple Leaf on his chest. The Olympics were just a little over a year away in Montreal. Even with his advancing age, Guindon still had some grim magic in his gloves.

Surveillance continued on him and Jones. In early June 1975, the officers learned that Jimmy Mulryan had built a new house on the Lake Simcoe shore in Keswick. He was living with a schoolteacher and was excited that she was expecting their first child. And Templain, meanwhile, was observed making numerous trips to his home in Sault Ste. Marie and often left packages in a locker at the Toronto airport.

Police with binoculars scanned his Oba lodge from a nearby island on June 11, 1975 and saw Templain and another man hauling garbage cans. The officers suspected the cans were filled with drugs or chemicals for making drugs. They saw men with other containers going by boat from island to island, dropping off more containers. The officers believed they had reached ground zero. This must be the lab.

A pre-dawn raid on the lodge was set for the first weekend of August 1975. Officers checked into the Oba Lake Lodge, posing as hunters. Templain was still in his bunk when the police burst in for what would prove to be the largest drug bust in Canadian history to that date, conducted jointly by the RCMP, OPP, Metro Toronto Police and U.S. DEA. They discovered less than fifty pounds of actual PCP, but 2,300 pounds of the chemicals needed to make the drug. They estimated that if it was all put to use, it would have been worth some $91 million on the street.

Even years later, Murphy insisted that Templain, Jones and Mulryan hadn't cut deals with investigators. And police simply hadn't bothered to charge Bould, Prince and Mulryan. Instead, they would be left on the street as starting points for future investigations.

Since he'd come into Murphy and Pospeich's view, the operation had focused intently on Guindon. Murphy thought he must be the mastermind, although he seemed unusually nice for a biker and was never seen packing a gun. He also didn't seem to have much money. Still, Guindon presented police with an appealing target. He wasn't wise to the ways of police surveillance after his prison stint, and he also didn't seem to appreciate that he was now a major trophy for police. "The cops have always got a police informant working around him," Kirby said. "It's a feather in some cops' hats if they can get a case against Bernie Guindon."

Police arrested Guindon in Toronto on the assumption that he was using his club to set up a distribution network. Police didn't find any guns, drugs or money. "I never got caught with any drugs whatsoever," he reflected. "There was no photo of me being at the property when he [Templain] was making the drugs or selling the drugs," he added. "He would sell all of the drugs and keep all the money. He didn't pass any on to me." When he was taken to the police station, Guindon got a chilling feeling when he saw Templain talking with police in a room. "He was there for a long fucking time."

Guindon was in the Sault Ste. Marie jail when Kirby and Frank (Cisco) Lenti of the Choice drove up to see him in the wintertime. "We froze our fucking asses off in a Chevy van," Kirby recalled.

Guindon felt that Kirby owed him money, which Kirby disputed. "I said, 'When you go to jail, you lose,'" Kirby recalled. "He said, 'We'll settle it up when I get back out.'"

Murphy was shocked to later learn that Mulryan's lifeless body was found hanging in the basement of his new home. Since he hadn't been charged, the bikers figured he was an informant. "We never charged Jimmy Mulryan and that is the biggest mistake we ever made," Murphy said. "They thought Jimmy Mulryan had been the rat in the whole thing."

Stewing in the Sault Ste. Marie jail, Guindon had problems with Templain, but he didn't know of anyone going after Mulryan. Thinking back, he didn't even remember Mulryan. And the only thing he recalled about that stint in jail was its lousy cold grilled cheese sandwiches. "I couldn't stand the fucking shit. That's why I don't eat it now."

"For the record, Mulryan was not an informant," Murphy said. Neither, he added, was Kirby.

Not yet.

CHAPTER 26

Body Seller

He sold bodies and information to the cops so he could get higher up . . .
That's how I got nailed.

BERNIE GUINDON on Garnet (Mother) McEwen

uindon's mother didn't go to his trial and that's what he wanted. She didn't need to see her boy sitting in court as a prisoner or hear prosecutors say how he was part of a massive drug ring that stretched down to Florida.

Special Crown prosecutor Frank Caputo characterized the ring as "a marriage of chemical expertise and a distribution system in both Canada and the United States."

The jury heard how U.S. Special Agent Kenneth Paterson of Buffalo infiltrated the group, and his description of how Templain brought drugs to Wisconsin several times.

Templain's lawyer Roy Youngson said his client "was nowhere near the top of the ladder in this system," even though the lab was on his island property and he travelled to the United States, Toronto and Montreal to distribute the drugs. "He is a self-styled big shot, a con man who has a broken-down airplane and who had the gall to tell a special U.S. narcotics agent he could deliver drugs anywhere in the world," Youngson said. "He was not the foundation of this thing but was a man who liked money and was a hopeful participant."

Without actually saying Guindon's name, Youngson pointed a finger in his direction, contending it would have taken a large group with the muscle and reach of the Satan's Choice to run the drug channel. Youngson also argued that the drugs were worth $63,000, not the mega-millions stated by police and splashed across headlines. In the end, Judge William Fitzgerald sentenced Templain to twelve years after he pleaded guilty to conspiracy to traffic in narcotics.

Guindon wasn't about to cut a deal. Like the fighter he was, he would tough it out in court and see where that left him. As he awaited trial, he didn't help his case when authorities intercepted a letter he wrote from behind bars, suggesting that his fortunes would improve if something happened to silence an American DEA agent who was key to the case. The fact that Guindon was the leader of one of the world's largest outlaw motorcycle gangs further tainted the court's impression of him. Police assumed that his status was proof enough that he was setting up a drug distribution network. "Guindon was the overall coordinator of everything," Murphy said, still convinced forty years later. "He was the overall boss of everything."

Guindon didn't believe the case against him was particularly strong, especially compared to the one against Templain. "I never got fuck all. That sonofabitch got everything. If he gave me anything, it wouldn't be more than a thousand bucks," said Guindon.

He was convinced he could also smell a sellout from Mother McEwen, somewhere in the background of the mess: "He sold bodies and information to the cops so he could get higher up . . . That's how I got nailed. He introduced me to Allan Templain." Whatever the case, Guindon bore the brunt of the operation. Ironically, the man who helped set and enforce the Choice's policy against hard drug use took the hardest fall in a major drug bust. In May 1976, he was sentenced to seventeen years for conspiracy to traffic in phencyclidine, five years longer than Templain, the man who drew him into the scheme.

Two months after Guindon's return to prison, Canada hosted its first-ever Summer Olympic Games. Without the drug beef, Guindon could well have starred on the Canadian boxing team. He would be into his forties or possibly even fifties by the time he got out of prison, depending on the parole board. His Olympic dream was effectively snuffed out. A tougher fight was just beginning.

In July 1976, Guindon returned to Millhaven. He didn't even bother watching the Olympics on television. It was as if the Games were in a far-flung place, in a faraway, inaccessible world, and not just a few hours down Highway 401, in Montreal.

Inside, time seemed to have stood still since Guindon's last mandatory visit. He was quickly reacquainted with his old cronies.

"It was like old home week," he said. A lot of the men were lifers, and some of them didn't really know how to survive on the streets, where they weren't provided with wake-up calls, meals, clothing, a job and a certain level of security. "You get fed, you get clothed and you've got a little money for canteen. You get institutionalized and they're bums on the street. They steal irons and toasters and televisions." The regimented life of a penitentiary suited them. "They've got three meals a day. They've got a roof over their heads."

Guindon didn't want his mother to visit him in prison, just as he didn't want her at his trials. "What are you going to say to her? She worked all of her life hoping you wouldn't go to jail." He focused instead on what was essential for his survival, like quickly determining whom he could trust. He heard that one of the Millhaven guards was a striker for the Choice chapter in Kingston. That broke the rules of both the bikers and the authorities. The guard clearly wanted to talk but Guindon wondered if he was working undercover against the club. Talking with any guard was always dangerous anyway, so he steered clear of the man. "You've got to be careful how you're talking to a guard. An inmate who might not like you might say, 'Look at him. He might be squealing.'"

During the first year of his sentence, Guindon heard that his former sidekick Big Jack (Bear) Olliffe had been shot dead. Big Jack had been working as a bouncer at the Cadillac Hotel, the notorious bucket of blood on Simcoe Street South in Oshawa where Guindon's father had once bounced and hung out.

On the last evening of his life, Big Jack made a fatal mistake. He tried to eject long-time Choice member Terry Siblock from the Cadillac for drunkenness. Siblock was the same man Big Jack had wrongly called a stool pigeon repeatedly over the past ten years. Such words aren't easily forgiven or forgotten on Simcoe Street South, and Siblock decided he had been hearing the insult long enough. He left the bar to pick up a .306 rifle, returned, and silenced Big Jack's slanderous lie forever. There were plenty of witnesses, but that just didn't matter to Siblock. As everyone there could plainly see, he wasn't willing to hear Big Jack badmouth him one more time. Guindon understood Siblock's feelings, even though he liked Big Jack well enough. "I don't know how the guy put up with it. He finally snapped. Said, 'Enough of this shit. Enough is enough.'"

Big Jack's death wasn't a total surprise to Guindon, even without the Siblock situation. "I figured that was coming sooner or later. He was acting as national president. It was going to his head. Nobody paid much respect to him."

Looking across the Detroit River from Windsor, Ontario, it's hard to imagine the Detroit cityscape is any more than a strong swim away, let alone in another country. In early 1977, the Outlaws and the Satan's Choice met secretly in Windsor to put even less distance between them.

On the Canadian side, only Satan's Choice chapters believed to be loyal to Mother McEwen were invited. As the Outlaws' war with the Angels raged on in the United States, the American club needed to boost its ranks, and it wanted to fill them with members of the Satan's Choice—and not the ones preoccupied with keeping their club Canadian.

Thunder Bay members took notice that bonds between clubs solidified when their old friend Howard (Pigpen) Berry hooked up with the Outlaws in the United States. "After Howard went to the OLs [Outlaws], it opened the door for even more association/biz," Verg Erslavas wrote in his reflections on the era. "By the mid-70s, we were tight with the OLs in many ways."

Not all Choice members had agreed to wear the Outlaw-Choice brotherhood patch, a sign that tensions were building within the Canadian club. "A lot of the guys were patriotic, surprisingly," Erslavas said. "'No Yankee shit on my colours.'"

There was a lot more to joining the Outlaws than just switching patches. For a biker, patching over to another club meant a profound culture shift. The Americans even rode a different model of Harley. Everything about the Outlaws was more rigid, aggressive, loud and in your face. "They were a different kind of club than the Choice. Some of the guys I met were from Detroit, Carolinas, Florida, Tennessee and other states. A lot of them rode rigid-framed choppers with open primary chains, which was a statement in itself by the mid-70s."

Behind bars, Guindon was livid when he heard about the meeting—and what happened next. In March 1977, the St. Catharines and Windsor chapters of the Choice joined the Outlaws, with Hamilton, Montreal and Ottawa following shortly afterwards. Toronto, Oshawa, Kitchener, Peterborough and Kingston remained loyal to Guindon's vision of an independent Canadian club. With that, the Outlaws beat the Hells Angels across the border and became the first international outlaw motorcycle club with Canadian chapters.

In the summer of 1977 the new Canadian Outlaws gathered to party with their American brothers at Crystal Beach, near Buffalo. They burned their Satan's Choice grinning devil patches and accepted the skull and crossed pistons patch of the Outlaws. They also adopted smaller patches that read, "RIP Satan's Choice MC."

Guindon fumed about Mother McEwen's betrayal. Frustrated at his own helplessness, he sat in his cell and pounded out leather craft with a little hammer. "I couldn't do nothing about it. Fuck was I mad. Especially at him. Stool pigeon motherfucker."

Guindon thought about his discomfort around McEwen since the first time they'd met in St. Catharines. "I had a negative feeling. I always get these feelings with some people. Maybe it's a natural feeling. Be careful. Be cautious." Part of the reason was that McEwen didn't even look like a real biker. "He looked like a fucking hippie. I thought, What's this guy looking for? He had a head shop."

The Hells Angels responded quickly to the Outlaws' expansion. On December 5, 1977, the Angels landed in Montreal. They patched over thirty-five members of the Popeyes, whose ranks included killers like Yves (Apache) Trudeau. The Popeyes had travelled south to party with Angels charters (the Hells Angels are divided into local charters, not chapters as other clubs are) on the Eastern Seaboard for years. Now they were part of something much bigger. They could dream now about expansion, not just survival.

The Satan's Choice had been the mightiest of the Canadian clubs when there were no international clubs in the country. Now, within only months of each other, the two most powerful American-based clubs had set up shop on Canadian soil, and the Choice's very survival was threatened. The dam was bursting and Guindon couldn't do a thing but tap away at his leather craft and hope the remnants of his club had the nerve to stand their ground.

CHAPTER 27

The Big Split

*I don't like to say anything bad about anybody, but Garnet McEwen—
he was a backstabbing fucking prick.*

Former Satan's Choice member VERG ERSLAVAS

Cecil Kirby quit the Satan's Choice in a dispute over pizza with a member named Billy the Bum. Shortly before the big patchover to the Outlaws, Kirby felt he was being threatened by someone who was involved with him in motorcycle insurance scams, and he wanted the Bum to watch his backside while he went into a home to sort things out. Billy the Bum replied that he couldn't at the moment because he had just ordered a pizza. That meant Kirby didn't get the backup (or any pizza), and he quit the biker club in disgust. Not long after that, the Commisso crime family reached out to him to do some work as an enforcer.

Around this time, someone pulled up outside Mother McEwen's home in St. Catharines and opened fire on him. McEwen considered his survival a miracle, and he credited it to a higher power rather than poor marksmanship. "That's when I seen the Lord," he later said.

Something bigger than patches was changing as international clubs were pushing into Canada. A love of motorcycles and riding wasn't always at the core of life in outlaw motorcycle gangs now. Clubs revolved around business. "I don't think the cops were ready for what happened afterwards, and they were certainly powerless to stop it," Erslavas said. "After 1977, it became a much different game."

Outlaw bikers had become an increased priority for police fighting organized crime. In June 1977, Inspector William Sherman of the RCMP told the press that 75 percent of drug trafficking in Ontario was controlled by biker clubs. As if to support his case, in August 1977, police seized more than a million dollars' worth of drugs during raids in Toronto, Kingston, Wasaga Beach, Hamilton and other communities. Most of the people arrested were Satan's Choice and Vagabonds.

Surprisingly, and to the chagrin of some of the remaining Satan's Choice, the club maintained relations with the American Outlaws, and their fugitive exchange program continued. It was an uneasy balance, as the remaining Choice members valued their independence while the Outlaws wanted to further their expansion onto Canadian soil.

While Guindon languished in Millhaven, a couple of American newcomers appeared in St. Catharines. They seemed to ask too many questions, with the story that they were fleeing American charges relating to vaguely explained gun crimes. They were turned away by other Choice members who weren't convinced by their stories. "You never know who the fuck they are," Guindon said. "They're going from chapter to chapter. They could be anybody. They could be a police officer. Undercover . . . He might be a pigeon . . . You always wonder."

One visitor who came to Southern Ontario under the mutual aid pact with the Outlaws was Harry Bowman of Detroit. He was known inside the biker world as "Taco" because of his Hispanic appearance, and authorities also knew him as Harry Bouman, David Bowman, Harry J. Bowman, Harry Joseph Bowman, Harry Joe Bowman, David Charles Dowman, Harry Douman, Harry Tyree and "T." Whatever the name he was using at the time, he was always recognizable by the multiple tattoos covering his body, including a skull and crossbones with crossed pistons and the words "Outlaws" and "Detroit," and a swastika and a Merlin the magician figure on his forearms.

Bowman became chapter president of the Detroit Outlaws in 1970 when he was just twenty-one, and rose up to become north regional president later in the decade. He moved about Motor City in an armour-plated Cadillac and later developed a war wagon with gun ports and bulletproof panels and glass. Often appearing psychotic and paranoid, he could also be charming and accommodating.

Bowman was at the Kitchener Choice clubhouse when Oshawa member Lorne Campbell got into a near punch-up with another American Outlaw named Brillo, who had ridden up from Nashville with a stripper. Brillo's Harley Panhead broke down, and Kitchener Choice members were rebuilding its engine when Brillo got word that an Outlaw had been killed in the United States. The news meant he needed to rush back to Tennessee. Before he departed, Brillo left his old lady with Campbell, telling him, "Look after her. I don't care if you fuck her. Just make sure she's not abused."

"I gave her a couple," Campbell said, referring to consensual sex. True to his word, he also found her work as a stripper and made sure nobody gave her any trouble. Brillo returned to Kitchener and started grumbling. "I left my old lady with Lorne and he ended up fucking her," he said during a visit to the clubhouse. Sitting in the television room, Campbell overheard the Outlaw's complaint. He stormed out of the room, grabbed Brillo and growled, "I'm gonna throw this mother-fucker down the stairs!" There was a certain amount of protocol involved even when tossing someone down a staircase, so Campbell added, "Go get Taco!"

As he waited, Campbell drove Brillo's head against the wall. Bowman quickly materialized, mollifying Campbell and saving Brillo from a bumpy descent to the main floor. "He was a nice guy," Campbell said of Bowman.

Though he wouldn't hear of the incident until much later, Guindon always appreciated how Campbell wasn't about to be pushed around by the Americans. There was a fine line to be walked with the Outlaws, and the imprisoned Choice leader could only hope that others like Campbell would keep their club alive until his return.

The Choice were far from finished after the big patchover. They were left with approximately two hundred members at the end of 1977, a drop of about a hundred from the club's heyday a decade earlier. Guindon had suspected the worst about Mother—"He was a stool pigeon"—and now those suspicions seemed confirmed. McEwen realized that the international Outlaws would be a more attractive target for police than the Choice, so he led his club there to improve the price of his co-operation. "That was why he went Outlaws."

In the wake of McEwen's treachery, feelings among the Choice were raw, akin to when a family is torn apart. "Every single chapter had to make the choice," Erslavas said. "Each chapter had to make the call, and each member had to make their own call." Some chapters, like Ottawa, split right down the middle, with an equal number of members deciding to keep their old patch and members deciding to switch.

"I don't like to say anything bad about anybody, but Garnet McEwen—he was a backstabbing fucking prick," Erslavas continued. "Mother was in it for his own personal reasons . . . his own gain. He thought there was a payday in it for him. Probably the biggest reason was [the Choice who switched] thought they had something to gain from doing business with the Outlaws. There was nothing noble about it."

Up in Thunder Bay, there were a half-dozen locals and three members from Ottawa in the chapter. It seemed to be fizzling away, and there was no return date scheduled for Guindon, who could revive things. "There was no way we were going to go Yankee, go Outlaw," Erslavas said. "We decided to fold up, up there . . . Maybe we felt after that there wasn't a future there. We let the guys know. They understood and respected it.

"I myself struggled. I loved the club. When I joined, I truly thought I had found my station in life. In 1977, I was only six years in and I didn't want to quit what I thought was the best thing that had ever happened to me. At that time, it was the toughest choice of my life. I then had to write the letter to Bernie, who was still in jail, and tell him about our decision. Believe me, that was tough. We all signed it, but I recall I wrote it. I looked up to Bernie, and it was hard to find the words."

Thunder Bay members made a trip down to Windsor during the time that was known as "The Big Split." They were in the border city to pick up a couple of motorcycles that were being worked on by a custom painter, and stopped by the old Choice clubhouse. This time, the familiar home-away-from-home feeling was gone. The clubhouse and the men inside it had been stripped of anything to do with the Satan's Choice, and the crest of the Outlaws, with its skull and crossed pistons, was everywhere. "Things were tense, to say the least," Erslavas said. "Some of the guys were packing side arms openly—the same guys who a couple of weeks before were our brothers."

Mother McEwen was at the clubhouse, which only made a tense situation tenser. "Some words were exchanged, but I couldn't really speak my mind," Erslavas said. "To do so then would have been foolish. I think the only reason we walked out without anything happening was because we knew some of the Windsor guys pretty well and there was certainly some mutual respect." That mutual respect didn't extend to McEwen, as far as Erslavas was concerned. "As for Mother, well, he was a piece of shit to sell out. I think everyone on both sides agreed."

Soon, there was word that Mother McEwen had fled west with a contract on his head. He had been kicked out of the club for embezzlement. Now he was considered a traitor, a stool pigeon and a thief—all good reasons for getting stomped on or shot in the biker world. Guindon heard from behind bars that Mother had weathered a severe beating, which made Guindon jealous. "They beat him with his wooden leg. I wish I would have."

Bernie Guindon, right, with his older brother, Jack.

Their father, bootlegger Lucienne Guindon.

A couple of French Canadians growing up in Oshawa. Guindon and Suzanne Blais, 1958.

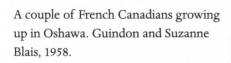

Guindon learning his notorious
left hook in the ring.

Guindon (lower right) in the Oshawa Boxing Club.

The Satan's Choice
Motorcycle Club
rides as one, 1969.

Satan's Choice motorcyclists shred chicken during field day

At one end of the farm field stood a very nervous chicken.

At the other end, 60 members of the Satan's Choice Motorcycle Club revved the engines of their machines, then at a signal, roared off.

It was a chicken race, a new game and a feature of the Oshawa Club's annual field day Sunday near Nestleton, north east of Oshawa.

The race was over in seconds. A motorcycle wheel killed the chicken and the cyclists dived for it. The winner came up with the prize: the largest chunk of bloody chicken—the neck and half the breast.

A number of chicken racers were bruised in a 30-cycle pileup during the rush for the fleeing bird but the blood that spattered them all came from the chicken. "A lot of people didn't want to eat afterward," a member said.

"I bet the humane society wouldn't like it," said Oshawa branch president Bernard Guindon, "but it was a lot of fun."

Bernard Guindon, 25, president of Oshawa chapter of Satan's Choice, holds result of chicken race at field day.

The Chicken Race makes the
news (*The Globe and Mail*,
August 6, 1968).

Wild Thing.

Guindon puts his fists to work representing his country.

Captain of Team Canada, touring Scandinavia in 1971.

Rod MacLeod (centre) and the Montreal Satan's Choice. (Ian Watson photo)

Garnet "Mother" McEwan, who led the SCMC in Guindon's absence, straight into the arms of the American Outlaws.

SCMC heavyweights Armand (In the Trunk) Sanguini and Howard (Pigpen) Berry, wearing his dead-skunk boutonniere.

Pigpen looking normal—and to his peers, more dangerous.

Montreal hitman Yves (Apache) Trudeau.

Training with a mountain of a man at Stony Mountain Penitentiary.

Boxing in Millhaven.

Out again, with Lorne Campbell (left) and Bill (Mr. Bill) Lavoie.

Growing up in Oshawa as ordinarily as possible, Harley Davidson Guindon.

Guindon marries the woman he could never forget, Suzanne Blais.

Two constants in a tumultuous life, Guindon's mother, Albini (Lucy) Guindon, and Suzanne Blais-Guindon.

Prison pal, John Mazzotti.

Harley, his dad and Montrealer Gregory Woolley.

The prison record Harley never wants erased.

Fighters and friends, Guindon with Canadian heavyweight champ George Chuvalo.

An enemy so long he became a friend. Johnny Sombrero died in 2016.

CHAPTER 28

Prison Blues

You just sit in the dark. It's just a hole. You're just in a square box. You wouldn't know what fucking time of day it was.

BERNIE GUINDON on prison punishment

Despite his extinguished hopes for Olympic glory, Guindon worked out harder than ever. Prisoners in Millhaven had at least an hour a day to work out in the yard, triple the time available during his days in the Kingston Penitentiary. "You had time to work out," Guindon said. "Put your mind in a different perspective. When you're getting yourself in shape, doing the exercise, you're getting away from the institution." He made a commitment to get in top shape for the distant day when he would again walk free. This would be his own personal Olympics. It would also help him cope with the upheaval in the Satan's Choice and survive until his sentence expired. "I'd try to mind my own business and watch over our own guys. What else could you do? I'd work out so I could take care of myself."

Guindon devised a punishing workout program to increase his core strength. It involved doing sit-ups while holding heavy weights and gradually decreasing the amount of weight. The most he managed was 350 pounds, almost 200 pounds more than his own weight. "Nobody picked up more weight than I did for a sit-up. Man, that was heavy. I'd have a guy sitting on my legs and I'd almost pick him up."

Like many boxers, Guindon avoided free weights. Muscle-bound fighters look tough, but their punches don't snap and cut as they should. In the Millhaven prison yard, free weights were also dangerous, in particular around the bench press. "Guys will come by and drop weights right on you. Drop a two-hundred-pound weight right on your chest. Whoop! Right on your chest. I've seen it."

Guindon prided himself on taking care of his own problems inside, like the time someone smacked him in the head with a steel bar. "I did get even with him. I think I dropped a weight on him." Guindon knew enough to mind his own business when trouble started in the yard, but sometimes he couldn't. Sometimes men he considered brothers were involved. Behind bars, bikers tended to hang together in the yard, even when they were from different clubs. "You'd look after them. They'd look after you. It works both ways." That sense of fraternity extended even to some Outlaw inmates he met inside. "I didn't have any problems with them. I had a good name."

One of Guindon's closest buddies was John Mazzotti, president of the Windsor-based Lobos, who served time with him in Collins Bay and Millhaven. "He was just a solid guy that watched your back if you watched his. A good biker." With friends like Mazzotti, Guindon would sometimes say they "had to hang T," prison talk for "stay cool and keep things together."

Guindon also knew the mob guys, from a distance. "I never paid attention to them. Most of them seemed to think their shit didn't smell. They didn't want to hang with you. Joe Dinardo (a boxer) used to be with those guys all of the time. He was always with the Mafia guys." During Guindon's first prison stint, mob guys were openly hostile toward bikers, but that had relaxed somewhat. Both groups had come to understand the other group had power and could be useful. "They had a lot of long arms, so to speak. They used to pay a lot of people to do their dirty work."

Danger behind bars often came at unexpected times from unexpected people. "There are a lot of crazy fuckers in there. They get paid by somebody else that don't like you. I had the problem once. I remember giving him a shot or two," said Guindon. The attackers were often addicts, paid in drugs, or men of little status in the hierarchy of inmates. "They send the idiots, the ones already doing life. They've got nobody visiting them, no family. They're just left in there. They're just vegetables."

About two and a half years into Guindon's sentence, his lawyer was able to reduce his sentence from seventeen to twelve years. It was now possible to think ahead to the day when he would be set free, and he pushed to upgrade his employment potential. He wanted to take a course to learn upholstery, and when he couldn't get in, he went on a hunger strike. That lasted a couple of weeks, but the smell of food was starting to get to him. Then he retched and coughed up a tapeworm, which mystified and disgusted him. "I was so fucked up. How do you get a tapeworm? It don't make sense to me. You wonder, *What the fuck's happening?*"

Despite the toll prison was taking on his health, it was bringing his leadership instincts to the fore. He was made an honorary member of the Allied Indian and Métis Society and was voted head of the prisoners' committee. There, he became friendly with prisoner and author Roger Caron, who served with him on the inmate committee. Caron was a fellow bootlegger's son whose father also beat him in his youth. By the time Caron published his Governor General's Literary Award–winning prison memoir, *Go-Boy!*, in 1978, he had spent twenty-three of his thirty-nine years behind bars. Guindon liked Caron but they didn't hang out together, Caron "being a straight john—somebody not into the motorcycle world."

Though he was separated from his Harley, Guindon never turned his back on the fact that he was a biker. He felt that bikers were discriminated against when it came to getting passes to leave the prison, and he raised his concern during a visit from Solicitor General Robert Kaplan. "I told him right straight out in front of the warden that if the discrimination didn't stop, we would start tearing the walls apart."

Not long after that, Guindon and fellow inmates literally did tear the walls apart. During a riot, they broke up bed frames and used the metal to carve holes between cells. There were eighteen cells on a range, and they busted a passageway between all of them. When order was restored, authorities installed quarter-inch steel between the cells to prevent it from happening again. Exactly what triggered the riot wasn't clear, but a precise reason wasn't needed. "It was just about stupidity. We didn't want to smash up, but you've got to follow the leader sometimes."

The riot landed Guindon in the box, a windowless cage in the middle of the yard, with a tin for a toilet and no light. It didn't take long in there before he lost track of day and night. The closest thing to a human interaction he experienced was someone slipping a bologna sandwich through the door. "It's not a happy place to be. All you do is think about what you're going to do. What you've been through. Are you going to behave? You just sit in the dark. It's just a hole. You're just in a square box. You wouldn't know what fucking time of day it was. You roasted. You had no clothes. You just had your shorts on."

On happier days, when he was back in his usual cell, Guindon resumed work on his crafts, making tap, tap, tap sounds on metal or leather late into the night. Sometimes, the persistent noise and his flashlight annoyed other prisoners and they asked him to stop. He did. Other times, when no one seemed to mind, he kept on tapping.

In May 1979, he was transferred to nearby Joyceville. There, he tried to teach others how to do leatherwork. One of his students was his cousin Maurice (Bullfrog) Guindon from Hull, who was serving time for theft. Guindon had become a sort of craft master, having won seven national awards for his leatherwork. Bullfrog was a rank beginner, who hadn't been the same since he caught a bullet in the head in a Quebec pool hall. He was further hampered by losing half the fingers on one hand to gangrene. While he remained a nice guy, Bullfrog was clearly not master craftsman material. "He was fucking useless, him and Tom the Wop," Guindon recalled. "He was in the Vagabonds. I'd just lose it on them. They drove me fucking nuts. I had a year in with them. It felt like five years."

While Bullfrog was a bust at leatherwork, he did have a black belt in karate and understood exercise. He helped Guindon with his physical training, using a broom handle to smack him in the stomach as he continued to obsess about making his abs preternaturally strong.

Some of Guindon's energy went into making leather key fobs with

"Free Bernie Guindon" on them for his brother, Jack, to sell. There was also something special for his daughter Debbie Donovan on her eleventh birthday: a matching purse and wallet set with a little tiger and "Debbie" on the strap. A string of roses adorned the wallet. He sent the gift to her grandmother's house in Oshawa. When Debbie opened the wallet, she found fifty dollars inside with a note explaining it was bad luck to give one that was empty. "Back in those days, my mom was a bootlegger," Debbie recalled, "and money was tight." At one point, Debbie's mother had two booze cans running, one on Elena Street in Oshawa, just a few minutes' walk from where Guindon's father had sold illegal liquor. Like Guindon, with whom she frequently corresponded, she didn't drink.

Debbie spent the money her father sent on new clothes. They had always been close, though at her age, she'd never visited him in custody and he never spoke about prison life in his letters to her. Instead, he told his daughter that he missed her and asked how she was doing. He never apologized. Without deliberate irony, he advised her to stay in school and behave. He signed his letters with "SWAKAH" for "sealed with a kiss and hug."

Debbie tucked the purse and wallet set away in a safe spot. "It's gorgeous but I never used it. I still have it. It was more sentimental."

In late 1979, Guindon was transferred again, this time to Collins Bay, an aging medium-security correctional facility in Kingston. It was unusual for a prisoner's security to be upgraded to Collins Bay from lower-security Joyceville as his sentence progressed, leading Guindon to suspect he was the target of a prison snitch. "Maybe they figured out I was selling drugs."

Prisoners had a choice of drugs while inside: hashish, cocaine, methamphetamines or angel dust. Marijuana was generally too bulky to smuggle in. "I used to have a guard bring in some of my stuff," Guindon said. "I'd have somebody pay the guard on the street." Sometimes, the payment was made with cheap companionship. "The guys would get them a broad," Guindon said. "She'd get him the dope and get lucky with him."

In addition to leatherwork, Guindon learned a new craft to help mellow out his remaining time inside. He called his serendipitous new creation "Frog Logs," cigarette papers drenched in hashish and marijuana oil. "It was an accident," Guindon explained. He was rolling hash papers to sell to prisoners when he caught wind that a guard was coming by. He quickly hid about a hundred papers, but when he retrieved them, they were hopelessly stuck together. "I had a hundred or so papers and I had to do something." He squeezed them together into a giant joint and then sliced it into one-eighth-inch segments, like coins. Extra potent and easy to hide, they proved to be a hit with customers.

A guard once told Guindon that he wanted everyone to quit smoking up. That was akin to telling senior management at Harley-Davidson to stop making touring bikes and focus on mopeds.

"Would you rather see everyone on Valium?" Guindon asked.

"Forget I ever asked," the guard replied.

Though Guindon's reduced living conditions weren't enough to push him to prison moonshine, he did indulge in hash oil. Even a devoted teetotaller needed some help, once in a while, settling his nerves. "Smoking relaxed me. You're doing big fucking time. You go, 'Holy fuck, am I ever going to get out of this?' You've got a lot of maniacs in there who don't like club bikers. It didn't take much to walk by and stick a knife in you." Guindon also dropped acid, a drug he only used in prison. "I only did it in jail. I never did it on the street. I used to go on my own vacation, so to speak. Go on a holiday. Take a trip. I probably did more drugs in two months in the joint than I ever did on the street."

Sports provided another outlet. He played defence on an inmate hockey team. "I was fairly good," he said. "In defence, you're in more fights than playing forward. You're hitting the guys more. I wasn't a fast skater." He was also a catcher on a baseball team. A high point in his prison athletics career was when he managed to score a home run on a bunt, through a combination of hustle, poor fielding and a thunderous collision with the opposing catcher.

Despite the drugs, sports, politics and crafting, Guindon was still best known behind bars as a boxer, and a dangerous one at that. "He had that killer instinct," Hamilton street gang member George McIntyre said.

"He had power, he had speed, and blood did not dissuade him at all. You had to kill him to beat him. There was no quit in him." McIntyre remembered Guindon particularly shining on Friday nights, when inmates would play floor hockey. "Anytime you played floor hockey, somebody was getting knocked out. On Friday night, somebody got knocked out, and the person usually knocking them out was Bernie. In an environment like that, Bernie was king. Nobody could touch him."

Back in Oshawa, Guindon's eldest child, Teresa, got her driver's licence when she turned sixteen. She also became the proud owner of a yellow 1969 Mustang.

She drove it to a friend's apartment, which was in a house that had been split into several units. Outside, a smiling stranger who looked to be in his early thirties approached her, saying he knew her father from prison and that he had a box of letters and cards from him that she might like to see. Her father was somewhat of a mystery to her, since she'd been raised in her maternal grandparents' home. "My mother wouldn't tell me a lot about my dad. I'm sixteen. I'm all excited. I'm finally going to find all about my dad."

Minutes after entering his apartment, she realized she was the victim of a horrible deception. "None of this was true. There were no cards and letters." The stranger surprised and overwhelmed her as soon as they were alone. "I put up a good fight but I lost it." He severely injured her wrist in the struggle, but other damage was far worse. "I was a good girl. I wanted to save my virginity for my husband. He stole stuff from me that I couldn't get back." Another man entered the apartment, and Teresa felt he was about to rape her too, but she managed to run away.

She could feel something changing inside her. It wasn't pleasant, but it did feel necessary. "After that rape, I was tough," Teresa said. "I wasn't a bully, but I didn't put up with crap. After you've had bad things done, you become hard. You shut your heart down. I didn't give a crap about anybody . . . I didn't tell my mom for the longest time. I didn't tell anybody."

She only told her mother after she heard a rumour that the man who raped her had venereal disease. Her mother took her to a gynecologist, where she learned she did not have the infection. The experience was humiliating, nonetheless.

Word of the attack filtered back to Guindon, who called her from prison.

"I'll take care of it," he said.

"Don't," she replied. "I don't want that man's blood on my hands. Don't do anything. Don't touch him."

Guindon had faced down some tough men for the honour of his club. He'd have done the same for his daughter in a heartbeat, so it wasn't easy to hear Teresa call him off. But he wouldn't want people making decisions about his life for him.

"I will respect your wishes."

CHAPTER 29

Quiet Expansion

He was a stand-up kid at seventeen.

BERNIE GUINDON on Oshawa Satan's Choice member Lorne Campbell

The first time Cecil Kirby saw Wolodumyr Walter (Nurget) Stadnick of Hamilton was in the summer of 1977 at Wasaga Beach. Stadnick had just graduated from a local teen motorcycle club called the Cossacks to the Wild Ones, who were making a name for themselves at the time with their mob ties. They had helped Mafia families undertake a flurry of bombings of bakeries and other small businesses, which earned Hamilton the nickname "Bomb City."

Kirby thought Stadnick was trying too hard to look like a badass biker. "I didn't like him," Kirby said. "I thought he was sort of a poser." It wasn't until later that Kirby realized his initial impression was wrong. Stadnick was the real deal, from head to toe.

Somewhere along the line, Stadnick picked up the nickname "Nurget." Usually, there's no mystery to biker nicknames. It's easy to imagine what inspired the likes of Pigpen, Tiny, Crash, Slash, Boxer and Skid Mark. But no one beyond Stadnick himself had a clue what "Nurget" meant, and he refused to tell. What is known is that Stadnick is the five-foot-four son of a tree cutter who worked for the City of Hamilton. Born on August 3, 1952, he had two older brothers, but neither was a hardcore biker. By the time he crossed paths with Cecil Kirby, Stadnick had settled into a solid home on East Hamilton Mountain, not far from where he grew up. He kept rock star hours, seldom rising before noon. He worked out regularly and was fit if not physically imposing. He abstained altogether from smoking and narcotics, and drank only in moderation. His icy stare rarely devolved into anger, and never into the psychotic flashes displayed by some outlaw bikers. Even to an enemy, Stadnick seldom raised his voice or even said anything memorable. Years later, a police officer was asked how Stadnick could function in Quebec when he didn't really speak French. The officer replied that Stadnick didn't speak much English either.

Stadnick preferred to listen and watch rather than talk over others. He was able to draw advice from a wide range of people, from drug dealers to professionals, without appearing threatened. He was clearly a man much bigger than the sum of his parts. As Guindon weathered his second prison stretch, Stadnick quietly set off a chain of events that would one day make the Choice leader's world nearly unrecognizable.

On the night of October 18, 1978, Bill Matiyek of the tiny Golden Hawks biker club was shot dead in a bar in Port Hope, east of Oshawa. Authorities called it a cold-blooded execution, but Satan's Choice members called it self-defence and a defining moment for their club, especially its Oshawa and Kitchener chapters. Lorne Campbell of the Satan's Choice said he shot Matiyek that day to protect his biker brothers, that Matiyek was about to open fire, and Campbell and others left the bar alive only because he was faster on the trigger.

After a sloppy police investigation and trial based on questionable testimony, a half-dozen bikers went to prison for the killing, but not Campbell, despite his confession. Guindon had known Campbell since he was a seventeen-year-old and was impressed but not surprised that Campbell stepped up and said he pulled the trigger. "He was a stand-up kid at seventeen . . . That took a lot of balls. That's why Oshawa had such a good name."

One of the men convicted for the Matiyek killing was David (Tee Hee)

Hoffman of the Kitchener Choice. He served a couple years for the shooting before police wiretaps surfaced that revealed he was far from Port Hope the day Matiyek was shot. Even though Hoffman was serving time for a crime he didn't commit, he didn't say a word against Campbell or anyone else.

Guindon was impressed by everything he heard about Hoffman, whom he considered quiet, extremely strong, popular and well mannered. Hoffman didn't use his status in a biker club to bully anyone either—something that was big in Guindon's books. "He was a helluva guy. Never bothered nobody. I don't think he used his patch." It was also a point of pride for Guindon that no one ratted on any other club member, and that Hoffman stayed quiet, even when he was wrongfully sent to prison. "How many guys would do that? I was very proud of them." They reminded Guindon of why he became a biker in the first place.

The year 1979 was shaping up to be a particularly tense one. On Saturday, June 23, 1979, police in Hamilton swooped in on the Outlaws, Wild Ones and Red Devils, seizing LSD, marijuana, speed, shotguns and rifles. Meanwhile, the Outlaws and Hells Angels continued to jockey for power in Canada. Staff Superintendent Bruno Dorigo, head of the OPP's criminal intelligence branch, didn't see peace on the horizon. "Our sources and undercover agents tell us these two clubs are battling for supremacy in the province," Dorigo told the press. "There have been several killings in Quebec [from biker rivalry] and now it's spilling into Ontario."

Tensions played out on both sides of the international border, as guns were sent north and drugs went south. Perhaps that explained why at least one hitman entered a small house on Allen Road South in Charlotte, North Carolina, sometime between two and five in the morning on July 4, 1979. The shotgun-wielding intruder managed to kill a guard who had been posted outside on a chair, and then made it inside to where three men and a woman connected to the local Outlaws were resting.

When the chapter president arrived later that morning, he found no signs of struggle on the lifeless body of the guard. He had clearly been caught by surprise. There were also no signs of resistance on the other four bodies inside the clubhouse, where they lay face down. They had been shot several times, and one of the men had also been tortured. The massacre was never solved.

Guindon read the news reports and wondered. He'd fought many a David and Goliath–type battle, but this time he was stuck in prison and his club was finding itself caught between a pair of giants. Two hundred members was still a serious club, but nothing compared to the forces now bearing down on the territory of the Satan's Choice.

A new visitor was shining some light on Guindon's time at Collins Bay: his daughter Shanan Dionne, who was born in January 1975 to a girlfriend named Wendy. Jack would drive the child down to Kingston so she could connect with her father.

In retrospect, Shanan resented being watched over by a guard, but she was impressed at how respectful the other inmates were toward her father. She had particularly fond memories of a huge Native inmate named Tom, who gave her a handmade suede vest. Tom clearly respected her father, as did the other inmates in the visiting room. As her dad walked over to see her, they would stop him to ask, "Hey Bernie, is that your daughter?"

"He's a showstopper when he comes into the room," said Shanan.

She didn't like being told their visiting time was up. But when she got back in the car for the drive home, she couldn't help but feel like a member of a very special family. What she couldn't have known was that everything that made her father seem like royalty was crashing down around him, and there wasn't a thing he could do about it.

CHAPTER 30

Reunited

I had the feeling that the only one who cared at all was Bernie Guindon.

Long-time Bernie Guindon friend SUZANNE BLAIS

Guindon had a realistic shot at parole in the mid-1980s, so he busied himself with learning new skills so that he would be able to make a decent living. He already knew how to be a cook, and now he set his mind to learning how to be a barber and an upholsterer. He also set his mind on an old fascination: Suzanne Blais. He even remembered a tiny bit of French.

Hi Sweets!

Just received your letter & as always it's really nice hearing from you. Thanks for the news clippings.

Started back hitting the bag this week & doing more exercises & feeling much better. A good way to relieve head pressure.

Been doing a lot of cell time of late & have been watching & listening to the ball games. Hope the Phillies win the Play-offs. They do deserve to win the way they're playing.

Yes I do think I've got you figured out pretty close & reading between your lines does help. Look if you are so worried why don't you write under your maiden name & give me another address at least you'd be able to get it all off your chest as you've been holding it in much too long. Am I right Sweets? Still awaiting answers to several of my letters I've written to top officials regarding my case. Mind you I have caused several waves which is the main thing. With luck I should be hearing some good news by the end of the mth of early Nov.

Well Sweets till next time do take real good care of yourself & best wishes. Goodnight, god bless, sweet dreams, many pleasant fantasies of me as I've of you & fond memories.

> *Love & Respect Always*
> *Bernie No #1 Frog SWAELKAHF OOO*
> *XXXXXXOOOOO*

Would you please get me Spectator clippings from Sept. 23/80 about Bikers. Thanks.

> *Ton amie pour toujour Suzanne*
> *Bernie No #1 Frog*
> *SWAELKAHF*
> *XO & much more.*

Determined to get out as soon as parole was available, Guindon made a bold decision and quit the Satan's Choice. The apparently life-altering decision didn't alter as much as he meant it to appear. Asking for early release while an active member of an outlaw motorcycle club would have been futile. "It wasn't really a quit," he later said. "I had a leave of absence so to speak until I had my act together." Even though it was just a sabbatical of sorts, even the guise of leaving the Choice bothered him.

He wrote Suzanne in another undated letter:

Thanks for the call much appreciated. I feel real bad that you no longer write. I've quit the club & finding it hard to adjust but I'll do it. Hope all is going well with your family. Got the Caron story. Again thanks.

Love in friendship forever
Bernie No #1 Frog
SWAELKAHF
XO

He was elated when she wrote him back in a card with a Christmas scene, a horse hitched to a sled and hauling a Christmas tree. The picture looked like something out of rural Quebec.

Just received your beautiful card & the lovely poems & can't thank you enough. You are one of my oldest & truest friends & I hope someday of getting together for long talks. Did I miss sending you a birthday card & if so I apologize & I'll now wish you a belated birthday wish. Sure would be nice if you could visit or if I could phone you at nights as I've access to a phone from 5:30 till 11 PM & on holiday wk ends 8 AM – 11 PM. See if you can give me a ph. # as I'd like to talk with you in privacy . . .

Love, friendship & respect always
Bernie No #1 Frog
SWAELKAHF
XXXXOOOO

His mood picked up as she wrote back yet again.

Hi Beautiful so how is mon sheri? Sure hope this letter does find yourself, family & friends all in the very best of health & in fine spirits. Thanks for the last card & etc. much appreciated. Sorry for cutting you off short the last time we were on the phone. Believe me I love to hear your voice & it just hurts me deep down that I cannot touch you or see your beauty. Theres so damn much to say & I just keep finding my mind going black. The poem in the last card was just beautiful &

I can't get over how so few words can mean so much. I'm just waiting anxiously for the 22nd so I can find out in which direction I can move in concerning my life. Well this one will tell all that for sure. As for me I'm still active in fact I even took a few more items on, like as if I didn't have enough on my mind. I only get into the Barber Shop once a day for one hr & then its Committee work. I'm (we) are finally making progress & we are getting a lot of backing which is something new in here. Hope all is going as well as can be expected at your end. Always remember that your always thought of & our memories will last a lifetime. So until next time do take real good care of yourself. Give my love & best wishes to your mom for me.

> *Love & Respect always*
> *One who Cares*
> *Bernie No #1 Frog*
> *SWAELKAHF OO*
> *XXXXXOOOO*

Guindon was guarded in what he wrote, especially after authorities had intercepted his letters from jail after his PCP bust. That intercepted message, with its mention of how his life would be easier if someone did something about a DEA agent, had most likely added a few years onto his prison term. "You had to be careful what you said in letters," he said. "They were listening to all of your conversations."

Suzanne's mother died of a heart attack on May 7, 1981, while visiting a Toronto weight-loss clinic. She was just fifty-six. When Suzanne went to her mother's home to clear out her mailbox, she found a card for her mother's birthday, which was May 18. It was from Guindon. "At that time, I had the feeling that the only one who cared at all was Bernie Guindon," Suzanne said.

Cecil Kirby was also feeling alone, though for very different reasons. He had become convinced that his former bosses in the Commisso crime family were planning to murder him.

By this time, Kirby had done some truly horrible things, including providing the gun used to kill Constable Michael Sweet at the Bourbon Street tavern on Queen Street West in Toronto on March 14, 1980. He had also planted a bomb at the Wah Kew Chop Suey House on Elizabeth Street in downtown Toronto, which killed cook Chong Yim Quan and injured three others in May 1977.

There were still some jobs Kirby refused, like carrying out a murder contract on mobster Paul Volpe. Compassion had nothing to do with it. Kirby worried that this job in particular would endanger his own life. Volpe's death would create a lot of heat in the underworld, and killing a hitman is cheaper than paying him to keep his mouth shut.

As Kirby's employers dragged their feet on paying him for past work, he grew convinced that he was next on their hit list and felt his range of options narrow. In the biker world, there's no greater crime than being a rat, but staying alive is a good thing too, so Kirby called the police for help. Soon, he was wearing a hidden recording device while working as a police agent. By the end of 1981, evidence obtained by Kirby had put the brothers Rocco Remo, Cosimo Elia and Michele Commisso behind bars.

Kirby also helped police jail more than a dozen others, including Charles (The Bike) Yanover, who was convicted of trying to overthrow the government of Dominica. Yanover was also pinched for bombing Harold Arviv's Toronto disco for insurance money, a crime that Kirby said he almost committed himself. He said that he asked for a high price for the job, and Arviv hired Yanover to bomb the disco instead. "I guess he did it cheaper," Kirby said.

He wasn't a member of the Satan's Choice any longer when he worked for the Commissos or the cops. He was also surgical about the evidence he shared with police, telling them plenty about the mob and nothing that put any bikers behind bars. He even warned former Toronto Choice member Frank (Cisco) Lenti that he should get out of town for a while, before all his information led to arrests. Soon, police heard of four separate contracts of $100,000 for Kirby's death and then another one for $250,000. The rumoured numbers may have been inflated, but the desire for his death was real.

From his vantage point in prison, Guindon had mixed feelings about Kirby. He had no sympathy for a rat, but he felt that the mobsters had brought grief upon themselves by not honouring their debts to him. "I never thought he would do that. For what he did for that family, they should have paid him instead of trying to kill him. He stood up to them."

Kirby also played a role in Ken Goobie of the Choice going to prison, but not by ratting him out. Back during his break-and-enter days, Kirby floated the idea that they would be less conspicuous in residential areas if they dressed up as postmen. "I said, 'Nobody pays attention to a mailman when you're breaking into a house,'" Kirby recalled. Goobie acted on the idea in Kirby's absence and was caught, earning himself two years inside Collins Bay Institution.

As Kirby faded into life in witness protection, Lorne Campbell and Guindon were reunited in 1984 in Collins Bay, after Campbell was convicted of violent gang-related crimes. Campbell quickly became the workout partner that Guindon had always wanted.

He didn't question Guindon's training techniques, not even when Guindon would whomp him in the stomach with a board while he did sit-ups.

The Choice reunion continued when Pigpen Berry was shipped north from a North Carolina lock-up. He had been convicted in the United States of a series of crimes, including trying to steal a tank from a military base. Exactly why the Outlaws felt the need for a tank was never explained. Already a skilled cook and musician, Pigpen proved to be an accomplished artist. Among his miniature prison creations was a stage-coach and horses, and a ship, all painstakingly carved out of wood.

The calm and focus of working on a hobby was a balm against the barrage of insanity behind bars. Recently, a kitchen helper at Collins Bay had repeatedly stabbed and almost beheaded an unsatisfied diner who had become rude when denied a second portion. (To prevent similar outbursts in the future, the service area was almost entirely closed off from inmates, so that food was pushed out through a narrow slot.)

Prisoners often used each other for crude amusement. One evening, after lockdown, a prisoner began screaming and making smashing noises, calling on fellow inmates on his range to riot. Campbell later noted that nothing was broken in the prisoner's own cell. He had only been making loud noises with a cup, pretending he was wrecking his cell. His goal had been to incite others to riot for his own entertainment. "Nobody fell for it," Campbell said. "He was removed from the range."

In the yard, talk occasionally turned to fantasies of escape. Two inmates tried to recruit Guindon to go over the wall with them. Perhaps they thought that Guindon's Choice buddies on the outside would help them hide out. Guindon bluntly declined. "I told them to go fuck yourself. I'm already doing enough time. Get caught and I have to do twice as much. I'm having a hard enough time doing what I'm doing."

Guindon didn't hear the shotgun blast that stopped the pair of would-be fugitives before they could clear the wall. He imagined they would have had a tough time crawling across the barbed wire at the top, even if the guards in the towers somehow didn't notice them. The two men recovered from their wounds behind bars. "I think they watched too many movies," Guindon said.

Now eighteen years old, Guindon's daughter Teresa was sitting at a common-room table with her father, his girlfriend Wendy Dionne and her uncle Jack. As they were chatting, a husky inmate came by their table.

"This is Pigpen," Guindon said.

"That's your name?" Teresa asked him.

"That's what they call me because I'm a fucking pig," Pigpen explained.

Her father laughed and kept on laughing after Pigpen made some sexually suggestive comments to her. She felt ridiculed and exploded, punching her father square in the nose. It was a hard, focused blow, worthy of a Guindon. He bled heavily on the table before being led back to his cell.

Not all of the women in Guindon's life were fed up with him. Though he continued his correspondence with Suzanne Blais, he was introduced to a woman by another female friend. In a short period of time, she and Guindon became a couple of sorts. Soon, she gave birth to yet another Guindon daughter.

CHAPTER 31

Reconnecting

I don't think any of us girls had a cakewalk of a life.

Bernie Guindon's daughter SHANAN

For a long time, Guindon hadn't expected to hear anything positive at parole board hearings, but he could at least hope for a few laughs. Once, he attended one with a tape deck and played a few bars of Johnny Paycheck's country hit "Take This Job and Shove It" before he was dismissed and ordered back to his cell. Even if he had gotten paroled that day, he figured he wouldn't have lasted long on the streets. With his reputation, he would've been scooped up by police for associating with criminals. "What's the sense of getting out if they're only going to get me for association or thinking of association?"

In time, he became more optimistic and his behaviour followed suit. In the fall of 1984, Guindon was granted parole. On November 19, his forty-second birthday, Suzanne Blais picked him up from a halfway house in Toronto's Parkdale district. She was sitting in a limo with a bottle of champagne and a green-iced birthday cake shaped like a frog. Guindon wasn't a drinker and he wasn't supposed to consume alcohol on parole anyways, but at least he could enjoy the cake.

Suzanne was still married, but that didn't bother her as she took him to a Burton Cummings concert at the Imperial Room in the Royal York hotel, a venue so ritzy that Bob Dylan was once refused entry because he wasn't wearing a tie. Guindon marvelled at the sight of the CN Tower a couple blocks away on Front Street. The world's tallest free-standing structure stood for eight years before Guindon saw it. "It was brand new. It was to me."

Guindon felt as warmly toward Blais as when they had shared their first dinner together almost thirty years earlier, but wondered how long she'd feel the same. "We had a great time, and he was really surprised," Blais remembered. "I felt it was the least I could do for all of the encouragement and support he had given me all those early years."

Much had changed in the decade Guindon had spent locked up. The old, seedy Yonge Street strip had been flushed away in the aftermath of the August 1977 sex murder of twelve-year-old shoeshine boy Emanuel Jaques. His body was found on the roof of Charlie's Angels body-rub parlour at 245 Yonge Street, across from the current Eaton Centre and a stone's throw from the old Venus Spa, where Guindon used to work.

Upon their former leader's release from prison, club members supplied Guindon with a Harley, and he used it to reconnect with his daughters. He hadn't been around to protect them, and now there was plenty of damage he wanted to repair. Estimates varied of just how many children he had fathered. Guesses began at eleven, and at least two of them were in the care of Children's Aid. "I think that it bothered him that a lot of his kids were in a lot of horrible life-changing situations that he couldn't take care of," his daughter Shanan said. She was just ten when he was freed, but most of Guindon's kids had grown up before he had gotten out of jail. "I don't think any of us girls had a cakewalk of a life."

Guindon climbed on the bike and took some long rides down some hard roads, seeking out his daughters and trying to find a place for himself in their lives. There were no sons, as far as he knew. "He basically had to go around the country, one by one, and collect them," Shanan said. "I remember going into a strip club with my dad to check on one of my sisters."

It wasn't easy growing up in Oshawa as Bernie Guindon's daughter. "I thought if I acted really tough, he would accept me," Teresa said. "It brings you in circles you don't want to be in . . . A lot of kids get in trouble because it's attention. It's not good attention but it's attention." She felt she was doomed to be rejected by her father because she was a girl. "My dad didn't want a daughter. He wanted a son."

Teresa worried that as long as she lived in Oshawa, she would never escape the taboo of her last name. Parents wouldn't let her play with their children. Boys seemed afraid to ask her out, for fear of what might happen to them if things went wrong. Employers were reluctant to hire her. "I was taboo, taboo. You go out with her and make a mistake, you end up in the river," she said. "My dad's reputation followed me."

Life seemed stacked against her from birth. "My whole life, I was living behind my dad's shadow and it wasn't good . . . My mother was young . . . I was told that I was a mistake. Nobody wanted me." Teresa thought seriously of changing her last name. "I almost did and then I thought, *Should I be ashamed of who I am?* I thought *no, no.*"

Guindon didn't want to force a relationship on his daughters, but he needed them to know that he was around now and that he cared about them always. His message was "I'm here if you need me," and it was painful to deliver. "I'm sure it wasn't any fun," Shanan said.

Aside from the girls' emotional reactions to their long-absent father, he struggled just to keep track of all his daughters. Each had a different mother except for the two from his second wife, Barbara Ann. Another two were born to different mothers in the same year. But Guindon took to the job with a newfound commitment, lecturing Shanan when he learned that the thirteen-year-old dropped acid on Canada Day. "This is going to lead to this and this and this," he said, lifting his nose like he was snorting something and jabbing at his arm as if sticking a needle into a vein.

Having returned to Oshawa, Guindon also took it upon himself to sort out the lives of friends and acquaintances in the biker world. "Every second knock on the door was usually drama," Shanan recalled. "He would complain he was stressed, but he couldn't turn away a knock at the door. They expected him to sort out the bullshit. Stripper bullshit.

Boyfriend bullshit." At times, she would get frustrated and tell him, "You're spending your time with the wrong people." With time, her tone softened: "Now that I'm older, I understand."

Teresa was already grown up by the time her father was paroled. She had married an ex-con whom Guindon knew from behind bars, though he didn't know his new son-in-law's offence. To ask while behind bars would have been considered poor form.

Teresa found work in palliative care, easing the pain of terminal patients. Then she became a professional clown, to bring joy to children. She also wrote a children's book called *My Gentle Giant*, which tells the story of a little girl whose love transforms a cruel giant into someone lovable, despite the barriers put in place by villagers. It was easy to imagine what the little girl in her story wanted. "That was my dream," Teresa said. "That my dad would lose the club. Become a better person. Have a happy life. Have a normal life."

When she was thirty, Teresa suffered a stroke and was no longer able to write well enough to put together a grocery list, let alone write more books. "I thought, *My life is over.*" Rage finally consumed her. "I got really mad at God, and I decided that I wanted to end my life. Commit suicide." She planned to use a cocktail of prescription pills but wondered if swallowing them would keep her out of heaven. She also wondered about the consequences of having a father who led the Satan's Choice. "I thought I might not get in because of my dad."

She started reading a bible that had been given to her by her maternal grandfather, and she marvelled as the paralysis began to leave her body. She also found that she had lost the need for approval from her birth father, who had never been there anyway. To Teresa's mind, he wasn't the father who had saved her. She felt cleansed and finally freed. "God healed me."

Guindon got a phone call from his old friend George Chuvalo in 1985, asking for a special favour. The boxing champ's son was in trouble.

Guindon suspected it hadn't been easy to live in the shadow of a famous father whose very name called to mind toughness and courage.

Certainly, that's what he was hearing from his own kids. Jesse Chuvalo's drug problems began at the age of twenty, shortly after he lost a kneecap in a motorcycle accident. The pain from the injury lingered and he turned to heroin to fight it. Soon, he was an addict, and his father, so indomitable in the ring, was worried and lost.

"Would you mind coming over and having a talk?" Chuvalo asked.

Guindon didn't hesitate, as his respect for Chuvalo ran deep. "He was always a nice guy. He's a gentleman."

Guindon tried to scare Jesse, just like he had tried to scare Shanan after she used acid. He did his best to explain to Jesse that drug users often end up in prison and there's no joy in that life. "I told him the truth. You don't want to go to jail. You ruin your life. You'll never get a job."

Guindon left the meeting thinking he had gotten through to Jesse. It was a good, hopeful feeling. "I talked to him a good hour. He seemed like a good kid. He listened. Two months later, he was dead."

Jesse shot himself in the mouth in his bedroom on February 18, 1985. Chuvalo said he appreciated Guindon's support throughout that horrible time, before and after the death: "He was very sympathetic. He was a kind guy. He was a nice guy. He would lend his support."

Guindon thought of his friend Davey Hilton and his sons. Hilton had been a high-level boxer, with a knee-buckling left hook, and he had close associates that included Montreal mobster Frank Cotroni. Hilton's sons had fallen into trouble, and Guindon suspected they were going through the same troubles as Jesse Chuvalo. "He [Hilton] was a good guy, good boxer," said Guindon. "The boys had to grow up in the old man's history."

Chuvalo and Hilton were tough men—Chuvalo famously so. But neither shared the kind of infamy that comes with being the leader of the Satan's Choice. Guindon wondered to what degree his history would continue to haunt his own family.

CHAPTER 32

Angel

She was untameable. He was madly in love with her.

Guindon's daughter SHANAN describes the
mother of his son, Harley Davidson Guindon

Angel was drop-dead gorgeous in an edgy, troubling way that was impossible for Guindon to ignore. The blue-eyed, teenaged stripper was also impossible to understand. She giggled often and said little. She was extremely public and painfully private all at the same time, dancing naked in front of strangers but painting the windows of her home black. Even her best friends didn't know her last name. And very few of them knew that her real name was Lorraine, or that her father was a big deal in amateur boxing circles, who had split from his wife for reasons that weren't quite clear.

Angel was less than half Guindon's age and younger than some of his daughters. It seemed hopeless from the start that he could rescue her from herself, but Guindon revelled in lost causes. "He pretty much took her right off the stage and into a fur coat," Shanan said.

Angel was small, but like her newfound lover, she radiated power and charisma. She also shared his mania for freedom. She would disappear and reappear and never explain where she'd been, then disappear again. She was also fearless, not letting his love or anger or authority control her. "She was untameable," Shanan said. "He was madly in love with her." Upon emerging from prison, Guindon had resumed leadership of the Satan's Choice, and Angel liked the power that came with being known around Oshawa as the old lady of Canada's most powerful outlaw biker.

She was still a teenager when she became pregnant. She appeared to be utterly devoid of maternal instinct, and thoughts of becoming a young mother overwhelmed her. "She was more of a big sister to me than anything," Shanan said. "Angel at the time was the link to my dad." Complicating Angel's pregnancy was the fact she had only one good kidney, which worried her further.

There were rumblings that the relationship between Guindon and Angel could crash even before their child was born. To take the pressure off their relationship, the pair reached an agreement: If they separated in the future and the baby was a boy, he would go with Guindon. If the baby was a girl, she would go with Angel.

Their baby was born on October 15, 1985, in Oshawa. Finally, at age forty-two, Guindon had a son he could raise from birth. In Teresa's eyes, her father was like some medieval monarch who finally had a male heir to continue his reign. So liberally had Guindon been procreating that three weeks later he would have another daughter when Sarah was born to a girlfriend. "My dad impregnated so many women because he wanted a son," Teresa said. "The only reason he wanted a son was because he wanted him to carry on the name."

On the subject of names, there was a rumour that Harley-Davidson might give a free motorcycle to anyone who named their child after its famous brand. The rumour turned out to be false, but Guindon joked that the name was still a good choice for his son since he could never forget it.

"He stepped down from the throne," Teresa said of her father, and of the ascent of his newborn heir, Harley Davidson Guindon.

Harley represented possibilities for his father. The boy was Guindon's chance to finally get parenting right. He was a perfectionist, though his track record as a parent didn't yet reflect that. "He was my dad's do-over baby," Shanan said. "He was the first child that my dad had on the street and got to raise on the street. I think he tried really hard to make up for a lot of things."

Guindon quickly learned that he wouldn't be able to count on Angel. Though the young mother remained in the family's circle for years to come, Harley has gently described his birth mother as "unmotivated, not ready for child-bearing," which was probably reasonable for a teen-aged street kid.

From the beginning, Guindon expected his son to grow up tough. When Harley was still a toddler in diapers, he fell over and hit his head on a coffee table. He started to cry and Teresa tried to comfort him, but Guindon jumped in.

"Don't do that," he said. "He's got to be a man. He's got to toughen up."

Teresa sensed things were going bad fast. She asked if she could become Harley's legal guardian. Guindon wouldn't hear of it. For better or worse, Harley Davidson Guindon was his father's son.

CHAPTER 33

Hospitality Industry

He challenged me and I knocked him out. I told his girlfriend that if
she woke him up, I'd knock her out too.

BERNIE GUINDON on customer relations at his resort

While in prison, Guindon had a new idea about how to make a legitimate living after he got out. He planned to establish a high-end trailer park where bikers could camp, drink beer and ride their Harleys. He also hoped to attract many people who he considered "common citizens." Guindon had his eye on a campground near Parry Sound, which he first spotted while out of prison on a pass. He had a smooth-talking partner who wanted in on the idea, but neither of them had the money yet. They did, however, have a name for their camp: Shan-gri-law, for the mystical, happy valley described in *Lost Horizon*, the 1933 novel by British author James Hilton.

In an attempt to raise money to purchase Shan-gri-law, Guindon and his partner ventured into real estate. They found a house they could fix up and resell, and bought it without a down payment by convincing the seller to add five thousand dollars to the selling price. It worked. Then they repeated the process several more times. "I swear on my patch that it was totally legit," Guindon said. Next, they branched out and set up a seafood shop on Ritson Road near Highway 401 in south Oshawa, called Frog's Fresh & Frozen Sea Products. "I didn't know shit about it," Guindon confessed. "I liked surf and turf."

Through the seafood and the houses, they scrounged up enough money to finally buy the Shan-gri-law, which offered more than 175 acres of private campsites. Their plan for the grand opening was to bring in John Kay and Steppenwolf, whose song "Born to Be Wild" became the ultimate biker anthem after it appeared in the movie *Easy Rider*.

Kay in person wasn't as much fun as his song. He seemed businesslike and a bit detached when he arrived, and Guindon wasn't about to act like some giddy fan-boy. "I don't like bugging people if I know they've got a job to do."

Kay wasn't impressed with the wooden stage that Satan's Choice members had built on the property, and he refused to perform on it. Lorne Campbell, one of Guindon's most loyal supporters in the Choice, stood up for the boss in the way he knew best. He stepped in, telling Kay, "All of your vehicles and instruments stay here. You can fuck off if you want.'" Kay played.

After the concert, Kay departed while some of his band stayed on and partied with the bikers and some of their female friends. Their tour was over and it was time to cut loose and celebrate. Steve Earle, the Grammy Award–winning country star from Texas, was far more accommodating than Kay and didn't grumble when he played Shan-gri-law. "He was a pretty good guy, normal type of guy," Guindon said. Things also went more smoothly with promotions like Kickass Country, a country jamboree; amateur boxing and charity toy runs.

Shan-gri-law was fun, but as a business, it was falling short of Guindon's hopes. For one, the public didn't feel welcome, and two, bikers worried that letting their guard down in such an obvious spot would leave them vulnerable to an ambush from enemies. That left few actual customers to pay Guindon's bills. "We were hoping that we were going to get civilians. Hardly anybody showed up."

The guests who did arrive often made Guindon re-examine whether his future really lay in the hospitality industry. Weasels kept poaching the chickens that Guindon raised for eggs and meat, and some customers treated the livestock even worse. Guindon ordered one wannabe biker to stop taunting his chickens and retire to his tent. "I did this with authority in a way the dumbest SOB would understand. He challenged me and I knocked him out. I told his girlfriend that if she woke him up, I'd knock her out too. The next morning, he came and apologized."

In an attempt to be family friendly, Shan-gri-law had a petting zoo. One of its residents was a goose nicknamed "Dog." "He acted like a watchdog. They are quite a watchdog, those things." The goose attacked little Harley and spat on him and put up a spirited fight when Guindon rushed to his son. That was the end of the goose. "We ended up eating him."

The pygmy goat and the dog in the petting zoo caused fewer problems, while the boa constrictor occasionally slithered away and hid. "My dad would have to give a red alert," Shanan recalled. "'If anyone finds a ten-foot snake . . .'"

Determined to make a go of the camp, Guindon soldiered on. He sweated to clear trees to expand the camp's usable property. One day, he hooked a chain from a tractor onto a stump and then let out the clutch. "As soon as I let the clutch out, that sonofabitch was on top of me. The steering wheel went right on my chest." Infuriated, Guindon thought he was going to die. He didn't talk to God. He stayed conscious by cursing the teenagers who worked there and who should have done the job themselves and now should at least be saving him.

His chest was in great pain and his left arm seemed paralyzed. He struggled to get his feet under an axle in hopes he could push the tractor off himself. A few of his young employees finally showed up and managed to pile up logs under the tractor to relieve the pressure. After about twenty minutes, he was freed but near death. Emergency workers arrived and inserted a tube into his lung to drain it.

"The nurse cut him open so he could breathe, because he was coughing up blood, and took him to Huntsville Hospital and gave him twenty-four hours to live," Harley said. His left lung was punctured. Six ribs were broken. "And he said fuck you to the doctor. 'I'll be out of here in a week.' Then he went home . . . He basically refused to die."

Once home, Guindon couldn't make a fist with his left hand and his left arm felt as stiff as a canoe paddle. He built a contraption with coat hangers and elastics that helped his hand recover.

He was barely out of the contraption when he got involved in a fight with a camper that centred around Angel. The man pulled a knife on Guindon, who put him hard against a wall. The incident landed Guindon briefly in jail again for assault. Shortly after he was released, he tested his fist with a left hook on a familiar face—his business partner's. "He didn't give a shit who he went over to get ahead," Guindon said of him. "I finally gave him a shot in the jaw and told him to stay away. He left." With that, Guindon did three more months in jail for assault, while the doors closed for good on Shan-gri-law.

CHAPTER 34

Nightmares

We saw the nightmares.

Bernie Guindon's FORMER GIRLFRIEND describes his son,
Harley, as a preschooler

Corky's bar on Park Road in southwest Oshawa was a popular spot for GM workers, bikers and strippers. It had large front windows, which allowed the bikers to keep an eye on their Harleys while they played pool. There were also good live bands, covering AC/DC and their like, filling the dance floor. Maggie Pearce-O'Shea went there sometimes as a sixteen-year-old and once saw Guindon swinging his motorcycle helmet at a man, which wasn't shocking, given Guindon's reputation and the Corky's crowd. "Not sure why or what happened. Kinda normal stuff for that bar," Pearce-O'Shea said. "I didn't hang out to watch the aftermath."

Guindon was at Corky's on a Friday night when a woman in her mid-twenties caught his eye. Things hadn't been going well with Angel, and Guindon always noticed good-looking women anyways.

She was on the phone, checking in with her office for messages, when Guindon introduced himself.

"You can see I'm busy," she told him. "You're interrupting me."

His reaction surprised her. "He was very apologetic. He ended up being very sorry for interrupting me."

Guindon was born the same year as her father, but he seemed young in a way, which she later chalked up to his lengthy stretches of prison time. "I believe that when they go inside, they're stunted inside," she said.

It didn't take long for her to realize that Guindon was someone special in the Corky's ecosystem. When he and other bikers rode into the parking lot, often after spending much of the evening at Dynasty's strip club, some of the female patrons rushed down to the women's washroom. "They'd be down there removing their panties," she said. "It was nasty, nasty."

Those women then hustled out to the parking lot at closing time, circling the bikes of Choice members in the hope they would be one of the chosen few to score a ride home. "These girls just didn't care," she said. "Some of these young girls had big-time daddy issues."

Guindon began giving her rides home. Soon, he was spending the night, although he still maintained an apartment on Simcoe Street South with Angel, where he kept some clothes. As she got to know Guindon better, she would sometimes stake her turf by putting itching powder on the back of his helmet. She would later check out which girls at Corky's seemed to be rubbing their eyes and faces suspiciously hard.

One day, when the woman went to Guindon's apartment to get some clothes for Harley, she stumbled on a situation there that she wouldn't later describe, except to say that it was totally unfit for a child. "There were some things going on in the house that weren't appropriate for children and Bernie didn't approve of," she said.

That was enough for Guindon to move with Harley into her basement full-time. The decision to leave Angel was necessary but still painful. "I think she's the only woman who crushed my dad," Shanan said.

Though the family won't give specifics, the demise of Guindon and Angel's relationship was as hot as its beginning. "She's got to live with her own demons," Shanan said. "It took a toll on both of them. I don't think he ever wanted bad for her. She went down some pretty crazy, dark, winding roads. She doesn't make a little bang. She makes a big *kaboom!*"

Whatever had happened in the home was clearly having an effect on Harley, even after he was taken away. "We saw the nightmares," the woman said. "We had to deal with the nightmares of that."

Harley was just four when he came into her life. She already had a boy of her own, who was living with her. She recalled one morning when Harley pleaded with the adults around him not to be sent to school. "He was terrified. Absolutely terrified. It was quite a scene." Aside from her, the house was full of male friends of Guindon, all of whom were pushing the child to leave for school. "It seemed the closer he got to going out the door, the more terrified he got."

She dropped to a knee so she could talk to little Harley face-to-face. That's when he explained why he was so afraid. "They had told him the day before that when they got to school, they would be doing the Eucharist. When they told him that he would be eating the baby Jesus and drinking His blood, he took it literally."

After considerable coaxing, she convinced Harley to go to school. "He was so cute," the woman said. "He needed a female there to look after him. He needed someone that was willing to listen to him rather than tell him. He was the littlest one in the house full of men and boys. He just needed to be listened to."

That morning marked a point of no return in her relationship with Harley. She decided then and there that she would become his step-mother. "That is absolutely the moment I fell in love with little Harley."

She still had issues of her own to sort out as she brought Harley into her life. She had been a foster kid and homeless at sixteen. At seventeen, she was pregnant from an abusive partner. "Bernie sobered me up, so to speak. I was getting involved in some things I shouldn't have done. He straightened my life around."

She wanted something that she had constantly heard about but never experienced. Now, she felt like she was on the verge of finally getting it. "I wanted to be a part of a family." She already loved little Harley to bits, but life with Guindon offered so much more. "It was a family accepting me," she said. "It wasn't just Bernie. It was his mother, his brother. I appreciated being part of the family. I grew up without a family and they took me in."

Soon, she was making contact with all of Guindon's progeny that she could find, which was no small task. She took it upon herself to help the children connect and develop some sense of family. With her care, relationships blossomed as much as they could. "I took note of the birthdays. It was fun. Bernie was always there for them. He just needed someone to tell him when and where."

The stepmother found herself constantly telling Harley that his birth mother, Angel, loved him very much "in her own way," which she believed was true. "He was such a cute kid and had such a big heart," the stepmother said. "It was heartbreaking to see what he went through growing up. I've done my best to pick up the pieces and give him some loving roots he can call home."

The stepmother had dreams for Harley, just like other mothers have for their birth children. "I wanted him to be a firefighter," she said. "I knew he would have helped people. He would have been fantastic. He's a very intelligent young man."

Harley and her son grew inseparable. Much of Harley's bonding came through play-fighting with his newfound older brother. "He was rough and tumble," his stepmother said. "The boys collected baseball and hockey cards. They learned how to ride dirt bikes together in the back field and were forever building and rebuilding forts and exploring along a nearby creek. They chased snakes and whatever else they saw in the woods, and often brought animals home, either as additional pets or rescue projects." They always seemed to have what his stepmother called "the most devilish grins."

Shanan found something familiar in Harley's smile: "He's got the little smirk. The Bernie smirk."

The boys also spent plenty of time roaming south Oshawa together. "They were mostly rowdy and boisterous, but it was when they got quiet that I dropped everything and went running to find them," Harley's stepmother said. "Mostly I would blow a whistle out the front door and the boys knew to come home. HD got smart and set up a line of kids outside and around the hood to extend his range. They relayed the info to him that it was time to come in, and he would race back without detection . . . until he got caught. One day, someone let him down and he was late. That was the end of the relay tactics."

Money was tight and Harley's stepmother took another tenant into their bungalow. One day, that tenant's boyfriend came by to see her. He was in an ugly mood and was carrying an axe. Guindon boxed him down the stairs, leaving a trail of blood to mark his exit path.

Despite growing up with chaos around him, Harley understood from very early on that his stepmother's love included plenty of rules and expectations. "She has always been the mother figure in my life," Harley recalled. "She was strict. I got my ass whupped. She made sure I stayed with the books."

In turn, she noted, he genuinely wanted to make her happy. If she was feeling depressed, Harley quickly picked up on her mood and would ask, "What's wrong?" The boy's concern bolstered her flagging spirits. "He was the sensitive one," his stepmother said. "He'd be sensitive to other people's emotions . . . He was a kid with a big heart."

As his son grew up under his stepmother's watchful eye and firm hand, Guindon often busied himself working on motorcycles in the downstairs living room, which opened onto the garage. He stored bike parts in the backyard, in a bomb shelter that he got for free from a Satan's Choice member.

"He often had guys hanging around to help him work on his bike, just to keep themselves busy, clean and sober," Harley's stepmother said. "They would show up first thing in the morning and leave at the end of the day. There were a few that would stay with him overnight too if they needed a 'dry' place to stay. We never kept alcohol here at the homestead. Just a bottle of wine with dinner for special occasions."

Guindon had begun sparring with Harley when the boy was only three. Not surprisingly, fighting was in Harley's nature, something Lorne Campbell discovered when he was enlisted as the preschooler's babysitter. Campbell had worked for a time as a drug debt collector and had a serious reputation as a fighter. "He came out with the gloves on and smashed me in the nose," Campbell recalled. "I thought, *You little fucker*. Then I sent him to bed."

Some of Harley's other male babysitters suffered a fate worse than a smack in the nose with a boxing glove. Harley targeted them for "bagging," his term for punching someone as hard as possible in the gonads.

While still a boy, Harley's fight training became serious. "The man lacks patience and scares the shit out of me," Harley said of his father.

"Throwing the wrong punch or throwing without using proper footwork was a serious issue. I hated it. The man would make me do sit-ups by the hundreds. Five hundred to seven hundred was a regular night at the gym at five to six years old . . . For the most part, I didn't like training. Very repetitive, extremely strict."

One of the family's neighbours was a martial artist who had trained police officers. His specialty was tae kwon do, and for several years, Harley trained with him privately before and after school. "Sensei Ron" didn't rank Harley's progress with coloured belts or enter him in tournaments. He told Harley that what he was learning was far more than a sport. "I was always told that my father may have enemies that may come after me to get at him and that the training may save my life one day," Harley said.

Guindon took out a life insurance policy on his son. It included specific payments for lost body parts, like his fingers. It was as if Guindon was gearing up for a war in the not-so-distant future, against an enemy who was yet to be announced. It was as if Guindon were fighting phantoms, who could attack at any time of the day or night, without warning.

There was no way for Harley to escape his father's eye, even when Guindon wasn't physically present. "Sometimes my dad would watch the sessions, but when there was lack of progress or lack of respect, the sensei would bring the videotaped footage to him," Harley later said. That meant Harley was constantly pushed and evaluated as a fighter. "Push-ups and jumping jacks were my life."

There was an assortment of boxing gyms for Harley to train in as well, including an old barn on Lake Ridge Road in Whitby and a gym on Bloor Street East, where Guindon volunteered in exchange for workout time for Harley and his stepbrother. When Harley was particularly boisterous, Guindon slipped a large boy five dollars to give his son an extra-tough workout in the ring. Back then, Harley was small for his age, but he could hold his own with larger boys.

For Guindon, it was as if a clock was ticking loudly on his happy home life. He was receiving constant reminders of life's dangers. A Durham Region bouncer smashed him in the head with a pool ball in his hand. A man with a shotgun showed up at the Oshawa Choice clubhouse, full of anger. Somehow, Guindon was able to talk him into going away, with no shots fired. These episodes didn't surprise Guindon, but they ramped up his anxieties for his son. It was as though Guindon could see dark shadows approaching their happy little home.

"I think he wanted to devote more time to him," Shanan said, "because he knew he [Harley] was going to have a difficult time later."

CHAPTER 35

Big Brother

He [Guindon] was like a big brother to everybody.

Former Satan's Choice member STEVE (SLICK) MCQUEEN

In the face of the Outlaws' and Hells Angels' push north, Guindon faced a daunting task in rebuilding his Satan's Choice, partly because he questioned the loyalty of some new Choice members who had joined up while he was in prison. "I was having my doubts as to how many were on my side," Guindon said. "I figured geez, I'd have a helluva time rebuilding the club."

Some rebuilding was sorely needed. In Toronto, the Iron Hawgs had patched over to the Outlaws in 1984, giving the American club a chapter in Canada's most prosperous city. The Windsor area was lost for the foreseeable future after warlike Harry (Taco) Bowman of Detroit was elevated to the post of international president of the Outlaws. He would keep a firm grip on the Canadian city just across the Detroit River. Guindon visited Windsor anyway, displaying no warm feelings when he met up with Bill Hulko, former Choice president there. Hulko had bulked up considerably during his time in prison. "He had pecs bigger than my arms," Guindon said. But he still had that left hook and wasted no time in letting Hulko know what he thought of the Windsor biker's decision to patchover. "I socked him in the fucking head . . . He did nothing . . . I just wanted to see where his balls were. He didn't have balls that fucking day."

The Hells Angels were also on the move inside Canada. The club got its first Maritime chapter as the result of a bizarre accident. Walter Stadnick had graduated to the Angels in 1982. In 1984 he nearly died after his Harley was struck by a priest who ran a stop sign near Saint-Pie-de-Guire, Quebec, in his rush to see the papal visit. Members of the 13th Tribe of Halifax helped guard Stadnick as he recovered in Hamilton's St. Joseph's Hospital. In return, they were promoted to membership in the Hells Angels.

The Choice was bleeding members, and was a far cry from even the two hundred members who'd been holding down the fort during their president's prison term. "A lot of guys went Outlaws," Guindon said. "Others quit and got married. Some guys joined smaller clubs. Some guys went west, looking for jobs."

Guindon wasn't impressed with many of those who stayed behind and still wore the grinning devil patch of the Choice. They seemed lax about attending meetings or club runs. Some seemed to want a patch just to look tough. What Guindon wanted were members like Lorne Campbell and David Hoffman, who were comfortable in their own skin and who "had parts"—his term for "balls." He didn't want anyone who needed a patch on his back to make him feel like a man. "They think the patch is going to save their ass. That's why a lot of guys join motorcycle clubs. They've got no balls."

In an effort to reclaim some lost muscle, the Choice opened four new chapters in Ontario between 1985 and 1988, which gave them ninety-five members in seven chapters. That was a solid number, even if it was just a third of the Choice's membership before Mother McEwen's betrayal. Many of the members were enthusiastic cocaine traffickers, and the Toronto chapter specialized in moving the drug from Quebec to Alberta, home of Canada's oil patch.

Some of the new members were solid, like ironworker Steve (Slick) McQueen, who joined the Kitchener chapter of the Satan's Choice in 1986. McQueen was a jaunty man given to wearing a custom-made bowler hat and who bore more than a passing resemblance to actor Jack

Nicholson. He was also a ferocious street fighter and could speak with authority about having an eye coming out of its socket because of a broken orbital bone while battling. He could speak with equal authority about inflicting that condition on an opponent.

McQueen respected Guindon's reputation as a boxer. "I was a different kind of fighter," McQueen said. "I did lots of street fighting in Hamilton." He also fought as an underground cage fighter near construction sites around Fort McMurray, Alberta. "I fought in barns and different types of places," he said. "That was craziness. It was a well-kept secret. I would always suggest, 'Let's make money. No rules. Just get up and get at it. Whoever wins gets all the money.'"

Like Guindon, McQueen wasn't particularly large. He stood five-foot-nine and weighed about 180 pounds, but he had the fighting spirit of a wolverine. "Size don't mean anything," he said. "When they're unconscious, they're only as tall as they are thick."

Like many members of the Choice, McQueen had some unresolved issues with his father. He ran away from home as an adolescent and made it all the way from the Niagara Peninsula to the Fraser Canyon of BC before he was caught and returned home. When police asked his father why he hadn't filed a missing person's report, McQueen's dad told them they should try taking him into their own house for a week and then they'd be able to answer the question for themselves.

McQueen recalled being impressed with Guindon's attitude at a motorcycle rodeo in Kitchener. Guindon struck McQueen as a proud, old-school biker, who was eager to participate in any event that was held, whether it was brawling for a chunk of a beheaded turkey or seeing who could ride the slowest without falling over. "There was Bernie, the living legend. He competed in every event. I don't remember him winning anything, but he was a goer. He just wouldn't quit."

George McIntyre of Hamilton's East End Parkdale Gang was at the same motorcycle rodeo. McIntyre had brushed up against Choice members in jails and at boxing matches. "Bernie's always been the same. Good-natured straight shooter. He treated everybody the same. Wasn't a bully. Didn't like rats. His word was his bond, and he was a tough boxer."

McIntyre noted that Guindon had definite ideas about how fights should be conducted: "He was Marquess of Queensberry rules . . . When the guy hit the ground, he didn't go for putting his boots to his head. He had already made them look bad enough. He had respect for people . . . It was honour among thieves. Call it what you will."

That weekend near Kitchener, McIntyre and McQueen found themselves competing against Guindon in an event called the "stick race," which was an outlaw biker version of musical chairs. It started with a dozen motorcycles slowly driving around a big circle of tires. Each motorcycle had a driver and a man on the back. A man standing in the middle of the circle held eleven sticks. The "road boss" threw the sticks in the air and the men on the back of the bikes ran to fetch one. "Then it's full-on fucking war and anything goes," McIntyre said. "There's no weapons involved, except the stick. You can do whatever it takes."

Once a stick is secured, the passenger jumps back on his ride and races across the finish line. It should have been a good event for Guindon, since he carried a striker from Sarnia on the back of his Harley, who, McIntyre estimated, was about seven feet tall and three hundred pounds. "He was a Goliath," McIntyre said. "He wasn't a person. He was a place."

That afternoon, it came down to just two teams vying for the stick race championship: Guindon and the massive Sarnia striker against McQueen and McIntyre. When the final stick was thrown, McIntyre saw he could easily out-leg the Goliath. "He was such a big three-toed fucking sloth." However, McIntyre thought it would be bad form to win in this manner, since he was an invited guest and not a Satan's Choice club member. So he did what he thought was the more polite thing: he drop-kicked, airplane-spun and body-slammed the Goliath into submission. McIntyre was just five-foot-nine, but he had beefed up to more than 220 pounds in the weight room. Years later, McIntyre still laughed at the memory of Guindon chewing out the Goliath after their loss: "You big fucking galoot! Look at the size of him! You had your chance to shine and you blew it!"

Despite Guindon's furious outburst, McQueen was impressed with how accessible he was with club members, including newcomers like himself. "Anybody could talk to Bernie. It didn't matter what your problem was. He was like a big brother to everybody."

Guindon also displayed some surprising life skills. McQueen recalled taking part in a brawl in a Kitchener bar that left him with a huge black shiner that shut his left eye, and an ugly gash in his face. "You could see the bone in my forehead. It was opened up." Going to the hospital wasn't an option, because that would mean certain arrest. "Police were involved in the fight and they didn't do so good."

McQueen and other bikers regrouped in the local Satan's Choice clubhouse, where Guindon was visiting. Guindon had seen plenty of ugly eye injuries in the ring and on the street. He was convinced that McQueen would lose the sight in his left eye if something wasn't done soon. He sat McQueen down in a chair, and a mammoth biker from the Oshawa chapter held him from behind while another biker sat on his thighs. Then Guindon splashed whisky on McQueen's face and commenced operating. He had no training whatsoever in medicine, but he'd practised stitching while in prison, doing petit point, and watched other boxers get stitched up. He reckoned he could handle the job as well as anyone in his circle.

First, he lanced the mouse under McQueen's eye and then sewed it up with three or four stitches. Next came another ten or so stitches above his eye until the bone was no longer visible. "He did the sewing. He knew what he was doing," McQueen said. "It was just like in the movies, buddy. They poured whisky on my face and started sewing me up. I was pretty much tethered to the chair by Bernie's helpers. I'm far from handsome, but I have Bernie to thank for the sight in my left eye. Unless you run your hand over my eyebrow, you can't tell."

It was around this time that McQueen met his future wife, Lucy. His life got immeasurably better from that moment on, he said. "I'm still enjoying my marriage as much as I did in the first day I met her," he said two decades later. "I won the wife lottery."

When Lucy was almost killed in a car accident in 1994, McQueen did not hesitate to quit the club to be by her side. "You're not allowed to quit, but I quit anyway," he said. Some of the members gave him grief, but McQueen didn't doubt for a second that he was doing the right thing. "It's what any man is supposed to do. You're supposed to take care of your family."

McQueen knew he'd have to tell Guindon of his decision. He wasn't sure what to expect. The president had been working hard to find good guys to rebuild the club; losing McQueen would be a blow to that effort.

"Go look after your family," Guindon replied, perhaps respecting McQueen even more for making the tough call to leave and tell him face to face. "That's the most important thing."

CHAPTER 36

Human

I'm sorry. I was a young dad. I didn't have the patience. You don't know how I grew up.

BERNIE GUINDON apologizes to his daughter

Ever since Guindon left General Motors, earning a legitimate living was complicated. His daughter Shanan said his resumé was marked by "great ideas, lousy partners."

There was his brief career as a barber after his second prison stint, when he worked for a time with a friend in Ajax, between Oshawa and Toronto. He had apprenticed at the trade while behind bars, but not all of that experience had been positive. He once accidentally gave an inmate a nasty two-inch gash while shaving him with a straight razor. "I wasn't bad. It's just it wasn't my cup of tea. I didn't feel comfortable."

On the outside, he practised on Harley. Little Harley sat relatively still for a variety of haircuts from his father, most of them of the pompadour variety. It was fun naming the haircuts his father gave him, but not so enjoyable actually getting them. "I never went to a barber until I was fifteen," Harley said. "I had the Rat Tail, the Step." Still, the price was right and it was an adventure. There was sometimes a lineup of neighbourhood kids at the house, waiting for haircuts that included "the Bowl" and "the Staircase."

Guindon also tried cutting Shanan's hair when she was eleven. At first she was happy for the one-on-one attention from her father, but then she became afraid as her hair kept hitting the floor. "It was lopsided, severely lopsided . . . I said, 'Okay, that's short enough.' He kept trying to straighten it up. I would have been bald if I let him keep going."

Guindon also did some work fixing transport trailers, but making custom motorcycles seemed more of a fit. This too presented challenges. Guindon was a perfectionist and not particularly businesslike, and many of his customers wanted *Easy Rider* magic on a moped budget. "A lot of people expected miracles," Guindon said. "They didn't want to give you the money to build a bike. They didn't realize the work and the money that goes into that."

There wasn't much money in leatherwork, as good as he was, since Guindon's craft was time-consuming and could be roughly imitated with cheap machinery. Few people want to pay a hundred dollars for a wallet, however well made it might be.

Guindon had plenty of other ideas for making an honest living. One particularly ambitious project was a fertilizer business run from a verdant property in tiny Baltimore, Ontario, north of Cobourg. Called Nature's Magic, the organic plant food was made by burning off silt and mixing in leaves and a special substance. The product was sold in bottles, and its makers believed it was so potent, it could grow crops on the desert sand. "We were convinced we were going to feed all of the poor people across the globe," Harley's stepmother said. "We spent day and night on that thing."

There were plenty of biker-related issues taking up Guindon's time in the early 1990s, and it was common for Guindon to answer his phone with "What's wrong?" That's how he answered it when his daughter Teresa called one night in a panic. She was unable to get into the room of her three-year-old son, Devin.

Guindon rushed over and took Devin's door off its hinges. Once inside, they frantically scanned the room but couldn't find the toddler. Devin wasn't on the bed or under the bed or in the closet. The boy had medical problems, so there was no time to spare. Could he have been abducted? Could someone have come in through the window? Guindon had always feared that his enemies might come after Harley to get at him. Had they targeted his grandson?

Finally, they found the boy, wedged between his mattress and headboard, curled up and sound asleep. What Teresa saw next was something she hadn't seen before and she wouldn't ever see again.

Her father was crying.

"Wow, that's a first," she said. "I've never seen you cry before."

"Well, I am human."

"Really? News to me."

"What do you mean by that?"

"You weren't the best dad in the world."

Perhaps the horrors of his own childhood flooded back to him as he said, "I'm sorry. I was a young dad. I didn't have the patience. You don't know how I grew up."

"I have an issue with men crying," Teresa later said. "I always look at them like they're wimpy or something. My dad was tough. I had never seen a gentle side of him."

She wasn't pleasant with her father as he shed tears over the thought of losing Devin to his enemies. "I wasn't being sweet and nice. I was being a bitch, basically. I was throwing in a dig.

"He cried and said, 'Teresa, I'm sorry.' I cried too. I said, 'I forgive you.'"

CHAPTER 37

Black Death Eyes

Being a Roman Catholic school, we don't choose Satan. We choose Jesus Christ.

PRINCIPAL at Harley Guindon's school

Harley couldn't understand why he was sent home from Holy Cross Catholic Elementary School in Grade 1 for wearing a black and orange T-shirt with "Harley-Davidson" written across the front. He tried to argue that it was just his name, but didn't convince anyone. He faced another shirt-related drama when he was nine years old and in Grade 4. That time, he was sent home for wearing a black T-shirt celebrating the thirtieth anniversary of his father's club with the message, "Support Your Local Choice."

His father didn't take the school's reprimand lightly. He took his complaint to the *Whitby This Week* newspaper. "I can't see anything wrong with the T-shirt," Guindon told a reporter. "It was never meant to be offensive. We went out of our way to design the T-shirt to be socially acceptable. It doesn't have the club's emblem. It doesn't have the word 'Satan' or anything like that. In my opinion, Harley was discriminated against because of who his father was, rather than the actual shirt."

Guindon and Harley's stepmother had met with the school's principal, but nothing was resolved. "We pointed out Satan's Choice was a motorcycle club," Guindon told the newspaper. "We represent an alternative lifestyle, but we're not a political or religious organization."

Principal Tisi wasn't impressed, calling it "inappropriate dress" that made an indirect reference to Satan. "Being a Roman Catholic school, we don't choose Satan," Tisi said. "We choose Jesus Christ."

Guindon took his protest up a notch—in volume. He began taking Harley to school on his motorcycle. The Guindons lived on a school bus route, near where Guindon had grown up, but Harley often deliberately missed the bus to get a ride on the back of his father's bike. "Most times when riding through the streets on our way to school, he would pop wheelies in front of my peers walking, leaving me holding on for dear life," Harley recalled. "I never got used to it. The back rest didn't give me that feeling of comfort one would expect. Every time he did it, even if I knew it was coming, it would still scare the shit out of me."

Harley was a naturally energetic child, and Guindon refused to allow him to take any medication to calm him. Booze and pills of any sort were foreign to the Guindon household. "People believe that because my dad had a beard and rode a Harley, he must have been a party animal," Harley said in 2016. "To this day, I have never witnessed my dad drink alcohol or do drugs or saw him under the influence." Guindon extended his own abstention to his son, whether he could use the medicinal help or not.

Years later, it irritated Harley's stepmother to hear people say that Harley was groomed to be an outlaw biker. She spoke instead of a birthday at Chuck E. Cheese's and family photos taken at the front of the house, under the "family tree." Another photo shows a grinning Harley in his Boy Scout uniform on a Santa Claus parade float. "He really wasn't exposed to a lot of it when he was growing up."

Harley was exposed to violence early, however. One day after school, he was getting ready to step off the school bus when he saw a man running up his driveway, carrying an axe.

"Fight!" kids screamed.

That's not a fight, Harley thought. *That's someone trying to kill my father with an axe in front of twenty-five of my schoolmates.*

Harley later recalled: "I can remember this as clear as day. The guy was . . . ready to cut his head off, and he [Guindon] slid like a boxer, throwing out a jab, and knocked the attacker out cold upon the lawn."

Guindon was so focused on his attacker that he didn't realize the school bus had stopped directly across the street. Harley and his friends stared as Guindon dragged the unconscious man from the lawn into the garage. Harley rode the bus for a few extra stops, giving his father appropriate time to dispose of the unconscious man. Then he walked home as if nothing had happened. "I didn't lay eyes on him [Guindon] until dinner and didn't even receive an explanation. Almost like I must have been dreaming." The police never showed up at the door, despite the many little witnesses. "Not even the bus driver called the cops that day," Harley said. "The kids at school used to tease me because my real name is Harley Davidson, but after that, things became much easier."

Harley didn't see much of his father's rough side. "For the most part, I was sheltered," Harley said. But when Guindon drove Harley around town, there was always a baseball glove, ball and bat on the back seat, even though they never went to the ballpark. "I've never seen him throw a baseball," Harley said. The bat was for self-protection, and the glove and ball were to make the bat look less suspicious.

On some special days, Harley got to escort his dad to work on film sets. Guindon's grizzled biker look was helping solve his employment problem by getting him work as an extra in movies and television shows such as *Jungle Movie, My Date with the President's Daughter, Kung Fu: The Legend Continues* and *Blues Brothers 2000*, when he got to visit inside actor John Goodman's trailer.

The most frightening sight Harley saw while growing up wasn't the man with the axe, or a Molotov cocktail crashing through the front window of his home for reasons his father refused to explain. It was the change he occasionally saw deep in his father's eyes, when they seemed to turn black with rage. Harley recounted a chilling pattern to his father's anger. When he started to lose control, Guindon looked up to the left. Next, he crossed his hands, rubbed his neck and tilted his glasses down to the tip of his nose. Then he shook his head. The final and most horrifying part of this metamorphosis followed. "When my eyes go darker, I'm at my worst," Guindon confessed.

Harley called the angry eyes "black death" and thought, *Black eyes, it's on.* Harley didn't remember the black death eyes from the many times he was suspended from school, although he did receive the occasional whupping for that. The pupils went black when someone challenged or disobeyed his dad. "The only person on this earth that can make me nervous is my father," Harley later said. "When he is mad, you can see his pupils capture all colour flaring black before you, almost like you can see death behind his eyes. It doesn't take much. The man lacks patience in a serious way."

The black death eyes were almost exclusively reserved for adults, but one time, they were aimed directly at Harley. "That was because a school friend stole nearly two thousand dollars out of his drawer and he thought it was me," Harley said. "There are countless times that man scared the shit out of me, but that day is etched into my mind forever."

The black death eyes could also make an appearance at family cribbage games, when Harley's uncle, Jack, dropped by to play a game or two. Cribbage was a game that Guindon mastered in prison and he didn't take losing gently. Harley recalled games punctuated by bouts of "choking, yelling, punching, smacking and wrestling."

"You would believe they despised one another, but there's a genuine love somewhere under the exterior," Harley said. "He's never flew across the table at me, and we've played thousands of games together. Then again, I know better than to raise my voice and his blood pressure."

During one game with his father, Harley was dealt a twenty-nine hand, the best one possible. "The odds are like a royal flush in poker," Harley said. "He always told me if I got a twenty-nine hand he would give me five hundred dollars. The day I did, I moved our couch set to my room, and he purchased a new one. He bragged for months about it to basically every visitor. We lived with the cribbage board on the dining room table, which made it a constant reminder. He used to say I was the luckiest kid he's ever met and I don't just have a horseshoe up my ass, I have the whole horse."

Whether they were watching the Toronto Maple Leafs on television or attending Scouting events, Harley got something his sisters never did:

Bernie Guindon just being a dad. Harley was always working on a new badge to add to his Boy Scouts sash, but the most noticeable badge was the one his father gave him: his name. "I used to tell him to behave," Guindon said. "They were teasing him all the time. 'Harley, can I ride you?' It's hard." Harley's last name was tough to miss, too.

He was just a Beaver Scout when he approached his big sister Teresa. He was clearly upset about something.

"You're my sister and you love me, right? Can I tell you a secret?"

Teresa told him that of course she loved him and of course he could confide in her. Harley explained how a police officer had approached him at Beaver Scouts.

"He came up and told me how bad my dad was and he was going to kill him," Harley said.

"I said, 'I'm going to pray,'" Teresa recalled. "He was scared to go to sleep after that. He thought they were going to kill his dad. He was traumatized. He was like five years old. He said, 'My daddy's a bad man and they're going to kill him, and if I tell anybody, they're going to hurt the family.'"

It was four or five years later when Guindon first took his son aside and spoke to him man-to-man. On a Wednesday evening, they stopped by a pizzeria before a Cub Scout meeting. Harley was nine or ten years old and not even tall enough to see over the counter. After getting their slices, the father and son walked out the door, and in an uncharacteristically grave tone, Guindon said he needed to speak to him. "That was different, and I knew from his demeanour that he was troubled and it couldn't be good," Harley said. "He gave me a real hug, not something I was accustomed to if I didn't initiate it, and he said, 'Harley, you know I love you. I may never be coming home again, but you will be looked after. Harley, when you're older, you'll understand that sometimes a man has to do what a man has to do, no matter the consequences.'"

Even at that age, Harley knew better than to ask questions. "It didn't register immediately. I remember trying to concentrate at Cubs while everyone played ringette, but I remained teary-eyed on the sidelines, not wanting to play or speak to the leaders about why I was upset."

Harley just repeated to himself what his father had said, over and over until it was burned into the boy's mind forever. He didn't share a word of it with any of his friends.

Harley didn't see his father for the next three days. Then Guindon reappeared and all was right in Harley's world once more. Two decades later, Harley could vividly recall the raw emotion of running up and giving his father a hug and seeing the look of love in his dad's eyes as he lifted him into the air. "We never spoke of this again," Harley said. "It was a repressed memory until I had my son . . . When I close my eyes. I can relive that vision of the joy, when I wrapped my arms around my father with relief."

Guindon's recollection of the incident was less emotional. "Sometimes you had to fuck off and you never knew if you're coming back."

Guindon was back, and he and Harley celebrated by building a soap-box racing car from a block of wood. At the Boy Scouts derby, Harley placed second, only behind the scoutmaster's son. Next, they tried something a little more complicated. Guindon and Harley ordered parts from California to build a kid-sized 1964 Harley-Davidson Pacer. It was a rare bike, and Harley used birthday money, allowances and whatever else he could to help pay for it. "I worked selling chocolate bars and used all my money and had the bike built by the time I turned twelve," he recalled. The bike was painted a candy apple red when it was finally completed. "I would enter my bike into all the Ontario bike shows and won a few trophies along the way when my father would enter his bikes. It was something we did, father and son." Guindon said he later wished they could have put the Pacer together quicker, so that Harley could have enjoyed it more when the bike was the right size for him to ride. "He was too big when he got it."

Spending so much time with his father meant experiencing life as he lived it, including the persistent police attention. "I can recall being pulled over three times in twenty kilometres on a regular day." Getting pulled over was such a constant that Guindon always had to factor it into his travel time when going anywhere, since he hated to be late. "He finally had enough one day and went into the cop shop and asked for the staff sergeant," Harley recalled. Guindon suggested that day that he was willing to blow up the police station and himself along with it, if that's what it took for them to halt what Harley called "the harassment and fake tickets."

"After that, they left him alone, which was leaving me alone too, because we were always together."

Even without the road stops, Guindon received enough police attention to turn it into a father-son game. "Our home phone was tapped regularly. Multiple times in the 1990s, he would get me to listen to the cops talking on the phone, clear as day." Harley was amused by how his father could make it all seem funny, giving fake orders for people to go to certain places, leading police on wild goose chases.

"Living that life felt normal," Harley said.

It seemed everyone in the south end of Oshawa had a story about Guindon. Shanan would hear men in bars talking of drinking with him and knew it was false since her father wasn't a drinker. Once, she walked up to men bragging about sharing drinks with him and asked, "Tell me, what does Bernie Guindon drink?"

"I knew he would not pick these two sloths," she later said. She also heard women talking of wild sex with him. She declined to ask them for details.

When Angel and Guindon were finally done, she found a young new boyfriend named Scott, who was determined to do her proud. On the surface, Scott wasn't much like Guindon. He was less than half Guindon's age and appeared to be even younger than Angel. He didn't have much money and he certainly wasn't a fighter, but he was cute and soft-spoken and he clearly had something that appealed to Guindon's fiery ex.

Angel wanted Scott to become a full-patch member of the Satan's Choice. Scott had always done what he could to please her. He had trimmed off a little flab and bought a black chopper from Guindon, which he needed in order to become a striker for the Oshawa chapter of the Choice.

He was still a striker one evening in 1990, when Angel was visiting the home of her friend Maggie Pearce-O'Shea. Scott rode up on his chopper, and Angel and Pearce-O'Shea watched through the window as two full members of the Oshawa chapter suddenly appeared in the driveway. One stopped beside Scott and the other came up behind him. After a few harsh words, one of the Choice members caught Scott with a solid punch in the face. "I stopped watching after that," Pearce-O'Shea said.

There wasn't really much of a fight for her to see, but it was enough for Scott to realize he would not be getting his patch. There was a rule in the Choice that any striker who failed to make the grade and gain a full patch would forfeit his Harley-Davidson to the club. When the women finally mustered the courage to look outside again, Scott's chopper was gone.

Guindon professed innocence when asked about the incident. "Probably he fucked up somewhere," he speculated with a smile. "You had to fuck up bad. He wasn't a happy camper, either. I don't blame him. I didn't do it [sell him the Harley] to make money out of it. Things happen. A lot of guys weren't ready for the club. They thought they were ready, but they weren't."

Angel kept her cool and stepped outside to give her rejected man a hug, which Scott needed more for his pride than for his body.

"He and Angie disappeared from the scene after that," reflected Pearce-O'Shea, signalling an end to one of the most confounding relationships in Guindon's complicated love life.

CHAPTER 38

Moving On

Be good for your mom, do as she says, she knows what is best for you.

BERNIE GUINDON offers advice to daughter Sarah Hodgins

n the final decades of the twentieth century, plastic explosives, rocket launchers and automatic weapons replaced Saturday-night punch-ups as the preferred methods of settling outlaw biker disputes. Bikers were more likely to be found pumping weights in a gym than quaffing ale in a bar. The more dangerous the outlaw bikers became, the more they looked like average citizens.

It seemed nostalgic to watch Vagabonds president Donald (Snorko) Melanson snort up ungodly amounts of cocaine. "He used to make lines about two feet long," an old friend and fellow Toronto cocaine trafficker said. "What a big nose he had. He was like a vacuum cleaner." The more cocaine Snorko hoovered, the more paranoid he became. The fact that the forty-year-old owed Quebec Hells Angels about $900,000 for the product stressed him out and drove him to snort that much more.

Snorko's body was found in a room he had rented in the Novotel hotel on Yonge Street in north Toronto on September 3, 1987, with two bullets in his head. The killing remains officially unsolved, but his old friend had no doubt about which of his former underworld contacts pulled the trigger. It had to be the Quebec Hells Angels, who would have entered the room with the promise of another deal, his old friend reasoned. If they couldn't collect the debt from him, they could at least make him serve as an example to others. "Who else would do it? He owed them a big chunk of money."

Some two hundred Harleys growled along Steeles Avenue West from the St. Paschal Baylon Church in what was the biggest Toronto biker funeral in memory. They rode in from as far away as Dallas, Edmonton and Chicago, and mourners wore the colours of the Lobos, American Breed, Penetrators, Scorpions and Outlaws. No Hells Angels were seen. The bikers at Snorko's send-off were mourning the end of an era as well as the death of a friend. Being popular was no longer enough to keep you alive—something Guindon already knew all too well.

Back in the mid-1960s, the Satan's Choice had held meetings in a second-floor apartment in Toronto. Now the club's Toronto chapter met in a detached brick home in Riverdale with security cameras, a steel-reinforced door, a tall protective gate and fence, and high-powered quartz lighting for the front and back. Bikes were parked in the back, out of public view.

As the 1990s approached, the Ontario clubs were able to keep the Hells Angels out of the province by presenting a united front, much like the old Amalgamated Riders Association had blocked Johnny Sombrero and his Black Diamond Riders back in the early 1960s. A Canadian police Organized Crime Committee report from 1989 states that the Satan's Choice, Lobos and Vagabonds clubs all co-operated in the operation of a lab for clandestine methamphetamine production. As long as the established clubs pooled their energy and kept a common front, it was tough for the Hells Angels to crack Ontario.

Meanwhile, Guindon and the Choice continued to recruit heavily, hoping to ensure safety through numbers. The danger hiding in those numbers was that they might contain subpar members who could easily be turned into police informers or traitors.

Cecil Kirby had disappeared into a witness protection program and was living under an assumed identity when he saw Ken Goobie on the other side of the street in Vancouver's Gastown district. Goobie was wearing a long, dark coat, prompting Kirby to think his betrayals had just caught up to him. Goobie and Pigpen Berry often wore such businesslike clothing when heading off to do their most violent deeds in what Pigpen called "the dark side of town." The executive-style attire helped them blend in and also concealed weapons.

Kirby saw no point in running. It was better to face his fate head on like a man than run ragged like a cornered rat. He crossed the street to meet his executioner face-to-face.

"Oh no, that's all forgotten," Goobie assured him. "I'm a lieutenant in the Salvation Army now."

Goobie was known for his keen sense of humour, but he wasn't joking. One of the toughest of the old Satan's Choice was now an officer in God's army.

Thank God, Kirby thought.

Goobie was the only member of the Choice to be lost to the Salvation Army. The Loners Motorcycle Club was a greater threat. In Ontario, some of the Satan's Choice hived off to join the Loners, including Frank Lenti, Jimmy Raso and Brian Leslie Beaucage, one of the inmates involved in the killings in the Kingston Penitentiary riot.

Guindon didn't let the defections get to him. Rivalries and personality disputes often caused biker chapters to splinter. "Maybe they were tired of the bullshit that was going on in our club. You can always feel there's tensions somewhere."

As it turned out, tensions were part of life in their clubs, too. Beaucage's life ended in a Parkdale boarding house in Toronto. He was forty-three and had spent seventeen of those years behind bars. Considering how violently he lived, it was a miracle that Beaucage had lasted that long. Years before, he had been shot in the heart at a London, Ontario, strip club. His wife rushed him to hospital in time. This time, there was no hope of medical heroics. When his landlord saw the body, Beaucage's head was almost entirely hacked off after he was stabbed repeatedly.

Guindon heard that his old nemesis Johnny Sombrero and the Black Diamond Riders planned to attend a Sudbury baseball tournament on the Labour Day weekend of 1992. There was also talk that the

BDR wanted to set up a permanent chapter in Sudbury, which the Choice considered their territory. The BDR had even already tried to recruit new members, right under the noses of the local Choice. Maybe Guindon and the Choice couldn't hold off the Hells Angels and the Outlaws forever, but Johnny Sombrero and the BDR were another matter.

Guindon had never gotten over the image of Sombrero gloating as Guindon and fellow Golden Hawks clubmates fled across the field at the Battle of Pebblestone decades earlier. He wasn't about to let any fresh insults from Sombrero slide. Then a lone Satan's Choice member in Sudbury was cornered by Sombrero's group. "He had his colours on and we took his colours off him," Sombrero recalled.

Guindon's group showed up hours later in cars, with knives and guns, two-by-fours and, of course, baseball bats. They attacked Sombrero and some of his boys in the parking lot of the Sorrento Motor Hotel, and by the time the last bat was swung, eight members of the BDR were in hospital. "There was about forty-five of them," Sombrero later recalled. "Attacked seven of us. They shot two of us. They shot him in the guts and shot me in the face."

The incident became known in biker lore as "Sudbury Saturday Night," a tribute of sorts to the Stompin' Tom Connors song of the same name. The action finally addressed the shame of the Battle of Pebblestone and ensured that Johnny Sombrero would never set up a BDR clubhouse in Sudbury.

By March 1986, Suzanne Blais's marriage of twenty-five years had ended. Guindon was proud of her for having hung in there until her kids had grown up. He urged her to remember the good times, for there had been some, and to try to forget the bad times, even though there had been many.

"He beat me up several times," Suzanne later said of her former spouse. A big problem was jealousy. "He'd accused me of doing things I wasn't doing. So finally, I said, 'If I'm being accused of it, I might as well do it.' So I went to see Bernie."

As she settled into single life, Blais offered a temporary place in her home to a man she knew through her job at Stelco. He was leaving his wife and needed somewhere to stay until he got back on his feet. Then he just wouldn't leave.

Finally, after much pressure, he agreed to a departure date. On the day he was supposed to leave, Guindon rode up at seven in the morning in full Satan's Choice gear and told him, "I'm here to make sure you leave by five o'clock."

The man left on time, after cooking them a nice meal and taking a photo of Suzanne sitting on Guindon's lap, smiling.

Suzanne and Guindon still weren't a couple. Whether it was Harley's stepmother or someone else, there was always at least one other woman in Guindon's life. Suzanne wasn't about to put her life on hold waiting for him to change. She remarried on February 10, 1994, at the Old Mill in Toronto, and her new husband didn't seem jealous when Guindon attended the wedding. He gave them a leather art piece of a sad-eyed clown lying on a bench, which he had made himself. Later, the new husband helped Guindon apply for a guaranteed income supplement.

Guindon's daughter Sarah Hodgins was eleven years old in 1995. She yearned to meet up with her father. She had old photos from when she lived in Oshawa, back when she was perhaps three or four years old, but she had no real memories of him. She decided it was high time they become reacquainted. Her mother and Harley's stepmother connected and agreed that Sarah should get some daddy time.

Guindon, Harley's stepmother and Harley all drove up to Callander, Ontario, about 87 miles north of Oshawa, to pick up Sarah. Once back in Oshawa, Guindon took Sarah for a twenty-minute ride on the back of his Harley. There were no wheelies, just a restrained tour about town with her dad. "That's one of my biggest memories," Sarah said. "It was the coolest thing." Even as she was getting to know the club's leader, she knew nothing about Satan's Choice. "I just thought he was the guy with the motorcycle," she said.

Her new-found half-brother, Harley, was friendly but rough. Harley was her big brother by just three weeks but he asserted authority over her. He told her something about taking boxing lessons and was being "just a little shit disturber. Testing me."

She was taken aback by what happened when she told her dad that Harley wasn't playing gently. "I remember him giving me shit for tattling on Harley," she recalled. Asked if Harley got in trouble for his roughness, she replied, "God, no. Not at all." Instead, she was told in no uncertain terms what was expected of her in her father's household: "Quit being a rat."

That aside, the visit was a success. Harley felt like a long-lost brother and love found its way amidst the scrapping. Guindon was a daddy with a motorcycle, and Harley's stepmom couldn't have been more welcoming. Not long after Sarah returned home, she got a letter from her father, dated September 15, 1995.

Dearest Sarah

Thank you ever so much for the beautiful motorcycle sun catcher. I heard you picked it out yourself, too. We have it on our living room window, so we can look at it & think of you every day. We also have a collage of family pictures & we were hoping you could send us a more recent photo of yourself to add to our collection.

It is a shame that you are so far away. We heard that you've been in Oshawa but we keep on missing you. Next time try & call before you come & maybe your mom will bring you for a visit.

By now you must be in grade five. How do you like it so far? Maybe you could send us a letter once in a while to let us know how you are doing. It would be nice if you could come to visit maybe for March Break or for some time next summer. We'll have to make some plans with your mom.

I'm sorry for missing your birthday & etc. I'm very forgetful to say the least at times & [name omitted] keeps a list of dates for me to remember but she didn't have your date. I think it might be Aug. 15? If so sorry again my fault. Let me know & I'll make sure not to forget next year.

I'm trying to keep myself busy building bikes so I do spend a lot of time in my workshop. I also spend a lot of time riding my Harley & going to Club functions & etc so I do keep busy.

[Name omitted] goes out to work & I stay with my son Harley. He is in grade 4 & he can be quite a handful. I hope you get along well with your mom & help her out around the house. You are very lucky to have a mother that loves you so much & takes such good care of you. Harley & some of your step sisters are not that lucky & I help those children out a little more because without me, they would not have the guidance that only a parent can give. This doesn't mean that I love some more than others, it only means that I must try to spend more time with them when they need it.

We had not had much time together because you are so far away. Please don't think that you are forgotten. Nothing could be further from the truth. We think of you all the time & wonder how you are too. Hopefully we can have you come visit & you will get a chance to see Grandma Lucy while you are near. Your Uncle Jack had two heart attacks last year but he has quit smoking & is doing much better now.

Please don't forget to send a letter & a picture if you have one. I love you very much & miss you always. Be good for your mom, do as she says, she knows what is best for you. Good behaviour at school is very important to you so that you will learn skills that will help you later in life.

We will look forward to hearing from you soon. Until then, we will miss you. Please do take care of yourself & do your best at home & school.

Say hi to your mom and Michelle.

Love Always & Forever
Dad & [name omitted] XOXO
Harley xo

Harley's stepmom encouraged more visits, and sometimes Sarah stayed for over a week. The Guindons tried to make their home as peaceful and welcoming as they could. Once, when Sarah's mom was en route to pick her up, Harley's stepmom noticed a hooker standing on "her corner." "I had to go out and walk the hooker up the street to get her away from my driveway before her mom showed up," she said. "Since then, I've acquired a high-pressure hose. You should see those gals run when I pull it out."

Guindon remained under constant police surveillance. A paid police agent with a lengthy record that included fraud and theft convictions approached Guindon at the bar of the Dynasty strip club in Oshawa and asked to speak with another biker. The agent later testified: "He [Guindon] asked, 'Why?' and rubbed his finger against the side of his nose. I said, 'Yeah, could you help us out?'" The agent also testified that another patron later came to his table to discuss a drug deal, and the evening concluded with the purchase of a quarter ounce of cocaine for four hundred dollars in a pizzeria parking lot.

Guindon was charged in April 1992 after a ten-month investigation by Durham Regional Police and the OPP called Project Overhaul. The police agent said under cross-examination by defence lawyer Howard Goldkind that he never dealt directly with Guindon over drugs. The police agent also dismissed Guindon as someone who might have mattered in the area at one time but now was just an "old has-been trying to make ends meet." The trial ended in July 1994 with Guindon being found not guilty of trafficking drugs. But the investigation was a reminder that he was still squarely on the police radar.

A month after the trial ended, Guindon and Harley's stepmother climbed onto his Harley. He'd heard that an old Choice member named Greg Bradley was dying of cancer in Moncton, New Brunswick. Bradley's pain was so intense and unrelenting that he slept with a gun by his bed in case he couldn't handle it any longer. Guindon often needed long rides on his motorcycle to sort out his life. Sometimes the rides were to get away from things, but this time he was going to confront the problem head on: he was driving to Moncton so that he could give his old friend one last ride on a Harley. The fact that Guindon was short on money didn't stop him.

One night during the ride to New Brunswick, a Mountie stopped by their motel room and asked him for an autograph, which threw him for a loop. The long ride gave Guindon a chance to reflect on friendship, loss, the absurdity of life and how some things just feel good. It was also a chance to get away from some of the phantoms that seemed to be constantly following him. Harley's stepmother described Guindon on that ride as "Quiet, quiet. We did a lot of miles. When things bothered him, he got on the bike and went for a ride."

Sometimes, to get away, Guindon climbed on his Harley and went to visit his daughters in places like Winnipeg and Northern Ontario. Other times, he rode south for adventure. During extended hauls, he and Harley's stepmother brought a saddlebag each for clothes and a "beer box" for maps, her purse and various emergency items and tools. For longer trips, they also carried a suitcase on top of the beer box. Halfway down the road, they'd mail their dirty laundry home to lighten the load and make room for souvenirs. "We never passed anyone on the side of the road broken down without offering help," Harley's stepmother said. "He was a very good man in many ways. Others might argue, but I know different."

When Guindon rode south, he taped a map over the Satan's Choice sticker on his gas tank to cut suspicion at the American border. During one trip to the United States with Harley's stepmother, they stopped at a ceremony where a priest was blessing motorcycles. The priest became animated when he saw the grinning devil of the Satan's Choice crest on Guindon's gas tank. The man of God couldn't shake the holy water fast enough onto the grinning devil's face. "He stood there just whipping it," she said. "He emptied it out on the patch."

CHAPTER 39

Unwelcome Guests

Bring your dancing shoes.

AN INVITATION to a Hells Angels party

Walter Stadnick rode out of Quebec in June 1993 at the head of a pack of some hundred Hells Angels and supporters. They descended on Wasaga Beach in a not-so-subtle announcement that they planned to move into Guindon's home province. Ontario was simply too big and rich to ignore.

In early 1995, Quebec Hells Angels met in Charlottetown, Prince Edward Island, with Ontario bikers from the Vagabonds, Loners, Satan's Choice and Hamilton Red Devils. The long-anticipated battle between the Outlaws and the Hells Angels for the Ontario drug market was on. The smaller clubs would have to pick sides if they wanted to stay alive.

Guindon was invited to a Hells Angels get-together in May 1996 in Halifax. Ostensibly, the Angels were celebrating their twelfth anniversary in the Maritime city. However, Guindon thought it sounded ominous when he was told to "bring your dancing shoes," and stayed home.

David Boyko of the Los Bravos club in Winnipeg decided to attend. Like Guindon, Boyko was fiercely independent and wanted to keep his club's Canadian identity. He maintained close ties to other Canadian independent clubs like the Calgary-based Grim Reapers and Rebels, the Apollos of Saskatchewan and Guindon's Satan's Choice.

Things seemed friendly enough when Boyko left his Halifax hotel with Donny Magnussen of the Hells Angels. There had been bad blood between Boyko and Magnussen in the past over a drug deal, but Boyko didn't seem nervous. He was a six-foot-two, 240-pound enthusiastic fighter. Before leaving, he told his wife he would be out for a little while.

Boyko never did come back. His body was discovered in a wooded area beside a Dartmouth industrial park. He had been shot behind the ear, execution-style. If Magnussen was the killer, he kept his secret to the end. Magnussen's bound, plastic-wrapped body was discovered in the St. Lawrence Seaway, amidst talk that he was eliminated by the Angels to signal to the Los Bravos that they didn't support the Boyko hit.

Guindon didn't regret turning down the invitation to Halifax. In fact, he'd had just about enough of life as a target. He retired from the Satan's Choice as an active member later in 1996. He was fifty-three years old and had been a member of outlaw bike clubs for more than two-thirds of his life, if you count his prison time.

He left in good standing, meaning he could still attend Satan's Choice social functions, although he couldn't go to meetings or vote. It also meant he could enjoy a party inside a Satan's Choice clubhouse without constantly having to monitor security cameras and make sure no one got out of line.

His retirement was marked with a long bike ride and farewell party, from June 28 to 30, 1996, at a twenty-acre farm outside Port Perry. At the end of the ride, Lorne Campbell got him to stop and look at the procession behind them. There were Harleys as far as the eye could see, as well as ten-year-old Harley play-fighting in the mud with the son of another biker.

In the crowd was Suzanne Blais, who was accompanied by her new husband, Grant. They pulled up in a 1928 Ford Model A, then promptly got stuck in the mud. Guindon was her white knight of sorts that after-noon. "He pulled us out with a tractor that he just happened to be driving at the time," Suzanne recalled. "His sense of timing is perfect."

In his retirement speech, Guindon announced that he was "stepping up to share more time" with his son, Harley.

It turned out to be a good time to leave. The OPP ran Project Dismantle from 1996 to 1998 in an effort to target every member, associate, wife and girlfriend connected to the Satan's Choice. Some 250,000 phone conversations were intercepted, 197 people were hit with 1,363 charges, and $3 million in drugs, property and cash were seized. The club's fortified Hamilton clubhouse was also seized, marking the first time police confiscated a gang's headquarters in Canada. The Toronto clubhouse was then taken under a bylaw crackdown. As a result of the sustained police pressure, membership dropped from 135 in 1995 to just over 70 in September 1998.

At the same time, the Choice fell into a bloody rivalry with the Loners over drug manufacturing and distribution in Ontario. Most of the Loners were breakaway members from the old Choice, including Frank Lenti, who was almost killed in a car bomb explosion in the driveway of his home, across the street from a Montessori school.

It was during this turmoil that the Choice took new member Steven (Hannibal) Gault into its Oshawa chapter. Club rules stated that an existing member had to know a prospective member for at least five years before sponsoring him into the club. Gault's sponsor, Bill (Mr. Bill) Lavoie of Peterborough, hadn't known Gault for five months. Soon, there were rumours that Gault paid Lavoie twelve thousand dollars for the favour. There was something about Gault that didn't sit right with Guindon. "He had a cocky attitude," Guindon said. "That's what I got from him. I always had a gut feeling about him. The questions he'd be asking me. You always had to be careful how you answered him."

Because Mr. Bill hadn't done his screening job, club members weren't aware of Gault's backstory. He had been part of a group called the Travellers, which targeted seniors living on farms in Eastern Ontario for renovation scams. One elderly farmer was bilked for $260,000 for renovation work that was never done. Gault's personality got even worse after he started wearing a Choice patch. "After he got his full patch, he thought he was king of the world," his former wife said.

The Choice had done a fairly good job of keeping informants out, but Mother McEwen's betrayal still struck a raw nerve with older members. Guindon wondered about Gault, and he wondered, too, if Mr. Bill was selling information about club members to police. "He hadn't worked but he always had money," Guindon said. "I always wondered where he got the money."

In 1998, police approached Cecil Kirby to ask if he was game for another undercover job. This time, their target was Gerald Michael Vaughan, the former Richmond Hill Choice member whom Kirby had done break-and-enters with back in the early 1980s.

Vaughan was no longer a Satan's Choice, and he had never been a high-profile member. Guindon and many former club members didn't even recall him wearing a patch when he was with the club between 1972 and 1974. After quietly quitting the Choice, Vaughan tried for a time to upgrade himself professionally. He studied heavy equipment operating, studied for his Grade 10 equivalency and then was certified as a gas fitter. He also bought a car licensed to operate as an airport limousine at the Toronto International Airport.

Then, over a five-week period in the spring of 1979, something inside Vaughan snapped. Using a knife and a gun, he attacked women on Toronto streets, in parking garages, in a car, in an elevator and in their beds. He didn't know any of his victims, who ranged in age from fifteen to twenty-eight, but he somehow still felt they had brought the attacks on themselves. He later called them "loose women" and declared that his attacks "help them straighten out their own lives and thereby society in general." He opined that "society was in a pretty bad state" and that the attacks were part of "a mission to purify the world."

On May 21, 1980, Vaughan was found not guilty by reason of insanity on four counts of rape, four counts each of attempted rape and choking, five counts of break-and-enter with intent and one count of assault causing bodily harm. He was sent for an indefinite term to the Oak Ridge maximum-security mental health facility in Penetanguishene, Ontario. Vaughan was a sick, unapologetic man, and it was only natural to wonder what else he might have done.

Inside Oak Ridge, Vaughan refused to take part in treatment programs. Cold, controlling, distrusting, narcissistic, paranoid and psychopathic,

Vaughan had the officers truly scared about what he might do should he be allowed to walk free in 1998. They suspected he was a serial killer but needed more evidence. Their idea was to send Kirby into the mental health facility to hook up with him and get him to open up about his other suspected crimes.

"Could you approach him?" an officer asked.

Kirby said he was considering taking on the job, but then the offer just went away. He was left to wonder if the woman-hating serial killer who once wore a Choice patch had been released into the unsuspecting public.

It was around this time that Frank (Hippy) Hobson hit rock bottom. The former Windsor Choice member's wife left him in Calgary for another man, taking their three children with her. He was selling dope one night when police caught up with him and two friends. "The police pulled their guns and my two buddies froze," Hippy recalled. "I got out and ran." The officers threatened to shoot but Hippy ran on. By the time they caught up with him, he had shed his .9mm Beretta and stash of marijuana. Fortunately for him, the police didn't check out his apartment, where they would have found a dozen sticks of dynamite and blasting caps.

His life started to rebound, finally, when he was allowed to work for the John Howard Society, which helps prisoners integrate with society. He was granted permission to take a job as a cook at a gold mine in Lupin, in the Northwest Territories, about twelve miles from the Arctic Circle. A librarian there showed him a self-help book called *Psycho-Cybernetics* by Maxwell Maltz, which had been drawn upon by elite athletes and personal development coaches like Zig Ziglar and Tony Robbins. At that point, despite all of his crime, Hippy had only spent about five days in jail. He now decided to clean up his act, had his record expunged and went off to university.

Within a few years, he found work as a parole officer, which eventually gave him access to highly confidential biker intelligence reports on his old Satan's Choice clubmates, as well as members of the Para-Dice

Riders and Vagabonds. He estimated he reviewed some one thousand files at the police station on Toronto's Cherry Street. "Those albums had all kinds of pictures of bikers. I was amazed at how many I knew," Hippy recalled. He was now in a nice position to do his former clubmates and rivals huge favours, or harm, while drawing a government salary.

Unfortunately for his old club, Hobson had truly changed. "I never said anything to anyone and just put the albums back."

Rick Gibson of Winnipeg had heard throughout his childhood that his father was none other than Bernie Guindon. The thought that he was the son of the Satan's Choice founder appealed strongly to him. Gibson had always felt an attraction toward motorcycles, as if the yearning to be on two wheels was in his blood.

When he was ten years old, Gibson inserted table legs into the forks of his bicycle so that it would look like a chopper. He and some like-minded friends called themselves the Hells Choice.

In 1998, Gibson heard that Guindon was in Winnipeg. He made a point of dropping by to finally meet him.

"When I walked in, he was drinking a tea," Gibson recalled. He introduced himself.

"Pleased to meet you," Guindon replied.

Gibson told him that he thought he was his son.

"Who's your mother?" Guindon asked.

Gibson told him.

Then he asked when Gibson was born.

Gibson replied that he was born in 1965.

"Yeah," Guindon said. "That sounds right."

When Sarah Hodgins was fourteen, Guindon broke off communication with her. There had been no argument and there was no explanation at all. Up to that point, Sarah had never even seen him angry. He just went quiet. "He didn't say anything," Sarah later said. "He wouldn't talk to me."

The problem, she heard, was that he had found out she was dating a young man from the Caribbean. "He had heard from my sister that I was dating a black guy, period. That's all. He knew nothing about any of it. Just that he was black."

They only dated for a month or two, and later, she even forgot his name. What she did remember was that it caused a split between her and her father. A couple of years later, when Sarah was about sixteen, Harley was upset that their dad still wasn't talking to her. Harley called her and left a message for her to call back. When she returned the call, she got Guindon instead. He said, "What are you doing calling here?"

"That's the only time I've heard him raise his voice to me," Sarah said. For reasons that perplexed her, Guindon, a rare biker president who had let black men join his motorcycle club in the brazenly racist seventies and defended his black boxing friend on the streets of Toronto, had frozen her out for the most insignificant of relationships, just because her boyfriend had been the wrong colour.

In 1999, Guindon was getting some work done on a car at a garage when harsh words were exchanged with the mechanic. The next day when Guindon returned, he was clubbed twice in the back of the head.

There was no thought of calling the police. "No, Bernie would never go to the cops," Campbell said. "Not Bernie."

He was left with a feeling of lingering dullness in his head, which would never entirely go away. There was no retaliation. Guindon might have been playing by rules only he understood, but there was no denying he was living life as a civilian now, outside of the pack.

CHAPTER 40

Biggest Party Ever

I don't think I'm a fucking idiot. I've done some things in my life.
I've had a big club myself.

BERNIE GUINDON

Police surveillance officers shivered outside the Hells Angels club-house in Sorel, Quebec, on the night of Friday, December 29, 2000. Inside, Guindon and three hundred or so others attended what many thought was the biggest party in Canadian outlaw biker history. Despite the magnitude of the event, just outside Montreal, Guindon wasn't particularly excited to be there on that bitterly cold night.

They were gathered on hallowed ground, as far as outlaw bikers went. The Sorel clubhouse was home to the first Canadian Hells Angels charter. It was here that the Hells Angels took root in Canada on December 5, 1977. Now, almost a quarter-century later, the Angels' winged death head flag flew over the clubhouse's roof as the club swallowed up members of well-established Ontario clubs like the Lobos, Last Chance, Para-Dice Riders and Satan's Choice. The Vagabonds in Toronto and the Hamilton-based Red Devils remained intact; they were considered friendly enough to the Angels not to be a threat and were not vital to the mass expansion.

The Ontario bikers inside the Sorel clubhouse were allowed to join the Hells Angels without having to go through any initiation process. For many of them, getting an Angels winged death head patch was a dream come true. Guindon's feelings were more complicated. Diehard Satan's Choice members had bitterly resisted the American-based Outlaws, and now they were joining another international club. Guindon was going in as president of the new Hells Angels Oshawa charter. Nationalistic feelings ran particularly strong in the Oshawa chapter of the Choice, and they had been the last to concede to the Angels. Guindon had been pulled out of retirement for the patchover, likely averting a war between the Angels and diehards in his old club.

The mass patchover to the Angels bolstered their Canadian position against the Outlaws, but it was more immediately a response to sudden moves made in Quebec by the Rock Machine, a rival club that had already folded into the larger, U.S.-based Bandidos Motorcycle Club. Just four weeks before the Sorel patchover, the Bandidos had shocked the biker world by expanding en masse into Ontario, giving forty-five members of the Ontario Rock Machine probationary Bandidos status at a ceremony in a banquet hall in Vaughan, north of Toronto.

The Angels' response in Sorel gave the club instant charters on both coasts and throughout much of the country in between, the Prairies excepted. There were three new Hells Angels charters in Toronto, and one each in Woodbridge, Kitchener, Sudbury, Oshawa, Thunder Bay, Windsor, Lanark County, Keswick and Simcoe County, as well as a probationary charter in the Niagara region. With one bold move the Hells Angels could boast 110 members in the Greater Toronto Area alone, the highest concentration in the world. Canada was now home to some 550 Hells Angels, which accounted for about a fifth of the membership of the world's largest outlaw motorcycle club. Angels' founder Sonny Barger liked to say that the sun never set on his Hells Angels, and now Guindon's old empire helped him solidify his boast.

If Guindon was going to wear the patch, he decided he'd live it as well. In 2003, he made a pilgrimage, riding down to Arizona to meet Barger for his sixty-fifth birthday on October 13. Barger ran the Cave Creek charter of the Angels and lived on a small ranch near Phoenix.

It was familiar territory for him, not that far from where he'd served four years of federal prison time for conspiring to blow up the Outlaws' clubhouse in Louisville, Kentucky, in the 1980s.

The year 2003 hadn't been a good one for Barger. That was the year he learned that his third wife had been a paid police informant. Also that year, someone put an up-close bullet between the eyes of Dan (Hoover) Seybert, president of Barger's Cave Creek chapter.

Not surprisingly, Guindon rode his Harley into a high-security environment in Cave Creek. Barger seemed uncomfortable, and not just because he spoke through a stent in his throat after a bout with cancer. His attitude, as Guindon summed it up, was one of "Yeah, okay, you're here. I have to put up with you." Guindon was particularly sensitive to the perceived snub: "I don't think I'm a fucking idiot. I've done some things in my life. I've had a big club myself."

Barger once had a bodyguard who drilled horns into his head to give himself an extra-intimidating appearance. That guard wasn't on duty when Guindon arrived, and he wasn't happy with the replacement.

"I wasn't impressed with his bodyguard or whatever they call him. Had this attitude. The guy had a fuck-you attitude. Things he'd say, like a rude remark all the time. I came all the way from Canada. I didn't stay long." With the Arizona desert beckoning, Guindon did what he always did when he didn't want to sit still. "I went riding . . . Got better out on the bike."

CHAPTER 41

Regrouping

I don't recall how we got to the topic, but he [Guindon] said if he ever heard I was doing pills or opiates that he would literally kill me.

HARLEY GUINDON

Harley left home at fifteen, first moving in with his older sister Shanan and niece Rori. "When I was leaving, my father said, 'You'll be back,'" Harley recalled. "That statement gave me the courage and strength to overcome every obstacle by myself to prove him wrong." They still loved each other, but Guindon's house was far too small for two alpha males.

Living with his sister also proved to be a challenge, though Harley loved her too. His next move changed his life forever. "After leaving my sister's on good terms, I moved right into the worst part of Oshawa, the real south end. There were times I drank hot water in the winter to stay warm and had migraines from not eating for days at a time. Then I started selling dope and stealing cars and got myself into some trouble."

Like his father, Harley was charismatic and he didn't do things by half measures: "We probably stole about three hundred cars. We'd go joy-riding." Once, when they were playing bumper cars with two stolen vehicles, Harley hit the brakes and was rammed from behind, flipping his ride into a ditch by a farmer's field. "We gathered our thoughts and went back and stole another one."

Dodge Neons were particularly easy pickings in the early 2000s, as were Oldsmobiles. All it took was a screwdriver, some nerve and a few seconds to get one rolling down the road. "We even took them from the police pound one day. They were easy. They were there." Once, Harley was riding in a stolen minivan on John Street in Oshawa, close to his grandmother's old folks' home. Music blared and the youths felt happy and at peace with the world, until a stranger's hand reached inside the vehicle at a red light and yanked out the keys. Then a voice shouted, "Call the cops!" The hand and voice belonged to the minivan's rightful owner, who was shocked to see his vehicle cruise past him with the radio cranked up. A slow-footed member of Harley's group did some detention centre time for the crime, but Harley and the others managed to bolt from the scene.

Harley was now living on Wentworth Street, about a half-mile from the Simcoe Street South residence where his grandfather had once sold bootleg booze out of the family home. On Harley's sixteenth birthday, Guindon took him shopping to buy him new running shoes and jeans. "I was a happy camper," Harley later said. His father changed the mood. "I don't recall how we got to the topic, but he said if he ever heard I was doing pills or opiates that he would literally kill me." Harley had only ever smoked a bit of pot and the like, so his father took him by surprise. "I took the threat seriously because he said it with such conviction I forgot everything else we spoke about."

As Harley watched friends he'd once respected succumb to Oxy-Contin addictions, sometimes fatally, he became grateful for his father's pre-emptive warning. "He was always adamant on carrying myself as a leader, and there was no room to dishonour our family name by shaming him with addiction. I truthfully believe that is what kept my head clean from the narcotics all these years." To this day, Harley rarely smokes even marijuana. He is reluctant to be caught with "a stupefied appearance and unable to share mindful conversation."

Harley picked up a couple of assault charges, which put him into the Brookside Youth Centre in nearby Cobourg. There he received a visit from Rick Gibson, who had relocated to nearby Lindsay from Winnipeg.

"This wasn't the way I wanted to meet you," Gibson told Harley.

They both welcomed the idea of finally having a brother. At one point, they tried to tally up the number of Guindon siblings they had, but were unable to reach a more exact number than somewhere between eleven and sixteen.

Once released, Harley decided to get his life back on track and moved in with his sister Michelle and brother-in-law Tony. "The deal was to stay out of trouble and go to school. Their daughter Danielle lived there, so I had to be on my best behaviour." He lasted a year.

Harley gravitated to a street crew that took a page from the script of the 1991 action thriller *New Jack City*, which featured Mario Van Peebles, Wesley Snipes, Ice-T and Chris Rock. In the movie, a gang converts an apartment complex into a crack house. Like the movie characters, Harley and his friends learned how to protect their turf in a rough business. "You have a group of white guys selling a black drug, crack cocaine, in a black area," Harley said.

His friends included Kyle James Odette, who did prison time for pistol-whipping a former friend over a $1,500 drug debt, then forcing him to strip in a field near Belleville, where he froze to death. Another was Christopher Dwyer, who would later do time for murder. That was par for the course, as seven of the ten members in Harley's group ended up serving adult time for killing someone.

Harley's new circle of friends fell into a routine of going back and forth between the streets and custody. It was part of the natural ebb and flow of their lives, with games being one of the few constants in both places. Once, Harley was at a party playing bridge when news came that a body had been found and that one of them was about to be charged with the killing. The soon-to-be-arrested friend just joked, "Here's my gun. Pack my pen bag"—a bag of items inmates are allowed to bring into custody, like a small television, stereo and clothing. With the bag packed, the game resumed.

Harley was with his father when he got the news by phone that his friend Brandon Saville had been murdered on Saturday, June 2, 2005, on a footpath by the Erie Street bridge in Oshawa. Harley turned to his father and said he needed a gun to protect himself. "He flat out told me no," Harley recalled. Guindon was always there with advice or support for his son, but when it came to helping him with anything illegal, he drew the line. "I was understanding but disgruntled because the streets were a wild place at the time and I wanted to protect myself."

Around this time, there was a weekend house party where, in Harley's words, "Some idiot hit a girl after already being belligerent with a friend of mine." Harley one-punched the idiot unconscious, hurting his hand in the process. While the idiot lay in a snowbank, Harley went inside to tend to his injury. "I could literally have slid a quarter into my hand wound."

Soon, police were everywhere. Harley called his father and told him what had happened. Guindon wasn't impressed with the 2 a.m. phone call but did suggest "pouring liquor on my hand and getting the fuck home before I land myself back in chains."

"That was the first and last time I ever called that man intoxicated," Harley said.

When the calls became more serious, Guindon never failed to answer. "He would visit me wherever I was incarcerated, which I knew was hard for him to do considering I was the only child he raised due to his prime-life prison stretch. Although he wasn't impressed with my lifestyle choices or his name getting dragged into the media for being the son of a Hells Angel, he remained by my side the whole way through."

When Harley was eighteen, he was charged with assault with a firearm. He faced a possible ten-year sentence. His father, knowing all too well what would be in his son's future if he lost his case, attended all his court dates, worried.

"I remember our smiles remaining on our faces for several straight hours after being acquitted. We went out for fish and chips, and he was even bragging about the acquittal to the waitress while I was wearing prison clothes, all embarrassed."

Even when police didn't become involved, Guindon seemed to always know what Harley was up to. "The man finds out everything," Harley later said. "Everyone knows him or claims to know him. I'd get in a fight and he would call me up and ask about it."

Harley had left home several years before, but he thought of his father often and with a particular strain of pride. "I didn't realize my father's street status until my early adulthood. I never ran around threatening people with him. Anyone that knows me knows it to be fact. I never had to because I was always the toughest on the block, still am. I learned to handle my own conflict using him as a template of right and wrong. Standing up for the weak. Never backing down. Remaining forthright no matter the consequences. These are a few of the characteristics instilled to my very core, principles that have heightened my sense of self-worth to the point no one can tell me shit."

His friend Saville's murder brought about a five-month undercover investigation by Durham police called Project Burn, which wound through Bowmanville, Oshawa and Whitby, then outward into Lindsay, Peterborough and Toronto. It dealt with a street gang police called the Baby Blue Chippin' Crew or Crippin' Crew. Police accused them of picking fights with uniformed police officers and attacking innocent victims.

The street gang changed its name to the Cash Money Brothers, but its business remained the same: dealing crack cocaine. Project Burn ended with almost five dozen suspects charged with offences that included extortion, drug possession and aggravated assault. Harley was just twenty and he was once again looking at the very real possibility of serious prison time. To focus himself, he thought of his dad. "I would take perspective by putting myself in his shoes and think, *What would his standpoint be with this behaviour? Would he become irate? Would he be proud? Would he give me a whupping? Am I honouring him? Dishonouring him?*"

Guindon had split from Harley's stepmother around the time that Harley moved out, although they both still spoke well about each other. Guindon moved out to the town of Orono, about a forty-five-minute drive east of Toronto, to live with a girlfriend who was around his age, which was a switch for Guindon. The new girlfriend was suspicious of Suzanne Blais and wouldn't let her call or visit. She was also a drinker and a gambler, and she constantly proposed marriage.

Guindon was a survivor of three failed marriages (if you count the prison annulment) and countless dalliances. He had more kids than he could count. He wasn't in the mood for more drama, especially a union with a gambling drinker who didn't like his friends calling or dropping by. But he also couldn't leave. Guindon was focused on someone coming back into his life: his estranged daughter, Sarah Hodgins.

Six years after he'd stopped speaking to her, Sarah made the effort to re-establish ties with her father. "I called him and told him I'd like to come for a visit." She couldn't understand how she could lose contact with her father for so long just because she had gone out with a black boy for a couple months. She wasn't aware that her father had let the first black bikers into the outlaw biker world in Canada. She didn't know that he had stuck up for Spider Jones when racist bikers were trying to goad him into trouble, not that her father's past seemed to have any bearing on his present state of mind. But she did know that it was wrong to break ties with your own flesh and blood over something so minor. "It hurt that he would just lose contact with me over a guy," Sarah said. "Why would he stop talking to me over a small thing? It just seemed so petty and insignificant to me. I had never known anyone who was racist at that time in my life."

Years later, Guindon said he couldn't remember the cause for the lengthy split with Sarah, but he allowed that it would have upset him if his daughter had a black boyfriend. "I wouldn't have liked that." He had befriended and defended black bikers and boxers in his past, but drew a line here, admitting to a qualified racism. "It's totally different being in the family and the club. The club, I can get away from. You can't get away from them if they're family."

Her dad acted as if nothing had gone awry, and he quickly invited her down for a visit in Orono. Sarah found her father's new partner unsettling, with her less-than-subtle wig and false teeth and overall tough attitude. The woman only spent an hour or so with them before heading off somewhere else, alone.

Sarah and her dad never mentioned the split, as much as it still gnawed at her. What he did talk about was troubling as well. He mentioned smacking a woman upside the head and putting some woman in her place, reminding her just how rough a man he was. "I'm extremely against it. It kind of made me lose a bit of respect for him."

It wasn't the homey reunion Sarah had hoped for, but at least they were talking again. "It was Thanksgiving," she added.

Even when distant from her father, Sarah had remained close to Harley, and she found herself constantly worrying about her half-brother's future as he became an adult. "I always tell him to smarten the fuck up," she said, ever mindful of her father's long stints behind bars. "He doesn't listen to me."

Suzanne Blais's husband Grant died of a respiratory illness in January 2006. When Guindon dropped by to help her clean up her place, he found Grant's diary. In it, he read that Grant had never really loved Suzanne. He'd married her only for her refurbished 1928 Model A auto-mobile and trailer. "I felt how many mistakes can I make?" Blais said. "In my life, that was the worst mistake."

Blais swore that it was only then that her relationship with Guindon had turned physical. "I didn't have sex with him until I was a widow," she said.

One night in April 2006, Steven Gault dropped by Guindon's home unexpectedly. Gault, another former Satan's Choice who was now in the Hells Angels Oshawa chapter, offered Guindon work but didn't spell out what that would involve. Guindon hadn't really trusted Gault back when he was in the Choice, and he certainly didn't trust him now. "He promised me five thousand dollars a month and I said no. I didn't know what he meant by 'work with him.' I just knew it would mean trouble."

Guindon still harboured doubts about Steven Gault and Bill Lavoie, the two former Choice members who now also wore Hells Angels patches. Long gone were the days when Guindon could expel someone with a left hook on a suspicion or because he didn't like his attitude. It was dangerous to call a Hells Angel a police informer, even if you were the charter's president. Eventually, Guindon would learn that his suspicions were right. Gault was a paid police agent who received more than a million dollars for his role in an eighteen-month police operation, called Project Tandem.

While Guindon was a reluctant Hells Angel, there were still some perks to being a member of the world's largest outlaw motorcycle club. One of them concerned his mother, who now lived in an Oshawa seniors' home. She liked it when her boy dropped by to see her, wearing his biker vest or something with "Hells Angels" on it. Guindon had been her protector since his mid-teens.

"She said, 'That's my baby,'" Guindon reminisced. "She wanted the old people to know that she was protected by her baby."

Being able to put fear into the blue-rinse set wasn't a strong enough inducement for Guindon to stay in the Hells Angels. There's a five-year pin for being in the club, but he never received it. He announced he was quitting at an Oshawa chapter meeting. "They didn't like it. I told them I wasn't staying. I can't afford it . . . Everybody thinks you're a millionaire because you belong to all of these clubs."

Guindon left the club in good standing after a respectful ceremony, in which he was given a metal plaque with his image on an Angels' death head. "I had made my decision. I had been thinking about it for a while. Quite a while. Thinking, *Where do I go from this?*"

Guindon was sixty-four years old and he had been an outlaw biker for almost a half-century. Since Gault was the secretary of the Oshawa charter, it was his duty to burn Guindon's patch to make things official.

CHAPTER 42

Culture Shock

It was a culture shock. It was gloomy. Rusting away.

HARLEY GUINDON on Millhaven Institution

Harley Guindon looked out from the courtroom prisoner's box in early 2007 and saw his father giving him the finger. The extended middle digit came after Harley pleaded guilty to extortion with a firearm, two counts of forcible confinement and two counts of assault causing bodily harm. For this, he was sentenced to a prison term of five years.

Seeing his father's gesture was a troubling sight in an already unpleasant environment. But for once, Harley knew something his father didn't. "He was unaware that my lawyer, Alan Richter, had advised me during trial that the Crown was charging me with attempted murder if I didn't take a plea bargain," Harley later said. "To me, I had no choice. The rat . . . got on stand during the preliminary hearing and said I shot him. How do you fight that?"

At this point, Harley had been held inside the Lindsay jail for almost two years awaiting trial, after initially being charged with attempted murder. He faced the possibility of ten years on the attempted murder beef and another twelve for the related charges. That added up to twenty-two years and he was only twenty-one years old. Five years seemed like a bargain, especially since he might be released on parole before that.

The Crown agreed to drop charges against some of Harley's co-accused if he, Brendan Mak and David O'Neil all pled guilty. "After explaining why we all pled, my father understood," Harley said. "Bottom line: we were ready for trial. No one snitched and my crew took it on the chin wilfully. Not many men group together and take five years each out of loyalty these days."

Just a decade earlier, Harley had been working hard to win merit badges as a Boy Scout to make his father proud. In March 2007, he followed more directly in his father's footsteps. Harley entered the Millhaven Assessment Unit, where his father had been processed three decades before. Harley's file noted he lacked a high school diploma, trade or profession and added that he also was considered to lack initiative. After he sat through a battery of tests, he was found to have a 9.3 grade equivalency in language, an 8.3 grade equivalency in math and a 10.2 grade equivalency in reading comprehension.

Harley had heard plenty of bad stories about Millhaven, and his buddy Scotty Jones was killed there just before his arrival. That said, there's no real preparation for walking into a maximum-security prison for the first time. "It was a culture shock," Harley later said. "It was gloomy. Rusting away."

After his assessment, Harley was transferred to medium-security custody in Collins Bay Institution, where his father was also once an inmate. Soon, Harley was phoning his father a couple times a month. The line was monitored, so conversations were predictable. One would ask how the other was doing. "Oh, you know," father or son would reply. "Same shit, just a different day." Still, it was always nice to hear the voice of a loved one.

Guindon once dreamed of turning his son into a fighting machine. Now he imagined Harley getting out of prison and finding a job with a pension. "He needs a good job. Some kind of a job that he likes to do and intends on holding onto it."

As Harley settled into prison life, assistant Crown attorney Paul T. Murray filed a blunt report on him on May 3, 2007, to the National Parole Board:

> *He has shown complete disregard for the rules of society or for authority. I have attached a number of police intelligence reports that highlights his audacity and attitude towards police, including threatening officers, as well as other gang activity and violence. If he is prepared to take this position towards law enforcement officials, one can only presume that his level of disdain for the rights of normal citizens is greater, as was evidenced in the facts underlying the present conviction. Mr. Guindon will do what he wants to get what he wants, and if such involves violence or guns, then so be it. He is a dangerous individual who will no doubt revert to the only lifestyle he has embraced if given the opportunity: that of a violent drug dealer; he revels in the violence . . .*

Murray was equally grim about the prospects for Harley's co-convicted, Mak and O'Neil, writing, "These three have had access to guns and are prepared to use them for their criminal activities. I have no illusions about these three 'turning their lives around' for the greater good."

CHAPTER 43

Home Fires

I was told that my house had been burned to the ground.

BERNIE GUINDON

On March 30, 2008, Guindon received a call from Orono while he was attending the Toronto Motorcycle Show. "I was told that my house had been burned to the ground." No one was injured, but all of the cash he had hidden under a bookshelf was consumed by the blaze. He didn't believe in banks and had kept all of his money close to him. Now it was all ashes. He also lost his jewellery, including Rolex watches, artwork that he had made in prison, club memorabilia including his old Satan's Choice patches, motorcycles, bike parts, clothes, boxing memorabilia, and phone numbers and addresses for his old friends. Worst of all, he lost freedom.

The house wasn't insured because Guindon had been in the process of buying another house and had just cancelled the policy. Either it was extremely bad luck or someone knew when to hit him to hurt him the most. All of his possessions had been boxed up, ready for the move, when the house burned down. "He was more bent out of shape about his pictures than pretty well anything," Harley said. "He had a lot of art. I'm sure that took a toll on him."

Harley's half-brother Rick Gibson tried to help out, but there wasn't much anyone could do. The structure had collapsed and there was four and a half feet of water in the basement. "There was nothing left," Gibson said. "He was devastated."

A disaster relief worker gave Guindon a cup of coffee as he stood by the ruins and stared. Soon, police forensics officers arrived and started to root about, suspecting they'd find a body under the water. They searched thoroughly but found nothing to turn the rubble into a homicide scene. Apparently, someone had called in with a crank tip about a body in the basement just to make sure Guindon had as miserable a day as possible. "He didn't sleep that night," Gibson said. "He just stayed there. He was completely in shock. Didn't know what to say."

For the next two weeks, Guindon worked on the cleanup, but there was precious little to salvage. "He was just completely run off his feet," Gibson said. Some biker friends organized a poker tournament called "Bernie's Burnout," which raised a quick $2,400 to help get him back on his feet.

Guindon suspected that the family of a spurned woman, not a biker club, was behind the attack, but he couldn't prove anything.

His relationship with his girlfriend died with the fire. Guindon was sixty-five and homeless. Had he stayed on at General Motors all those years ago, his pension would be just kicking in. People close to him noticed that something happened inside him that he just couldn't fight. "I think when he had that fire, that's when age really kicked in for my dad," Shanan said. "He lost everything in the fire. Everything that made him."

"I was in bad shape," Guindon said.

He moved in with Gibson and his wife, Vanessa. They had been his sureties after he was charged for a domestic against his former common-law wife in Orono, which was dropped to a peace bond after taking two years in the courts. Guindon busied himself with working on Harley's motorcycle, which had sustained four thousand dollars in damages in the fire.

Gibson had always sought a tighter connection with his father, and now they were living under the same roof. There was certainly love there, but Guindon still felt awkward. Once, he had been president of the second-largest outlaw motorcycle gang in the world. He had been the go-to member of the inmate committee in one of Canada's toughest prisons. He had been captain of Canada's amateur boxing team. Now he felt like he was in the way and not even the man of the house. "It's hard, trying to fit in," Guindon said. "You can't just go into the fridge and get what you want. You've got to wait until dinnertime."

"He's not a man for change," Shanan said. "He likes routine. He's happy with a set schedule he likes to follow."

Despite the upheaval, one thing remained a constant in his life: Suzanne Blais seemed to be forever in the background, cheering him on. She and Guindon rode out east to the Maritimes in the summer of 2008. The trip marked the fiftieth anniversary of their first meeting.

A lot of time had passed since Guindon first climbed onto a motorcycle. He had lost friends to road accidents and gang violence. Now, natural causes were taking a toll too. On September 29, 2008, Sarah's mother, Marlene, died after a ten-month battle with lung cancer. She had remained close with Guindon since their early teens, and he often visited her during her sickness. At her funeral, attended by hundreds, Guindon was the first to shovel dirt onto her grave.

Guindon's mother was also frail. She had kept her spirit intact through a brutal marriage and seemed somehow unstoppable. "She was just there forever," Shanan said. "She was always there." She also knew she was loved in Oshawa. Guindon saw to that. In the final years of her life, Guindon and Suzanne got her groceries and took her to medical appointments, and Guindon wrote all of her Christmas cards out for her. "He was very much in his mother's life," Shanan said. "He was there once a week."

Her sickness was a profound blow to Harley, now settling into his first federal prison term. When she was younger, she had taken her grandson swimming every Wednesday. Now, Harley wasn't allowed passes from prison to be with her, and she wasn't healthy enough to visit him. "My grandmother was my heart," Harley said.

Albini (Lucy) Guindon died in November 2008. She was eighty-five. Harley was permitted to attend her funeral, escorted by three guards and shackled and handcuffed "like Hannibal Lecter," in Harley's words.

Suzanne gave a prayer and a speech for "Mom" in French. Then the francophones present joined hands and sang a drinking song that had been her favourite, even though she wasn't a drinker herself. Fitting the life of a woman who had done with so little, and whose infamous son found himself with so little after so many years of fighting, the lyrics included: *"Tu prends un verre, tu m'en donnes pas/J'te fais des belles façons/ J'te chante des belles chansons/Donne-moi-z-en donc,"* which translates roughly to "You take a drink, you do not give me any/I'm looking good for you/I'm singing beautiful songs for you/Give me some of that."

CHAPTER 44

Prison Reputation

I've heard about you.

Mafia leader JUAN RAMON FERNANDEZ PAZ

A personal drama played out quietly behind locked doors in Penetanguishene. At the Oak Ridge mental health facility, former Richmond Hill Satan's Choice member and convicted rapist Gerald Michael Vaughan began a series of treatment programs after being diagnosed with "narcissistic, antisocial and paranoid traits, and paraphilia [psychosexual disorder]." At first he co-operated, then after a few years in custody, he began refusing all forms of rehabilitation. His counsellors considered his growing obstinacy a psychological battle for control. Instead of trying to get better, he set out to better conditions for himself.

Vaughan wrote to his Member of Provincial Parliament, complaining that he should have the right to smoke and watch cable TV in his room. He already had a computer with Internet access. He also demanded privacy from female staff while in the shower and began to sponge-bathe himself using a bucket in his own cell. Then on July 14, 2004, Vaughan tried to kill a fifty-nine-year-old employee by clubbing him with a pot. The attack was nothing personal. Vaughan just reasoned it would get him transferred to a prison, where he would have more rights.

Vaughan learned he was suffering from more than psychosexual disorders. He was diagnosed with colon cancer and was often out of the facility for medical treatment. He began requesting a change of doctors, often with no apparent reason or warning. Cecil Kirby wondered if he was just scoping out the security of various medical offices. "He might have been looking for an escape route," Kirby said. "That's a game we all play."

Colon cancer killed Vaughan on May 5, 2008, at the age of fifty-seven, before he could make his escape bid. He drew his final breath in the Huronia District Hospital in Midland. The man who was perhaps the least stable, least known and most dangerous member of Guindon's old gang had been in maximum-security custody for twenty-eight years.

Harley Guindon was released to a Hamilton community residential facility two years after he was sent to prison. His limited freedom didn't last long. Hamilton police called him a key suspect in a June 2009 stabbing and also believed he was trafficking drugs. He was returned to Collins Bay later that month on a parole violation, and that's where he was on November 18, 2009, when his son was born.

The birth announcement read: "Our dear 'Junior' came out punchin' on Nov 18th, 2009 at 5:39 pm weighing 7 lbs 15ozs, 21 inches tall with an 8 inch reach." Harley appealed to prison authorities to give him an open visit, so he could hold his boy. He couldn't stand the idea of seeing him for the first time while behind a thick wall of Plexiglas. They refused.

"After this, I went haywire, punched a few guys out and went to the hole for being a threat to the safety and security of the institution. I spent six months in the hole and requested to be sent to Millhaven maximum penitentiary." His parole file states he was placed in administrative segregation for what authorities called "the safety and security of the institution." The experience made him despise the parole officer who yanked his freedom in the first place. "I still have dreams about that woman and they're not healthy," he said.

Harley's next stop was Millhaven's ultra-tough J-Unit. A lot had changed there in the few decades since his father had helped tear apart the walls between cells in a riot, but an inmate could still kill his time with a game of bridge.

To play bridge well, you have to be able to count cards. Strong bridge players often graduate from the ranks of lesser skilled games like cribbage and bid whist. "Bridge is the game for focus and concentration," Harley explained. "You don't play cribbage when you know how to play bridge."

In Millhaven, serious bridge players sweetened the pot by playing for money. Putting actual money on the table wasn't possible, but prisoners could arrange for friends and family on the outside to make bank deposits and settle debts. "I made lots," Harley said. "You just play with the people who have money." Bridge meant Harley could pay for a 1999 Harley-Davidson Softail custom ride that his father was building for him. "I gave him $10,500 while I was in custody because I always wanted a bike built by my father."

Harley was winning at more than bridge. He fought in cramped cells and he fought in wide-open hallways. Fighting in a cell meant close quarters combat, which favoured strength. Harley had that. Fighting in the open rewarded speed, and Harley had that too. "In a cell, you're using the wall, you're using everything," Harley said. "In the open, you can dance. You're not tripping over chairs." In both cases, most prison fights were settled quickly. "It's pretty well a hockey fight," Harley said. And when it came to "hockey fights," Harley quickly distinguished himself from the hated "cell warriors." A cell warrior is comfortable shouting out tough statements from his cell, knowing the steel bars and the guards are there to protect him. If confronted, he screams early and loudly, knowing this will summon the guards to save him.

Some of Harley's fights were over money. Others were over curiosity about who was the better fighter or because of an inflammatory comment. Sometimes it seemed as though guards enjoyed the fights as much as the inmates. "I've had a lot of them [guards] watch. A lot of them walk away."

As Harley's prison fight record improved, he decided to celebrate it with tattoos. Prison tattoos are etched onto an inmate's skin by using the "e" string of a guitar as a needle and the motor from a radio or an old Walkman cassette player. Getting a tattoo is a time-consuming affair, sometimes softened with prison moonshine. One of Harley's new tattoos read, "Before I PC I'll die in the yard." It took eighteen hours for Harley to have "GLADIATOR" etched across his shoulders. It was a reference to Millhaven as "gladiator school." His next tattoo was "2005–2009" and his fight record of 41-0. The thick needle left a ridge of scar tissue, an unspoken challenge to other prisoners. "It didn't make life easy for me," he said.

Harley was in the weightlifting pit at Millhaven in 2010 when a heavily built Hispanic man walked up to him.

"Hi. I've heard about you," the man said, his face betraying no sign of whether this was a friendly approach. "My name is Ray."

"Ray Fernandez?"

"Yeah."

"I've heard about you," Harley replied.

Fernandez was the right-hand man in the Toronto area for Montreal Mafia boss Vito Rizzuto.

Harley and Fernandez were soon getting along well, and Harley also became friends with Fernandez's associate Daniel Ranieri. "He was my workout partner, him and Danny. We walked a lot of miles around the yard. He was a gentleman. He didn't carry himself like a gangster."

Harley and Fernandez talked of plans for business once they were free again. Harley had every confidence they would become reality. "Ray's not a storyteller. If he says he's going to do something, he does it."

Harley also met up with Gregory Woolley from Montreal. The Haitian-born gangster ran Montreal street gangs and also had tight ties to the Hells Angels and Vito Rizzuto. "He was always smiling," Harley said. "He was always laughing. He was the best chess player I've ever played." When Harley wasn't working on vehicles destined for the army, physical training and school work, he was facing Woolley across a chessboard. Over a four-year stretch, Harley estimated that he and Woolley played 2,500 games. Harley also estimated that he won one of them. "We'd play all day, every day, for four years," he said.

As Harley sat in prison, he thought about how many people blamed his father for the time Harley was doing. He took this as an insult to his father and himself. His father wasn't a puppet master. Harley wasn't a puppet. "I chose my own path of life, one I never witnessed from under my father's thumb," Harley said.

Guindon couldn't tell his son what to do as a kid, and he couldn't tell him much of anything now. Harley was incensed that he couldn't have visits from his father because of an order barring him from connecting with criminal associates. Harley grieved this, and eventually he was granted a ten-minute phone call every second week with his dad. It wasn't much time, but enough for Harley to realize that despite his father's age, Bernie Guindon hadn't much changed.

CHAPTER 45

Remarriage

I don't know what the fuck she sees in me. She knew I was a fucking whore.

BERNIE GUINDON **on his upcoming marriage**

Guindon moved more slowly and deliberately now than in his prime boxing years, but as he slipped into old age, he still wasn't soft and cuddly. Rick Gibson recalled being at a motorcycle show when his father was somehow irritated by another man whose name was also Bernie. Gibson didn't see the incident, but he caught up with his father in time to see the result.

Someone called out, "Bernie just knocked out Bernie."

Gibson didn't have to be told which Bernie he would find still conscious.

"I'm the Bernie," Guindon announced.

"Fuck, that guy raised his cane at me," recalled Guindon, "so I gave it to him."

Stories like this didn't surprise Harley. He had seen and heard much to make him marvel that his father was still alive. "I could understand why rival clubs disliked him," Harley said. "He walked right up to two dozen members and told them what he thought, which wasn't good. I witnessed him losing his lid at a Toronto bike show, calling on one percenters [outlaw bikers] while foaming at the lips, solo. These guys were in their twenties to forties while he was pushing sixty all alone. This happened because a man looked at him and smirked. When it came to him being disrespected, he would swing first, ask questions later.

"A larger, in-shape guy not listening to my dad's direction to leave, unaware of who he was, turned to him and said, 'What are you going to do about it, Grandpa?'

"Not a second thought, and whammy!" Harley said. "There's a helmet in the mouth and you're missing eight teeth. The man just never cared. He's going to die the same way he was born, an alpha male."

Guindon was nothing if not a survivor. After his Orono home burned down, he stayed with friends and family for two years before he once again found some stability. He and Suzanne Blais married on September 11, 2009, at a resort motel in scenic Kawartha Lakes, north of Toronto. It was her third wedding and either his third or his fourth, depending on whether you counted the annulled prison one.

Harley had been released from prison but remained under strict parole conditions. His request to attend their wedding was denied by his case management team, who reasoned that going would bring him in contact with criminals.

Suzanne was as giddy as a blushing schoolgirl as the wedding approached. Guindon was in good humour himself, though no one would mistake him for Keats or Byron when speaking of the ways of the heart. "I don't know what the fuck she sees in me. She knew I was a fucking whore. I'd fuck anything that walked the streets. The more the merrier. You only live once."

Their nuptials were celebrated with 529 fellow bikers and other friends, and at least twenty-nine uninvited guests. Police surveillance officers carried binoculars, cameras and notebooks around the property, and it seemed a biker couldn't piss in the bushes without tripping over an officer spying on the event. Other officers stood on ladders for a more panoramic view, calling out licence plate numbers of guests for another officer to write down. Annoyed, Suzanne approached some and sarcastically thanked them for making them all feel safe.

During the ceremony, Guindon, wearing a black shirt and white tie with a black leather vest, rode his FLHT Harley Decker through a gauntlet of bikes onto a white stage. Suzanne, dressed head to toe in white, appeared riding side-saddle on a Harley Road King tricycle.

The bride and groom each held live white doves as the assembled guests and police surveillance officers heard that doves mate for life. The bride and groom released the doves, then set free another ten for good measure.

At the end of the ceremony, the newlyweds climbed onto Suzanne's Road King to ride off, with fellow bikers revving their engines and beeping their horns in a salute. Then everyone dined on burgers, corn on the cob, beans and pickled eggs long into the night.

Married life would require some adjustments for Guindon. Suzanne had a cabinet full of Paul Anka CDs and memorabilia. "I hear it every fucking day," he grumbled. Still, even a daily earful of Canada's beloved crooner beat sleeping on someone's couch. "If it wasn't for her," said Guindon, "I'd be hitchhiking."

CHAPTER 46

Gladiators

I'll never forget him getting stabbed in the top of the forehead and this guy struggling for a legitimate three seconds, trying to pull the blade out of his head, while I'm being sprayed in this guy's blood.

HARLEY GUINDON describes a prison attack

Harley missed his father and Suzanne's wedding. A parole condition banned him from associating with criminals, but he couldn't avoid those connections for long. He was arrested again in February 2011. That meant a trip to the Kingston Penitentiary Transition Department, a holding-processing area that's a particularly unpleasant place to do time. "You have no idea what crimes the other inmates were there on or revoked for, and it is entirely integrated." In the holding area, an inmate like Harley, destined for the general prison population, is kept with those bound for protective custody. Harley felt like he was constantly being goaded. Fortunately, he didn't have to share a cell. "Believe me, coming from the Millhaven max, the only institution not integrated, it's impossible to turn an eye when in knowledge of a diddler or baby killer. I always had an issue putting on my blinders."

Already emotional because he felt police had framed him on the charges that had brought him to Kingston, Harley deeply resented the separation from his family. Aggravating him further, his new surroundings were spartan at best. "The windows were smashed out due to previous riots, leaving the extra blanket to do no justice during the winter months. I remember my toes frozen together and seeing my breath each time I exhaled, sleeping with a toque on my head and my hands in my armpits."

Next came three months in J-Unit, which Harley would later call "extremely character building." J-Unit remained home for the bad apples of the penal system, who had stacks of institutional misconduct charges against them. Like his father before him, Harley rioted there. "We burned the range down." He and other inmates were hosed down three times in a week with OC spray, an intensified form of pepper spray. They were sprayed so often that the prisoners seemed to become immune to it, like cockroaches who aren't slowed down by weak pesticide. As the noise from live gunshots carried on during the riots, Harley slept on the webbing of a goalie net.

The day the riots and the OC spraying ended, Harley and his bridge partner Michael Swift were walking back to their range when "he was rudely approached by a guard with an ego problem," Harley said. The guard announced he was taking Swift to segregation for arguing, and Swift responded with a one-punch knockout. "The guard literally lay unconscious, stiff as a board, snoring on my foot," Harley recalled. Then they were overcome by a cloud of "enough OC spray to drop an elephant."

Violence among inmates was frequent and bloody and lasted long after the riots ended. "There were too many stabbings to count or be able to remain solid if I spoke about the details," Harley said. "It was rare to see a fist fight, and even when those are in action, nine times out of ten there's a shank on someone's hip." Prisoners couldn't expect anything resembling a fair fight. "A pack of wolves will tear the meat off your bones with sharpened steel—like teeth biting through an apple," Harley said.

Harley was able to talk about two stabbings that took place during his time in J-Unit without violating the inmate code of silence, because they were swiftly dealt with by prison authorities. In one case, Harley was talking on the phone under a guard tower when he saw a cluster of inmates throwing on their institutional green jackets, even though they were indoors. Something bad was about to go down and it would be hard to identify who had done what because the green jackets made them all look the same. "Sure enough, they start running towards me, and for a second, I ask myself, *What the fuck is this?* and then it happens: eight to ten bandana rabbits stabbing this one guy from a rival crew that just landed in the jail the day before, literally two feet beside me." He called them "bandana rabbits" because of the odd, animal-like way they hopped about, although there was nothing funny about their actions. "I'll never forget him getting stabbed in the top of the forehead and this guy struggling for a legitimate three seconds, trying to pull the blade out of his head, while I'm being sprayed in this guy's blood."

A few weeks later came another night Harley would never forget. He'd gotten to know an inmate from Toronto called Little John. "He had been on my range for a couple weeks and we'd shared some good conversation," Harley said. "I thought he was a good, solid guy." Harley and Little John had each formed a negative opinion of an inmate who they thought acted like a tyrant. "Little John and I had something in common as we attempted to fight the same man that populations feared."

A rumour began circulating about Little John. Prisoners were saying he was staying out of the yard because he was dodging a beef with another inmate. Left unanswered, talk like that could get an inmate killed. Making matters worse, the man Little John was rumoured to be avoiding belonged to a group Harley called "one of the fiercest groups of men in the Canadian federal system."

There was still a prison code—although it wasn't as strong as it had been in Guindon's day behind bars—that a prisoner had to be considered solid to be respected. "The solidest place that carries a code is J-Unit," Harley said. Prisoners there constantly evaluated who was solid and who wasn't. "People get killed for making a mistake like talking to a guard." It was time for Little John to prove himself.

Harley told him about the rumour. "I said, 'People are saying that you're hiding out on our range, and we can't be having that. If you have a problem, it's either you face it or you have to leave.'"

Little John answered back sternly, "I'm not hiding from no man. I'll be in the yard tonight."

He was true to his word. That night, on March 20, 2011, 230-pound

Little John stood off by himself against the gymnasium wall, one foot up on a cinder block. A beefy black man who looked a bit like UFC fighter Kimbo Slice, Little John didn't seem like he should be afraid of anything, but Harley knew that waiting like this was nerve-racking for him. Though Harley was supposed to stay out of it, he was anxious too. "I sat down with three people to play bridge with my back to the wall," said Harley.

A group of inmates flooded into the gym. They had their green jackets on. An unusual silence fell over the men inside. Out of the corner of his eye, Harley noticed Jordan Trudeau, a twenty-nine-year-old aboriginal inmate from Manitoulin Island, Ontario, separate himself from the pack. Trudeau was serving a life sentence for second-degree murder. He made a quick approach toward Harley's table.

"He began driving his jail shiv four to five times into the side of my bridge opponent's neck. I knew what he had just done was the biggest mistake he ever made." The target of Trudeau's assault was a lifer who had just been returned to Millhaven and happened to look a lot like Little John. "The worst case of mistaken identity I have ever seen," said Harley. Trudeau had accepted the job of killing Little John, not knowing his victim, only what he looked like.

"The card room went wild, yelling at Jordan," Harley recalled. "The people in the room began to congregate, pacing towards Jordan as he walked backwards, palms out in protest." He still didn't understand his error. At least a dozen men stepped in to defend the bleeding inmate, who'd been quietly dealing cards to Harley only a moment before.

The miscue gave Little John time to make a decision. He landed a right hand squarely onto Trudeau's chin, knocking him cold. The pack of men in green pulled back.

"The man has to go," one of them said about Little John, and the mob concurred. To let him live because of a case of mistaken identity would be an embarrassment.

Twenty-one-year-old David Bagshaw was beginning a life term for first-degree murder for a particularly cowardly offence that disgusted many of his fellow inmates: he had stabbed fourteen-year-old Stefanie Rengel of Toronto, then left her to die in a snowbank on New Year's Day

2008. Taking up where Trudeau had left off was Bagshaw's chance to earn some much-needed prison stripes. "Bagshaw truly was trying to stay out of trouble, but sometimes when it's you or him, animal instinct takes over and you eat or be eaten," Harley said. "The parole board would say he had a choice, but they weren't there."

Bagshaw sprinted in Little John's direction "knife out, cornering him . . . behind the heavy bag and swung with purpose, landing every blow," Harley recalled. The shank sank deep into the target's leg and midsection. "You could see Little John was refusing to go out faint-heartedly."

Sensing wounded prey, the pack surged forward, but Little John kept fighting. With a flurry of punches, he broke away from the group, and then abandoned any thought of his immediate safety and waded back in, "throwing and punching until he was pushed to the ground and dug out by multiple weapons."

A guard fired down from the tower, hitting Bagshaw in the leg. "He hopped in my direction to avoid any more wounds, and to me, it appeared that the bullet went in and out, and I told him he needed to get medical attention," Harley said. Bagshaw hopped out of the yard through an open door to the weight pit, and through that space to another door, opened by staff. "Once he skipped through that door, I never saw his face again."

The gunfire had backed the mob off Little John. One of them noticed Trudeau stirring. He awoke from his stupor, an eighteen-inch puddle of blood around his mouth. He struggled to his feet and a friend counselled him to "just finish what you were doing and everything will be all right."

Trudeau advanced on Little John, shiv in his hand. Little John clutched a side wound, leaning against the same wall where he was first attacked. The pool of blood around his feet was visible from across the room. "Little John couldn't believe his eyes," Harley recalled. *How could this not be over? What did I do so wrong to deserve this?* I could only imagine how he felt."

Fear and adrenalin were keeping Little John on his feet. He sluggishly eluded thrusts of Trudeau's shiv as the guard fired down again. Trudeau paid no mind to the warning shots. If he didn't scar his target and fulfill his duty to his peers, his life wouldn't be worth much anyway. Harley recalled: "Then there was a shot that echoed and sounded like two. Little John went back to the wall while Jordan folded like a chair."

Though Harley was friendly with Little John, he believed the rules of the range had to be respected, and so he didn't take sides. He and another inmate ran to the fallen Trudeau. Someone grabbed the shank from his hand and tossed it away. "The guards shot tear gas at us like we were trying to hurt Jordan," said Harley, so they tied T-shirts over their mouths and carried Trudeau's slackened body through the same route Bagshaw had just taken to get to the hospital. "As we got him to the back door, a number of guards answered with assault rifles aimed at our chests, screaming to 'Get away from the door!' . . . They looked at us like we were next."

Harley and the other inmate slowly lowered Trudeau to the floor. "We both felt him go lifeless in our arms, and we looked at one another that very instant, knowing what each other had felt."

Blood was sprayed on the gym walls, the floor and a card table in the aftermath of the struggle. "If you grabbed a dry mop, you could have filled a wheelbarrow," Harley said. A negotiator in the gun tower asked the prisoners' range representative to either get the prisoners to clear the gym or convince Little John to walk through the medical doors. "Some called him names as he exited. I clapped with respect, knowing ninety-five percent of the people in that gym would have taken an easier road that day," Harley said. "If I ever see him again, I look forward to shaking his hand."

He also felt bad for Trudeau. "It wasn't Jordan's beef, so there are no sides to have. They both were warriors that unfortunate evening."

Harley was released as planned three weeks later, on April 15, 2011.

"This is where you're going to go when you're bad," Lucienne Guindon had told his sons, introducing them to the penitentiary decades ago. He'd meant it as a caution, not a legacy. But here was the grandson he'd never met, walking out of that same institution and about to enter another family legacy.

As Harley reflected back on that horrible night, he thought he wouldn't even have been there in the first place if not for a Durham Regional

Police officer saying that he was a Hells Angels prospect back in 2005. That was a lie, Harley said.

"I was always told that once you get in the club, the police never stop surveilling. You're always outnumbered and they never sleep. It's too much heat, it's too much hassle and it's not all what it's cracked up to be."

Harley had been a street gang member, not a biker, when he went into prison. He left prison thinking he had nothing to lose by wearing the patch of an outlaw biker club, as his father had before him. The Satan's Choice no longer existed, but the Hells Angels were alive and well. In March 2014, he got his Angels' patch. "Why not join? It's my life story. I'm now a federal offender anyways. I understood that I'm already a marked man."

From childhood, Bernie Guindon seemed destined to travel a hard road. He hadn't reached its end when his son was born, and now Harley followed in his tracks, seeking his own destination but ending up in the same place.

CHAPTER 47

"A Little History"

I've never done a bad thing to a good person and have always stuck up for the weak.

HARLEY GUINDON

Durham Regional Police Constable James Ebdon came calling to an Oshawa crack house in 2011 with questions for Harley's friend Bradley Cox. The patrol officer escorted Cox outside and said, "You give me attitude and I'm gonna fucking drag you uptown. I'm gonna say you assaulted me. I'm gonna say you threatened me."

Cox stayed silent while Ebdon had plenty to say, including: "I hurt people . . . and then I make their cocaine fucking appear." Ebdon, who was armed and standing close to two other armed officers, invited Cox to assault him: "Shut your fucking mouth and do something . . . do something please, do fucking something." Cox declined the invitation and Ebdon gave instructions on what Cox should say the next time they met: "Yes sir, no sir, three bags full, whatever the fuck you want. Can I suck your cock, sir? Can I do a backflip?"

That was an unpleasant enough story for Harley to hear, but it actually got worse. Ebdon, speaking into his police radio, gave a possible reason for why Cox generated so much interest and vitriol: "We think he is associated to Harley Guindon."

———

In the summer of 2012, Guindon and Suzanne rode from Ontario to Vancouver Island in nineteen days. Harley, who was out on parole, followed along in a trailer but didn't make it far. His friend was handcuffed and put in the back of an OPP cruiser somewhere around Wawa in a dispute over a payment for gas. Suzanne raced back and covered the bill, but by this time, police dogs were sniffing through his truck and marijuana was discovered in a ski boot.

Erslavas rode west with Guindon and Suzanne from Thunder Bay. "It was a fantastic ride," Erslavas said. "We stopped at all the provincial borders for pictures, and most of the Harley dealers, where Bernie was often overwhelmed with attention. Most of all, for me it was an opportunity to take 'the long ride' with Bernie. We had talked about it, but because of circumstances and timing, it never worked out, so taking that ride for me was something really special. Let's face it: none of us is getting any younger.

"We rode on, motoring across the endless prairie, just enjoying the miles, the wind, the burble of the pipes and the easy lope of the Harley engines. It's euphoric, almost Zen-like as one day flows into the next. The best rides always end with a certain level of regret, and that was the case, for sure, when we parted company."

Later in 2012, a telephone call from Harley hit Guindon like a stiff punch in the kidneys: Harley would be representing Ontario in a Hells Angels boxing match against a former pro in Vancouver.

"Can you give me some tips, Dad?" Harley asked.

There was only time for a twenty-minute lesson, and Guindon ran over the basics of footwork and punching combinations. Then Harley was off to fight the pro in a six-round match. Harley was a veteran of scores of prison and street brawls, but he had never actually boxed in a match before.

"I was fucking going crazy," Guindon recalled.

The pro Harley was supposed to fight had a cut under his eye from a bout two weeks earlier, and his trainer wouldn't let him take the fight. Another fighter stepped in to face Harley.

The next thing Guindon heard about the bout was Harley describing how he won it in the fifth round, after the ref called the fight on a standing eight count to protect his battered opponent.

"He was a man," Harley later said of the boxer. "He was strong. He was tough. He went three rounds toe-to-toe."

Harley was just twenty-six when he was back in the news in August 2012, as Durham police announced the results of a sweep called Project Kingfisher. The operation, which also involved Peterborough police and the OPP's biker enforcement unit, resulted in the arrests of twenty-eight suspects and the seizure of drugs, including heroin, cocaine and marijuana. Harley, who was on parole at the time, was now facing the possibility of a fresh prison stint for trafficking cocaine.

Harley often faced misconceptions about his name and upbringing. "People ask what it was like growing up with the last name Guindon and believe it to be a luxurious upbringing full of fun, adventure and respect. I did not inherit his respect. I inherited a name to defend, and honour, through the toughest times and protect it with my life. The life I knew was motorcycles and a crest with a devil on the back, with one parent, my father, with a mother on the run. I have been through a lot growing up, being kidnapped twice, held at gunpoint, etc.

"I look past how I was brought up and believe it to have instilled a moral compass to differentiate between right and wrong. I've never done a bad thing to a good person and have always stuck up for the weak . . . I love my father. I have earned his pride in me."

The little boy who once cried at having to receive the sacrament of Holy Communion at Catholic elementary school was facing charges that threatened to put him behind bars for seventy years. Harley wasn't about to blame fate or his father for his predicament. He also wasn't about to give empty apologies to his father for ending up back in jail. "I don't need to continue to think about what my father would think, because I am my own man now."

CHAPTER 48

Criminal Duties

I went to give him a hook. He moved. I hit him with the right.

BERNIE GUINDON on troubles with a motorcycle painter

Guindon was at a bike show called Classy Chassis in the Kawarthas, north of Oshawa, in 2012, when he heard a familiar gruff voice. "Hey buddy, come over here."

Guindon turned to see none other than Johnny Sombrero looking at him. His long-time nemesis was selling antique guns from a booth. Neither man was tempted to exchange punches for old time's sake. "That's past tense," Guindon said. Instead, they swapped business cards and then, later in the year, sent each other Christmas cards.

"I never disliked him, ever," Sombrero said of Guindon. There was absolutely no hint of apology from either side, just memories that somehow seemed good. "He wasn't the one who shot me," Sombrero said. "He's a good guy. He's a good kid. I don't look at him like the enemy anymore."

Sombrero said he always looked forward to getting Guindon's annual Christmas card with smiling photos of him and Suzanne wearing Santa hats. "It was always the first one to come."

———

Back in custody, Harley was anything but a model inmate. On December 14, 2012, a security intelligence officer at Collins Bay penitentiary wrote:

> *Overall while in institutional custody GUINDON's conduct can be described as very poor, and he was noted to be heavily entrenched in the criminal, gang and drug subculture of the institution, with ongoing connections to these elements in the community. It is noted that this behaviour continued despite the highest routine security controls available to an incarcerated offender, present in a maximum security environment. GUINDON established himself as a key figure in the institution, and relied on violence and intimidation to conduct his business and garner status. Numerous reports from his CASE Management teams throughout his period of incarceration note anti-social tendencies, and that his ties to organized crime and gangs served as reinforcement of his image and character. In preparation for GUINDON's release to the community on Statutory Release, his Parole Officer at the time noted: "He appears to regard this lifestyle with some degree of reverence . . ."*

In the spring of 2013, Harley learned that his Millhaven prison friend Ray Fernandez had been murdered by a Mafia hit team outside Palermo, Sicily. At the time, Fernandez had fallen into disfavour with his boss, Vito Rizzuto, for not taking sides in a Montreal underworld war that had killed Rizzuto's father and eldest son. Harley said the news upset him. "I had a lot of plans with Ray. For him to get taken out, it kind of hit home."

Guindon was getting frustrated. He'd been waiting months for a custom paint job on Harley's white 1999 Softail. It was the motorcycle Harley had financed with his prison bridge earnings, and Guindon was impatient to get it ready for his son, should he get out on parole.

The painter and tattoo artist was six-foot-five, 235 pounds and in his thirties. Guindon was about ten inches shorter, more than sixty pounds lighter and in his early seventies. As Guindon described it, "I went to give him a hook. He moved. I hit him with the right." That punch dropped the younger, bigger man, who later apologized for the delay.

Guindon's old friends from his club days were dropping from natural causes, like long-time Toronto biker Larry McIlroy, who passed away in October 2013 after a long bout with cancer. The sixty-seven-year-old had been a member of the Road Runners club back in the 1960s before joining the Satan's Choice, and he was an East Toronto Hells Angel at the time of his death.

Guindon's fearless nature didn't always help him, as it had with the bike painter. He got into trouble in the biker community for an interview he gave to the History channel, in which he said that the Hells Angels had absorbed some members from "Mickey Mouse" clubs in the 2000 patchover. Feelings were still raw when he and Suzanne drove to McIlroy's funeral to pay their respects. "A guy came up to me, probably one of the heavies, said, 'You're not wanted here,'" Guindon recalled.

Fighting at a funeral would only make an ugly day even uglier, so Guindon and Suzanne left, fuming. "I felt sorry for Bernie and Suzanne," Steve (Slick) McQueen said. "To me, I thought that was in bad taste. A funeral is not exactly the place to start bringing up stuff like that.

"I was saddened for Bernie. That a guy who played such an important role in the whole biker growth or development in Canada was forbidden from paying his respects. I just don't understand that . . . I saw him trying to leave. He had a hard time navigating his car through the traffic of Harleys."

Soon, Guindon was told he was "out bad" from the club, the biker equivalent of banishment.

The History channel broadcast didn't help Guindon's eldest child, Teresa, either. She was living in Windsor now, away from the Oshawa crowd. A pastor's wife approached her with a concerned face and mentioned the broadcast. "Is that your father? I feel so sorry for you. I will keep you in prayer."

"I just can't get away from it," Teresa said.

The world was also closing in on Cecil Kirby. The former Richmond Hill sergeant-at-arms had been living under assumed identities for more than three decades. Kirby confided in an interview for this book that he thought the end was drawing near for him. "I'm still waiting for a bullet in the back of the head. I'm just waiting for it. It's going to happen. I've got a bad feeling about it. Something should have happened by now." Kirby also had lots to say about the RCMP and none of it sounded positive. "I wish I would have taken a bullet in the head instead of cooperating with those bastards."

Kirby complained that it was increasingly hard to hide out in a world of instant messaging, digital photography and social networks. "It's a small world, believe me." As his physical strength waned, he came to regard anyone with a cellphone and a Facebook account as a potential threat.

"All of a sudden, I heard this click." He was in public one day and startled to realize that a woman he didn't know had just snapped a cellphone photo of him. "I flipped on her," he said. "I said, 'You're invading my privacy.'" He demanded that she immediately delete the photo and she balked. The man she was with could see that Kirby was deadly serious and his insistence was on the verge of turning ugly. The photo was erased.

Kirby makes a point of covering up the camera of any computer he uses before signing on. "I put a piece of paper over it [the lens], just in case. You never know. You gotta always be careful."

From his hiding spot, Kirby spoke well of Guindon, although they hadn't interacted in decades. "Bernie Guindon was pretty well known all over the place. Like the Sonny Barger of Canada. Really well known and really well liked."

For his part, Guindon didn't worry about cyber security or much else. He didn't have a smart phone or computer and had stayed off the Internet after a brief foray into online card games. "I used to play solitaire on the Internet and quit."

Like others of their generation, Harley and his friends treated the Internet as a natural part of life. Some of them had secretly videoed Constable James Ebdon's threat to frame Bradley Cox for assault and cocaine possession, and that video had gained more than a million

YouTube views by September 15, 2015, when Harley was scheduled to stand trial on Project Kingfisher, the massive drug bust targeting cocaine and heroin trafficking.

Just weeks before his trial date, Superior Court Justice Laura Bird released a ruling that changed everything about Harley's situation. After viewing the video, she concluded that the police officer had "committed several criminal offences in the course of his duties" and dismissed him as "not a credible or reliable witness."

With that, the Crown stayed all of the charges against Harley and several of his co-accused. After facing the possibility of several decades in prison, Harley walked free.

CHAPTER 49

Fathers and Sons

*I worry about Harley all the time. I told him, "Quit trying to walk in
my footsteps. Try not to be like me or you'll be in jail the rest of your
life." I did most of my best years in jail.*

BERNIE GUINDON gives advice to his son

L ife was full of surprises for Guindon as he settled into his eighth
decade. One of them was that he was still alive. He had a knuckle
that was out of kilter from a long-ago street fight, and his nose was
multidirectional after nineteen breaks in and out of the ring, including
one from Teresa's punch in the Collins Bay visiting area, and another
from a supposedly accidental shot from a female Special Olympian
with Tourette syndrome, also at Collins Bay. "That one really hurt,"
Guindon said. "I just had my nose straightened, for fuck's sake."

Guindon and Teresa remained in contact, despite their profoundly different outlooks on life. The eldest daughter of the founder of the Satan's
Choice was now doing God's work as an ordained minister with a special
interest in street people. There was something sadly ironic for her in the
name of her father's old club. Teresa knew how Guindon had slept in an
abandoned car after he'd fled his father, and heard the perhaps apocry-
phal story of how he had tossed Guindon's mother through a window.
She tried to understand. She really did. But as horrible as those stories

were, in her books they still didn't excuse everything that her father had done. "Just because you started out in a bad place doesn't mean you had to stay there," Teresa said. "My dad made a choice. Unfortunately, he made the wrong choice."

Emboldened by faith, Teresa had the courage to tell her dad things that others wouldn't dare. During one particularly heated conversation, she revealed that three Satan's Choice members had come on to her decades earlier at one of her father's birthday parties. After she'd rebuffed their sexual advances, they called her father "a washed-up nobody."

"They wouldn't say that," Guindon replied.

"Dad, they're not your friends," Teresa told him. "Family comes first. You have to choose your family."

Like her father, Teresa went for knockouts. Once, she told him, "One day you're going to wake up from this dream and you're going to realize you screwed up your life."

Despite the dust-ups that inevitably occur between forceful personalities, she is proud to possess some of her father's better qualities, like resiliency and leadership and a certain charisma, all of which help in her ministry. She also shares his fearlessness. "Do I hate him? No. I don't hate him. Do I love him? There's parts of him that I love. I wouldn't be here without him. I have empathy for him."

Teresa sometimes wondered how things might have turned out differently for her half-brother Harley if he had grown up with a different name, or if she had been allowed to adopt him when he was a baby. "He didn't have a prayer growing up with his dad," she said.

Once, Teresa pointedly asked her father if he even knew what love is. Guindon kept his infamous temper in check and made a point of telling her he loved her at the end of their talks, however rough they became. Guindon wasn't quick to tell people he loved them, but Teresa could draw it out of him.

One of Teresa's sons grew up to be a hip-hop artist, and her other son, Devin, became a successful construction subcontractor in Alberta. Guindon had once been reduced to tears with the fear that Devin had been kidnapped by his grandfather's biker enemies. Now, Devin had a son of his own, making Guindon a great-grandfather.

"The last time I visited him was in '08 and we went for a bike ride together," Devin said in 2016. "I love him as my grandpa, but he's definitely made my life hard carrying his last name." One of the reasons Devin moved west was because he grew weary of being pulled over and interrogated by police in the Oshawa area for no reason. Once, when he was seventeen, he parked on King Street in Bowmanville with his girlfriend and began counting out change to buy candy from a convenience store. "Then a cop pulled up behind me and ran my plate," Devin recalled. "That's when he called in for backup and K-9 units. They arrived very quickly. I asked what all this was about, and they said it was suspicious that I was pulled over to the side of the road. I asked him if it had anything to do with my last name, and they refused to comment on that."

Devin said that his mother tried to keep him away from Guindon, but he grew up wanting to be like his grandfather and uncle Harley anyway. They had a certain magnetic pull that was hard to explain or resist. "I was very young at the time and didn't know better," he said, adding that he can't help but have mixed feelings about his grandfather.

There's love but there's also something darker. "He always treated us good, but that doesn't mean he was a good person."

Harley's stepmother was planning a family get-together for his thirtieth birthday on October 15, 2015. Those party plans were ruined, however, when Harley was arrested six days before his birthday after a high-speed chase. He faced fresh charges of robbery, impersonating a police officer, pointing a firearm, possession of a military-style submachine gun, forcible confinement and three counts of assault with a weapon relating to a home invasion.

Four months later, he was transferred from the Lindsay superjail to the much smaller county bucket in Napanee, near Belleville, after he was given a Security Threat Group rating. That move came as prison authorities investigated a rash of stabbings in the Lindsay jail and concluded that things would be safer for Harley's enemies if he was somewhere else. He spent a night at Ottawa jail, when he shared a cell with a member of the Rock Machine, a gang that had been locked in a bloody war in Quebec with the Hells Angels in the late 1990s and early 2000s. The Rock Machine member gestured toward a sketch of a man urinating on the number "81." For Hells Angels, the number "81" is a club nickname of sorts, as their initials are from the eighth and first letters of the alphabet. Words were quickly exchanged, and Harley was hauled off to the hole after smashing the prisoner's orbital bone. With that, Harley was returned to Lindsay.

Guindon had long been worrying about Harley's fate. "Don't try to live on my history," Guindon said in a message to his son. "Get a fucking job. I quit GM. Kicked my ass ever since. After that, I've had mediocre jobs. I worry about Harley all the time. I told him, 'Quit trying to walk in my footsteps. Try not to be like me or you'll be in jail the rest of your life.' I did most of my best years in jail."

As Harley adjusted to life behind bars, Guindon maintained a relationship of sorts with his brother, Jack. Among other things, Guindon couldn't abide the fact that Jack insisted on riding a Japanese motorcycle. He didn't just consider it the wrong bike; he saw it as an attack on an entire belief system. To make matters worse, Jack once got a ticket from police for riding too slowly. For Guindon, that was an affront to nature. Jack eventually came around and got a Harley 1200 Roadster, but not before a wild public brawl with Guindon that began with a debate on motorcycle merits. "He almost choked me to death at a car-bike show," Jack recalled. "I made a comment: 'Bernie, all you think about is Harley-Davidson. You don't think about anything else.' Then he got really pissed off. He had me by the neck. He was choking me." That said, Jack had to admit that his 1200 Roadster was a fine ride.

Now in his slower-paced senior years, Guindon has time to daydream. Sometimes his mind drifts to revenge fantasies, even though many of his targets have predeceased him. "Sometimes in my sleep, I get some pretty bad thoughts going through my mind. If I ever get sick and I am dying, these guys might pay."

He doesn't miss the biker politics that once consumed him. "I don't get involved in that anymore. I just say, 'Enjoy your life. You haven't got much left.' I look at life like a bingo. It turns around and around and all of a sudden, there's a number for Bernie Guindon. When your number is up, it's up."

Like many seniors, Guindon sometimes thinks about his funeral. He knows for sure that he wants Frank Sinatra's "My Way" played. Suzanne approves, since its lyrics were penned by her beloved Paul Anka. Guindon is particularly moved by the song's ending, which goes, "The record shows I took the blows / And did it my way."

Some days that funeral feels closer than others. His memory, once so crisp and focused, sometimes fails him. "I go down the street and I think, *How the fuck did I get back here?*" Once, he found the drive back home from Canadian Tire unusually quiet. He had left Suzanne back at the store. He often struggles to remember the names of old friends, even though he can picture them. "The cops could hit me until tomorrow and I couldn't give them any name."

Guindon got a phone call from a Black Diamond Rider in November 2016, inviting him and Suzanne to a special event. His old nemesis Johnny Sombrero had died at the age of eighty-one, after suffering from diabetes and heart disease. It was a singular ceremony, as befitted Sombrero. The funeral cards referred to "Johnny Sombrero aka Harry Paul Barnes" as "The man who was larger than Life / who walked to the beat of his own drum . . . in silver toed boots . . ."

There were some Outlaws, Amigos from the U.S. and about forty or so Black Diamond Riders. Guindon was taken aback to see that some of the mourners wearing BDR colours were women.

Some of Sombrero's old clubmates stood as an honour guard by the casket, which was draped in a Union Jack. At the gravesite, two women passed out glasses of Scotch. Guindon joined in as they said "Goodbye, Johnny" and quaffed down their Scotch. Guindon drank his too, as a show of respect. "It was for him. Otherwise I wouldn't have drank it."

A week later, Guindon had another reminder of his mortality, as he turned seventy-four. Harley arranged from behind bars for him and Suzanne to have a special table at a United Boxing pro card at Mississauga's Hershey Centre.

His old buddies Steve (Slick) McQueen, Paul Gravelle and Lorne Campbell, and Guindon's daughter Michelle slipped through security to join him, Suzanne and his son Rick Gibson at their ring-level table, with McQueen sporting a herringbone bowler hat to mark the occasion. Michelle beamed and joked about how the biker landscape might have been transformed, had she been born a boy.

Gibson gave him a card and said, "Happy birthday, Dad," then spoke proudly of how he had worked himself into top shape with a good-paying construction job.

As the fog rolls in between Guindon and his past, he wonders sometimes if he was too harsh in judging his own father. His dad did deserve credit for cleaning himself up. If alcoholism was in his blood, he had at least quelled those fires. "My dad, he was an alcoholic. But he gave up drinking the last fifteen years of his life. He was probably a better father than I ever was. He raised us. What the hell? Put clothing on us and food in our mouths. What else do you want? He worked hard. You don't realize that when you are a kid."

Guindon now feels an unexpected kinship with both his father and son. Like it or not, they are all part of a family line, with shared challenges. "He [my father] didn't like me having a motorcycle club. Holy fuck. He was trying to keep me on the straight and narrow. That's the same as my kid."

Guindon doesn't condemn his father as a hypocrite just because he was a criminal. "He wasn't a straight-up guy. He made money the only way he could, I guess. Sometimes you've got to take the curve on the path and make a few extra bucks. A lot of people were bootleggers in those days."

Whatever Guindon has decided, his father is no longer around to hear it. The Satan's Choice Motorcycle Club is gone too, all but the memories, for as long as he can hold on to them. "I lost a lot of those days."

Sometimes he goes to his craft room in the basement and fashions leather copies of old Satan's Choice crests. Other times, he works on belts, wallets, cellphone holders and images of sad clowns. More than once, he's vowed that he will never again make a complex leather piece, as the tough material leaves his fingers and joints aching. But then someone comes along with a request or a hint, and he starts tapping away on the leather again. Even though his craft room is windowless, like a cell, he loves the quiet there.

Gone is the raw adrenalin of Guindon's youth, but a man in his seventies appreciates that there is more to life than adrenalin. Excitement was something in the past. Perhaps some peace is in the future. "You try and get rid of the bad memories and live on the good memories. All of the bad memories I've had . . ."

And so he taps away on his leather projects, struggling to hang on to any good times while hoping the rest will finally blow past him, like scenery or phantoms on the open road.

ENDNOTES

CHAPTER 1: **Beginnings**

Bernie Guindon was interviewed repeatedly for this book. His brother, Jack Guindon, helped here too.

CHAPTER 2: **Local Celebrity**

Suzanne Blais spoke at length and in detail about her life, including her early years.

After World War II, the southern area of Oshawa where Guindon's family settled was a magnet for thousands of workers from Europe and economically depressed areas of Canada, such as the Maritimes, rural Quebec and Northern Ontario.

Suzanne Blais came to the Oshawa street corner where Guindon worked with a tangled backstory that rivalled that of Guindon. Her father had been a draft dodger who changed his identity to avoid conscription into the Canadian military. She said she had two sets of identification papers after she was born on September 6, 1946, in the former gold rush town of Kirkland Lake in Northeastern Ontario, 440 miles from the Quebec border. Her father was Reo Blais and her mother was the former Juliette Neveu, and Suzanne was a "Blais" for Ontario and a "Lacasse" for Quebec.

Suzanne's father worked for a time in the gold mines of Kirkland Lake, and then as a bouncer and bartender at a local hotel. In the early years of her marriage, Suzanne's mother waited on tables in the nearby mill town of Iroquois Falls and its scruffy neighbour, Ansonville. Ansonville was a poorly planned sprawl of cabins and shacks with no water or electricity, and attracted many French-Canadians, as well as Russians and Ukrainians. Ansonville was roundly condemned by many of the inhabitants of Iroquois

Falls as a dark den of foreigners preoccupied with brawling, boozing and God knows what else.

The description of Ansonville "as a dark den of foreigners engaged in regular street brawls, illegal alcohol consumption, and other unsavoury activities" is from a report quoted by Kerry M. Abel in *Changing Places: History, Community, and Identity in Northeastern Ontario*, McGill-Queen's University Press (Montreal, QC and Kingston, ON, 2006).

Suzanne's mother left her with Suzanne's grandfather for a time, while she cooked in a bush camp in Temiskaming. Suzanne was the apple of her grandfather's eye, and he was a tough man to please. She would ride on his lap on the tractor like a little princess. "I was spoiled. I got on my grandfather's knee." She would play him like a Stradivarius, asking, "Are you sure you love me?"

Suzanne sorely needed to be loved and her grandfather appreciated that. He would always reply with words to the effect of, "Of course, Suzanne. You're my favourite little girl."

So strong was the spell that little Suzanne cast over her grandfather that her aunt and uncle would ask her to approach him when they needed two dollars for the movies. She would then ask her grandfather, who would invariably give them the cash.

Boxing bouts in Oshawa were held at the former Avalon Dance Hall on King Street West, the former Community Recreation Association building on Gibb Street, the United Auto Workers hall and the Civic Auditorium.

CHAPTER 4: **Supreme Commander**

I interviewed Harry (Johnny Sombrero) Barnes on June 22, 2015. He was cheerful and proud and didn't let on that he was suffering from diabetes and heart disease. He died of those conditions in November 2016 at the age of eighty-one, leaving behind five children and seven grandchildren. He had been married for fifty-eight years. Long-time clubmates wore black and white club shirts to his funeral at the Ward Funeral Home on Weston Road, near his old stomping grounds. His casket was draped in the Union Jack, as befitted his pro-monarchist views.

Sombrero's Black Diamond Riders weren't officially an outlaw club like the Hells Angels and Outlaws, as they didn't have a diamond patch on the left breast with "1%" on it, signifying they were the 1 percent of bikers who go by their own rules. Still, diamond patch or no diamond patch, Johnny Sombrero did pack a wallop for any new clubs on what he considered his turf.

In July 1963, Sombrero announced in a Toronto courtroom that he was shutting down his Black Diamond Riders. With a dramatic flair for words, Sombrero told Magistrate Joseph Addison that he was tearing apart the Riders' clubhouse in Davisville and disbanding the club because "the papers have massacred us."

He made his statement after being charged at the time with threatening the wife of a club member, which he dismissed as an unfortunate misunderstanding.

"Are you breaking up the club?" Addison asked.

"Yes," Sombrero replied.

With that, Addison gave Sombrero a compliment of sorts, saying that club members are "a pretty crummy bunch and you appear to be the only man of intelligence among them.

"You're the obvious leader and you cut quite a figure as you drive down the street in your big Cadillac, sometimes with a big beard, sometimes without it.

"There's not much doubt that you're using this group of illiterate, smelly-looking people."

Sombrero reassured the judge that he planned to spend his free time with his wife and three children, and that he realized now that he had been playing a dangerous game.

With that, the magistrate set him free on two hundred dollars' bail despite howls of protest from the Crown attorney. Perhaps the judge believed Sombrero when he said he was disbanding the Black Diamond Riders, but no one in Guindon's world believed him for a second.

During the Black Diamond Riders' ride down the Gardiner, a rider in the front had a club flag flying high above his bike. They all wore matching black shirts, looking like cleaned-up cowboys in the Rose Parade. Sombrero chose cotton for the club's black and white dress shirts, a break from the garb of the Humber Valley Riders. "I didn't want to get into this silk bullshit."

CHAPTER 5: **Fight Club**

I benefited here from interviews with Bernie Guindon, Jack Guindon, Spider Jones and George Chuvalo.

Chuvalo was impressed with Guindon's attitude, as well as his ring skills. Chuvalo understood heart and boxing, as he earned a 79-15-2 career record as a pro and managed to stay on his feet in bouts with heavyweight champions Muhammad Ali, Joe Frazier, George Foreman and Floyd Patterson.

The late Daniel R. Wolf, a sociologist and motorcycle enthusiast, did an excellent job of making sense of why people choose to be bikers in *The Rebels: A Brotherhood of Outlaw Bikers*, University of Toronto Press (Toronto, 1991).

Yorkville during the hippie days is analyzed at length in "Making the Scene: Yorkville and Hip Toronto, 1960–1970" by Stuart Robert Henderson, a thesis submitted to the Department of History in conformity with the requirements for the degree of Doctor of Philosophy, Queen's University, Kingston, Ontario, October 2007.

CHAPTER 6: **Expansion**

I benefited from an interview with Don Shebib and greatly appreciate his insights.

There's a police history of biker gangs in Canada in *The Gazette*, Vol. 65, Nos. 7–12, 1999, a Royal Canadian Mounted Police publication. It's a good look at the situation as it stood just before the Hells Angels patchover.

The original Satan's Choice included Don Norris and others named Spaceman, El-Pot Hole and Black Pete. The club was started in 1957 by teenagers and men who hung out at the Army Navy Club on Spadina Avenue in Toronto. The first members were called Sharkey, Jim Corbett, Frank Donnelly, Scotty, Big Ted and Red, according to Norris, with Sharkey acting as president. They later shifted their hangout to Aida's Restaurant at St. Clair and Stop 17 on Kingston Road.

When the Choice was forced to fold, Spaceman started a club called the Nomads in Highland Creek.

In the 1950s, the Black Diamond Riders hung out at a Queen Street restaurant. The BDR had a clubhouse on Steeles Avenue near Bathurst Street in northwest Toronto.

The Para-Dice Riders appeared around 1961, wearing a crest with a pair of dice. It was black and white and looked a lot like the BDR crest, which angered the BDR.

Another club of the late-1950s was called the Beanery Gang.

Lots of information about the Montreal chapter of the Satan's Choice can be found in Bill Trent's article "Riding Against the Square World," in *Weekend Magazine*, No. 38, 1967, with photos by Ronald Labelle.

Information about the Satan's Choice while Guindon was in prison the first time was provided by the *Toronto Daily Star*, *Canadian Magazine*, Paul King's "Chicklet Gets By with the Help of His Friends—Satan's Choice," (January 2, 1971.)

The rude ending to the first Satan's Choice convention is described in Eddy Roworth's "85 policemen break up 'convention,' nab 64 motorcyclists in farmhouse," *Toronto Daily Star*, September 25, 1967: 1.

CHAPTER 7: **National President**

Guindon guesses that it was his attitude that caused him to be locked up a couple of hours down the road in Guelph rather than close to home. He said he was told to expect a rough time, but it wasn't so bad. "Everybody said they would attack me down there. I had a couple of fights in there. I held my own."

Guindon was fired from General Motors in 1966 after refusing to stop riding his motorcycle to work. It didn't help that he wore his club colours on the assembly line.

Guindon said that biker club election campaigns generally lasted about a week and weren't a particularly big deal. There were secret ballots.

Carmen Neal once ran against Guindon for president. When he lost, he wasn't particularly upset, Guindon said. "I tried to run it as straight as I could," Guindon said. "Everybody has an opinion. If they think he's better, let him run it."

The leaping left hook was a punch to be used sparingly, especially against an experienced fighter like Gray. "You've got to be careful that the guy don't hit you with a right when you're leaping," Guindon said. "It's not one that I could use three or four times. The only time you'd use it is if you know the other guy . . . You've got to be careful of the right hand. If you're dropping your left hook, your hand goes down so you're leaving your head open to a right hand."

CHAPTER 8: Pigpen

I had a series of interviews with Howard (Pigpen) Berry and Cecil Kirby. They were conducted separately and not in the same area.

Baldy Chard is remembered in Paul Rimstead's "Tough Guy with a Heart of Gold," *Toronto Sun*, April 17, 1983, Jim Kernaghan's "Parker's Death Recalls Another Era," *London Free Press*, June 27, 2006, and Nicki Cruickshank's "'Barrie Bomber' James Parker Moved to City in 1930s," *Barrie Examiner*, September 28, 2012.

Chard lost thirteen fights as a pro heavyweight, although he did once level the third-ranked heavyweight in the world. There was also a fight against James J. Parker, who had a title bout against Archie Moore. That fight between Chard and Parker was the stuff of underworld legend, when the two men went bare knuckles in a closed-off ring in west-end Toronto, until Chard won in forty-eight minutes. That brawl was almost stopped when a friend of Moore's pulled a gun, only to be overpowered by the ring-side mob and hustled out the back door.

Nazi Martin Weiche is described in Jennifer O'Brien's "Infamous Ontario Neo-Nazi Dies," *The London Free Press*, September 6, 2011, and also in Jane Sims's "The Last Stand of an Old Nazi," *The London Free Press*, January 11, 2014.

Cecil Kirby is described in "How Does a Hitman Say He's Sorry?" by Cal Millar and Peter Edwards, *Toronto Star*, September 22, 1991, D1. He is also co-author of *Mafia Assassin: The Inside Story of a Canadian Biker, Hitman, and Police Informer* with Thomas C. Renner, Methuen (Toronto, 1986).

In the years after he was released from prison in the 1980s, Howard

(Pigpen) Berry became increasingly reclusive, vanishing from the biker landscape. There were stories that he had glued a jewel to the middle of his forehead and was wandering about telling people he was from India. Other stories had him living out of a small truck, or living off the land in the woods, occasionally foraging for food like a feral cat. The least probable of the rumours came from Lorne Campbell, who jokingly suggested he had married and was quietly running a charming bed and breakfast back in his hometown of Peterborough. I met with him and he had no jewel on his forehead. Out of respect, I won't say where we met, except that he was not running a bed and breakfast, charming or otherwise.

CHAPTER 9: **Yorkville**

The comment about Harley-Davidson having a trademark growling sound is from "Harley-Davidson Declares Victory in the Court of Public Opinion—Drops Federal Trademark Application," *Business Wire*, June 20, 2000.

Frank (Hippy) Hobson (he spelled his nickname with a y and not ie) and I corresponded on and off for several months. He graciously allowed me to quote from his unpublished writings on his life. He had gotten into the Satan's Choice through friends in the Kingston chapter, including Charles (Chuck) Grey and Wally High. One night in the summer of 1968, they went to a field meet, where there were also members from the Para-Dice Riders and Vagabonds, as well as Rod MacLeod from Montreal. This is how Hippy described it:

> There were two Ontario Police Officers sitting in one car watching everything we did. It was a hot day and I recall one of the Choice going over to the car and offering the officers a cold coke. About ½ hour later I remember seeing those police with their sirens roaring and doing donuts. Apparently there was a hit of acid in each coke. We were hysterical watching them carry on.

It was particularly steaming weather, underscored by the hit song on the radio by the Doors, "Light My Fire." He said that the song, with its line,

"Gonna set the night on fire," was playing in his ears as he watched from across the river the city of Detroit go up in flames during race riots. He wrote:

> I had a front seat row view of Detroit from a park bench in Windsor. The Detroit River separates Windsor and Detroit it is not that wide. It was nighttime and you could hear gun shots echo through the smoke from the fires. Both the bridge and the tunnel to Detroit were closed to the public. Tanks were clanking up Woodward Avenue as the National Guard had been called to help crack down on the rioting.

CHAPTER 10: Darwinism

In February 1968, Satan's Choice biker Michael George Nichols, twenty-one, of Toronto was convicted of common assault for using a jackknife to cut off the shoulder crest of a jacket worn by a member of the London Road Runners Motorcycle Club at a Thanksgiving weekend biker hill climb attended by six thousand people at the village of Heidelberg, ten miles west of Kitchener. Three other Choice members held the Road Runner relatively still as the crest was cut off.

I interviewed Mark DeMarco on July 5, 2015.

The Cross Breeds survived in Niagara Falls until the mid-1970s.

The family of Louis Iannuzzelli owned the House of Frankenstein wax museum on Clifton Hill in Niagara Falls. Iannuzzelli had ties to the California mobster Dominic Longo, who had been close to Hamilton mobster John (Pops) Papalia's father. He infuriated Papalia by putting money out on the streets to loan. Papalia didn't do anything about it while Longo was alive, but when he died in the fall of 1985, his protection evaporated. Iannuzzelli disappeared. There was a widespread belief that he was killed by Carmen Barillaro and an associate and that his remains were deposited in the foundation of a building in Welland. Barillaro was murdered in July 1997.

The Vagabonds and Black Diamond Riders were both long-established motorcycle clubs, although neither was an outlaw club in the strictest sense of the term. Members of these clubs did not wear the diamond-shaped patch with "1%" on it over their hearts, in the fashion of true one percenter clubs. (That "1%" stood for the 1 percent of bikers that the American Motorcycle Association would not admit.) The Vagabonds did something unique instead: they wore a patch with "100%" for 100 percent biker.

The convention weekend also included a "memorial service" for Guindon's long-time associate Carmen Neal, who was killed in an industrial accident at age twenty-six in western Canada the previous summer.

CHAPTER 11: Shock Value

Again, I benefited from interviews with Howard (Pigpen) Berry.

CHAPTER 12: Big Apple

I benefited from interviews with Frank (Hippy) Hobson and portions of an unpublished manuscript he provided to me.

There were happy times in the Guindon household when his father and mother danced. Guindon liked doing waltzes and imitating Elvis and Jerry Lee Lewis.

CHAPTER 13: Ring Wars

Walter Henry was kind enough to give me an interview.

The Hells Angels had a head start on the Satan's Choice, starting in San Bernardino, California, on March 17, 1948, and moving to San Francisco in 1954 and Oakland in 1957.

CHAPTER 14: Eye on Montreal

The Satan's Choice had a clubhouse in the 400 block of King Street East in Kitchener, while the Henchmen gathered inside a clubhouse on Highland Road in Kitchener.

The Dubois brothers rose up in the hardscrabble Saint-Henri district amidst rail yards and factories. They later bitterly recalled how they had been mocked by other children because they wore second-hand clothing and sometimes had to skip meals or eat molasses sandwiches. By the time they reached adulthood, the sons of Napoleon (Paulo) Dubois were feared by the Cotroni mob family and biker gangs alike.

The Devil's Disciples controlled the emerging crystal meth business around Saint-Louis Square in Montreal. What had once been magnificent Victorian manors had been converted into boarding houses as it became a hippie haven in the 1960s, with students, flower children and the trendy offering a potential customer base for the growing drug trade.

Allegiances constantly shifted in Montreal. In time, the Montreal chapter of the Choice lined up with the Devil's Disciples against the Popeyes. The Popeyes sold drugs, stole cars and broke into houses on a regular basis and used knives, guns and fists to get their way. But that didn't make them unusual. What made the Popeyes really stand out was their ability to use explosives against their enemies, who now included Guindon.

CHAPTER 15: Skin Beef

Armed robber Richard Mallory was a massively powerful 275-pound man who sometimes collected drug debts in the Ottawa area. He recalled how powerless he felt when he heard the Kingston Penitentiary gates slam shut behind him in 1968. "I was scared. That was my first prison bit. You hear the big gates close behind you. When the first gate closes, you hear the bang! I said, 'What did I get myself into?'"

Mallory quickly learned why gangsters in old movies often talk funny, as if their lips are stapled shut. That was because conversations were often forbidden in the old prisons like Kingston Penitentiary. "You couldn't even talk," Mallory said. "You had to talk out of the side of your mouth."

There actually was an official club position for someone who hung around a club but wasn't a full member. The position was called "hangaround" and is a common one for outlaw motorcycle clubs.

Another rule for prisoners is not to check yourself into segregation to dodge a beef or a debt to someone. Don't ask to be transferred, saying you are in danger, when you really want to move because you owe money. And don't peek into a cell when you're walking down a corridor. Prisoners don't like to be snooped on, like they're nothing more than animals in a cage.

Toronto Star writer Paul Hunter wrote an e-book for the newspaper called *Life after Life*, which tells of prison justice and the unsettling use of wheelbarrows.

Paul Gravelle gave me an interview for this chapter, as did Paul Henry.

Born on March 15, 1947, in North Bay, Gravelle was the eldest of twelve siblings, half boys and half girls. "I had to set the example," he said.

Gravelle had been a jailhouse and prison inmate for some time. At sixteen, he was arrested for car theft, break-and-enters, joyriding and weapons possession. "I was amassing a collection of guns," Gravelle said. "When they caught me, I had about thirty or forty guns in the crawl space of my house.

"I used to carry one all of the time—a .357 Magnum. When I was sixteen."

Gravelle's views about how he actually enjoys crime seem to fit into the thesis of Nicole E. Ruedy, Celia Moore, Francesca Gino and Maurice E. Schweitzer's "The Cheater's High: The Unexpected Affective Benefits of Unethical Behavior," *Journal of Personality and Social Psychology* Vol. 105, No. 4 (2013): 531–48.

There are family connections between the Gravelle family and the Guindons in the Buckingham, Quebec, area, as one of Guindon's uncles married a Gravelle.

CHAPTER 16: **Proud Riders**

Paul King wrote the article "Chicklet Gets By with the Help of His Friends—Satan's Choice" for the January 2, 1971, issue of *The Canadian Magazine*, while Marci McDonald covered the filming for the Saturday, October 3, 1970, *Toronto Daily Star*.

CHAPTER 17: **Thunder Bay I**

Verg Erslavas was extremely helpful here. He even went to the great trouble of writing out his memories as well as speaking about them on the phone.

There had been a club called the Road Agents in Thunder Bay before Guindon showed up. The Road Agents were based in Minnesota and weren't a one percenter club. They also had a chapter in Duluth. They left Thunder Bay about a year before Guindon's arrival.

Erslavas hadn't been a Road Agent.

CHAPTER 18: **Riot**

A commission of inquiry was set up in an attempt to make sense of the madness. Even before it concluded its hearings, Solicitor-General Jean-Pierre Goyer announced on July 20, 1971, that reforms for prisoners' living conditions were underway. Now, reforms included the new right for prisoners to elect committees and take part in work programs. Convicts would be given work clothing with their numbers on the inside and not the outside. Inmate committees would have a voice on treatment, training, recreation and community service projects. These reforms would apply to all thirty-two federal prisons, and not just the Kingston Penitentiary.

CHAPTER 19: **Olympic Contender**

Frank (Hippy) Hobson and John Dunbar lived in a farmhouse on the outskirts of Windsor and worked together at Chrysler.

Richard Mallory was in Millhaven in 1973 for the armed robbery of a Dominion store in Ottawa. "It was a folly of errors. We held up the place. We didn't get no money . . . They caught me under a porch somewhere. They said I never seen a big guy clear a fence like that."

Mallory knew future biker Brian Leslie Beaucage of London, Ontario, well and considered him a good lifter.

George Bradley was transferred in June 1972 to the maximum-security mental hospital in Penetanguishene for a psychiatric assessment. On June 28, 1972, a man who said he was Bradley's brother paid him a visit. They held a gun on an attendant and fled. Police suspected a third man acted as driver and lookout.

Banks and trust companies in the Toronto area were placed on special alert for the next few months, until Bradley was re-arrested at gunpoint in Toronto.

Richard Mallory was convicted in 2000 of being one of four men involved in the 1990 shotgun slayings of twenty-four-year-old Michel Giroux of Ottawa and his pregnant, common-law wife, Manon Bourdeau, twenty-seven. Mallory was arrested in 1990 and held in an Ottawa jail for almost ten years before the conviction. The case became known as the "Cumberland murders."

Mallory won a new trial on appeal after the original trial judge was criticized for not properly cautioning the jury about "disreputable witnesses" and certain "hearsay evidence." Mallory and his co-accused argued the Crown and police knew they were relying on "false evidence" from key witnesses, including a drug dealer, who received more than $400,000 from the Crown. That witness demanded more money if there was a new trial.

Charges were stayed in 2007 instead of having a new trial. The trial had cost more than $30 million and was called in the press the longest and most expensive trial in Ottawa history.

CHAPTER 20: Expansion Troubles

Joe Dinardo's real name was Gabor Magasztovics and his parents had brought him to Canada when he was twelve, in the aftermath of the 1957 Hungarian Revolution. His troubles with the law in his new country began almost immediately. Dinardo made national headlines in 1974 when he was a central character in the murder trial of millionaire Mississauga developer Peter Demeter, who was charged with hiring someone to beat his wife, Christine, to death in the garage of their home. Dinardo testified that he declined when Christine Demeter offered him ten thousand dollars to break her husband's legs and arms a week before her murder. Demeter was convicted of hiring a hitman to kill his wife, but the identity of that killer for hire was never determined.

I interviewed Cecil Kirby several times for this book in the spring and summer of 2015.

By 1974, the border chapters of the Satan's Choice associating with the Outlaws included Windsor and St. Catharines.

Kirby told of a trip in the winter of 1975, when about twenty Satan's Choice members were guests of the Detroit Outlaws on a bus travelling from Dayton to Georgia, with plenty of Coors, dope and women.

In 1976, there was a formalization of the association between the Outlaws and Satan's Choice with the creation of a patch showing a Choice pitchfork and an Outlaws piston.

According to the online obituary of Garnet Douglas McEwen, he was born on September 25, 1945, in Campbellton, New Brunswick, and died in hospital on Friday, January 27, 2012, in Saskatoon, Saskatchewan.

CHAPTER 21: Thunder Bay II

The late Daniel R. Wolf, who rode as an outlaw biker as part of his research, explained the difference between extreme recklessness and suicide on pages 216 to 217 of *The Rebels: A Brotherhood of Outlaw Bikers*, University of Toronto Press (Toronto, 1991). Raleigh's death wasn't suicide, although it was obviously behaviour that tempted death. Bikers hate the very mention of suicide and tend to shun the funerals of its victims. While Raleigh's death definitely was reckless, bikers often celebrate recklessness.

Wolf started his study while a doctoral student in anthropology at the University of Alberta in the mid-1970s, and his work captures the mindset of Canadian bikers during that time period. He went on to become a psychological anthropologist at the University of Prince Edward Island. The Rebels nicknamed him "Coyote" because he wore a coyote skin on his helmet.

Wolf explained how bikers react when a member dies while pushing life's limits:

Members who die by vigilantism, riding hard or law enforcement have a good chance of becoming martyrs. Rather than take the death as a warning that they should change their ways, and start riding safer or living more peacefully, instead the death is taken as a reaffirmation of their lives, as if there is a point to running head on into a truck while high on speed. Running smack into a truck while high on speed isn't taken as something cautionary, but rather as a romantic expression of life on the edge, where the ultimate epitaph is: "He lived and died like a biker."

Funerals for men who die in such ways are emotional, sometimes grandiose affairs. Wolf continued:

Such funeral runs are often accompanied by acts of defiance, like ignoring helmet laws, firing weapons at the graveside and draping a casket in the club's colours. In such a way, the surviving members don't become demoralized. Instead, they see their rebel values celebrated. The Choice would doff their helmets, daring the police to do something about it. Giving way to good sense, officers would instead accompany the bikers to the gravesite to make sure nothing worse happened.

CHAPTER 22: Pigpen Goes South

Regarding Florida, articles that helped include Michael Griffin and Jim Leusner's "Woman Recalls Life as 'Property' of Outlaw Enforcer," *Orlando Sentinel*, December 17, 1995.

There's something paradoxical at play about outlaw bikers and the military. While bikers love the outlaw image, they also see themselves as genuine patriots and the embodiment of freedom, and each wave of military service provides a fresh jump to biker ranks, from World War II to the present.

Rod MacLeod was close with Jacques (Sonny) Lacombe of the Choice, a well-off biker with a big estate, Bouvier guard dogs and a chemical factory. They made enough money that they would take vacations in the Caribbean together. "They'd ship their bikes down," Kirby said. "That was expensive."

Stairway Harry Henderson's obituary reads:

HENDERSON, Harold 'Stairway Harry' Age 64 of Dayton passed away Saturday Jan. 3, 2009. He was a 42-year member of the Dayton Outlaws. Survived by his wife, Sandy, 3 brothers Robert, Michael and Danny Henderson, and one sister Helen Caudle. There will be a viewing at the Outlaws Clubhouse Friday Jan. 9, 2009 starting at 6:00 PM. The funeral will begin at the clubhouse Saturday at 12:00 PM followed by the procession to Woodland Cemetery. If desired, donations can be made to 'Stairway's' wife Sandy in care of the Dayton Outlaws 272 N. Lansdowne Ave. Dayton, OH 45427. Condolences can be sent online at www.RogersFuneralHomes.com

CHAPTER 23: Last Olympic Hope

Lorne Campbell, Bernie and Jack Guindon described the UAW hall fight.

CHAPTER 24: Strange Clubmate

One of the more frightening Montreal Satan's Choice members was Mike French, who was born in 1950. French, who was nicknamed "Crazy Mike," was a product of the Queen's School in lower Westmount and the Weredale House boys' home in west-end Montreal. The boys' home was closed in 1977.

French was very active in the biker wars against the Popeyes. He was found murdered in November 1982 in Kahnawake. He was said to have boasted about killing Sharron Prior in Pointe-Saint-Charles seven years earlier.

Sharron Prior was sixteen and pretty. She disappeared from her home on March 29, 1975, after going to meet a friend at a Pointe-Saint-Charles pizzeria, a five-minute walk from her home. She was found four days later in a Longueuil apiary. She had been raped and beaten repeatedly and suffocated on her own blood.

French's suspected killer was a hitman in the West End Gang, but the murder was never solved. The killing was considered by many to be "sort of community service."

CHAPTER 25: **Mountie Radar**

Retired RCMP officer Mark Murphy was great here, as was his book, *Police Undercover: The True Story of the Biker, the Mafia & the Mountie,* Hushion House (East York, 1999).

The police operation was confused when a caterer named Tony was found in the hallway of the Venus Spa, with a .22 calibre bullet hole in his head. That murder was never solved.

CHAPTER 26: **Body Seller**

Guindon later heard that the Outlaws wanted to take his life around this time, even though he was off the streets anyway. "They were quite pissed off about what was going on. They thought we might be going HA [Hells Angels]. There were rumours to the fact that they weren't really pleased."

CHAPTER 27: **The Big Split**

Cecil Kirby said he quit the Satan's Choice in March 1976.

Kirby had been active in the mid-1970s with Duke in robberies, including one of a Willowdale gambler's house. By that point, they had things down to a science of sorts. They would phone the house and if no one answered, the plan was afoot. "You can go through a milk box if you know how to do it," Kirby said, describing how a smallish and flexible man like Duke could tuck his right arm on an angle and wiggle in.

The plan was to go into the gambler's home and get what they could in twenty minutes or so. The gambler kept about $15,000 in a wad in his jacket pocket, which was convenient. They had heard he sometimes kept $100,000 in the trunk of his car.

Later, when Kirby hooked up with the Commisso crime family, he said he was asked, "Did you do a house?"

He answered, "Oh yeah," but no money was returned.

By 1977, the Hells Angels had already expanded out of the United States into Australia and England. Now, they had their first francophone charter and the promise of more expansion, as they were close to other small but tough Quebec clubs like the Missiles in Saguenay, the Sex Fox in Chibougamau and the Marauders of Asbestos.

On the night of Saturday, June 8, 1999, a police tactical team moved in on a house in the upscale Detroit suburb of Sterling Heights and arrested Outlaws leader Harry (Taco) Bowman on multiple charges of murder, murder conspiracy and drug dealing. He had been on the run for two years and was on the FBI Ten Most Wanted list.

He was accused of the 1982 murder of a member of his club and the 1991 murder of the president of a rival club, the Warlocks, in Orlando, Florida, as well as plotting to kill officers and members of Hells Angels.

On Friday, July 27, 2001, in Florida, Bowman was sentenced to two concurrent life prison terms plus eighty-three years for ordering the murder of rival gang members, drug trafficking and fire bombings. Jurors concluded that Bowman used Outlaws clubs in Tampa, St. Petersburg, Orlando, Daytona Beach and Fort Lauderdale to further his racketeering.

CHAPTER 28: **Prison Blues**

George McIntyre of Hamilton's Parkdale Gang helped here. He was sent to prison on October 27, 1983—his twenty-fifth birthday—when Guindon was finally preparing to come out. McIntyre was heading for a three- to five-year manslaughter stretch. Since he originally faced the possibility of a life sentence for murder, the manslaughter term looked pretty good in comparison.

His legal troubles came when his buddy Mike Watson was trying to defend his title in the Canadian Amateur Bodybuilding Championships in their hometown of Hamilton on August 16, 1980. When Watson was ranked in second place, the hometown crowd erupted.

McIntyre quickly heard about Guindon from other prisoners. "He had a ridiculous reputation in Collins Bay," said McIntyre, who used the word "ridiculous" as a compliment. He said Guindon earned respect by stepping up and pleading guilty to misdeeds that other club members had actually committed. "Anytime he did, it was because he decided to. Sometimes he made sacrifices for his brothers. Sometimes shit happens and that's just the way it was."

McIntyre replaced Guindon on the inmate committee, where his responsibilities included settling conflicts between inmates and the system, picking movies and organizing social events. There were some drugs then, but not nearly the level there would be decades later. There was also some general feeling about what was right and what wasn't. "The prison is a totally different place now," McIntyre said. "The rules of the street had some bearing then. It's not like that in prison now. They don't have the ethics. It sounds silly to talk about ethics, but they did have them then."

McIntyre recalled some soldiers coming by once to play floor hockey with the inmates in Collins Bay. "They quit halfway through." The problem was the inmates were bodychecking everyone, not just the opponent with the puck. "They said, 'We can't do this. If they think the puck's going to you, they hit you.'"

He also recalled a prisoner bringing a knife with him to play prison hockey. "He didn't use it, though. I said, 'What are you trying to prove? We'll never get hockey again if you pull a knife. If you want to beat the guy over the head with your stick, that's fine, but don't use a goddamn knife.'"

That said, it was tough to put fear into some inmates to watch their behaviour. "They don't care," McIntyre said. "They are doing life anyway. They're not going to get out."

Brian Leslie Beaucage, one of the wilder prisoners in the Kingston Penitentiary riots, was also in Millhaven. "Brian was well liked in jail. A pretty solid individual. He didn't back down from nobody," said Guindon. "He was an all-round good guy, as far as I was concerned."

CHAPTER 29: **Quiet Expansion**

A youthful Walter Stadnick showed ability in auto shop at Hill Park Secondary on Hamilton Mountain and hung around the Cardinal variety store in the city's Birdland district. He and some teenaged friends rode Triumphs and BSAs and formed the Cossacks, a youthful Hamilton biker gang. Their most notable feature was the tufts of hair sticking up out of their helmets, which was an effort to give them a Cossack-warrior look. Stadnick's Cossack club of Hamilton had no connection to the Cossacks Motorcycle Club of Texas or a club by the same name in the former Soviet Union.

By 1978, Stadnick had graduated from the Cossacks to the Wild Ones, who had a clubhouse on Hamilton Mountain on West Avenue. The local Satan's Choice chapter had just patched over to the Outlaws, much to Guindon's chagrin. There were no Hells Angels in Ontario, and it was a lonely time to be part of a smaller club like the Wild Ones, even with their serious mob ties. Stadnick and two Wild Ones rode off to Montreal, hoping to attract Angels support. Only one of them would ride out of Montreal alive.

At the time, the Montreal Hells Angels chapter president was Yves (Le Boss) Buteau, the former Popeyes boss. He was seeking allies like Stadnick to counter the Outlaws expansion.

Stadnick knew he was riding into a war zone. In March 1978, Montreal Outlaw Gilles Cadorette was killed instantly when a bomb was placed under his car while it was parked at a Bordeaux Street bar. In April, Athanasios (Tom Thumb) Markopoulos of the Outlaws was slain by two hitmen.

The Outlaws caught wind of Stadnick's trip, and a pair of killers from Detroit and Miami tagged along behind them to Le Tourbillon bar in the east end, near Jarry Park, on October 12, 1978.

Stadnick settled into a booth with fellow Hamilton Wild Ones Guy (Gator) Davies and George (Chico) Mousseau. Sitting with them were Hells Angels Louis (Ti-Oui) Lapierre, Bruno Coulombe and Jean Brochu. Two clean-cut men who looked like cops approached them. Cops are generally annoying for bikers, but even they can have their uses. Sometimes, their very presence makes things safer. Who's going to attack while two members of the *Sûreté du Québec* are in the room? There was no great concern about the two strangers walking toward them until one of them pulled out a sawed-off shotgun and the other drew a pistol. Within minutes, Davies and Mousseau were dead while Lapierre and Coulombe were injured. Stadnick was able to slide under the table and was the only target left unscathed.

Stadnick was now in the Hells Angels fold and in the centre of a war. Soon, Guindon would hear of Stadnick's rise, but he was in no position to actually meet him. "I didn't see too much of Stadnick . . . You knew of him."

The wrongful conviction of the Satan's Choice bikers is described in detail in the excellent book *Conspiracy of Brothers: A True Story of Bikers, Murder, and the Law* by Mick Lowe, Random House Canada (Toronto, 2013), and in a chapter of my own book with Lorne Campbell, *Unrepentant: The Strange and (Sometimes) Terrible Life of Lorne Campbell, Satan's Choice and Hells Angels Biker*, Random House Canada (Toronto, 2013).

CHAPTER 30: **Reunited**

Some of the violence involving the Wild Ones was from their own hands, like when Derek Thistlewaite and Peter Michael Urech blew themselves up in a quiet residential neighbourhood early in the morning of Wednesday, May 23, 1979, in a botched attempt to intimidate a woman who was scheduled to testify that she had been gang-raped. Pieces of their van ended up on a rooftop three houses away, and others flew two hundred to three hundred feet.

A week later, on Wednesday, May 30, 1979, more than sixty police officers from five forces raided twenty Hamilton homes and clubhouses connected to the Outlaws, Wild Ones and Red Devils. They didn't come up with much, as charges ranged from unpaid parking fines to possession of explosives and restricted weapons. Some of the bikers taunted the police that they should have come earlier in the week, when they might have gotten more of what they were seeking.

Goobie was in Collins Bay in 1975, where he was reunited with bikers. Regarding the prison cafeteria attack, the same kitchen helper who almost beheaded a disgruntled diner also brained a suspected human rat with a putter taken from the mini-putt range.

CHAPTER 31: **Reconnecting**

After his son Jesse's suicide, George Chuvalo told CBC Television: "It's like everything you breathe in is grief [and] you just can't believe your son is dead. You just can't believe your son has died." Things only got worse for Chuvalo. In 1993, another son, George Lee, was found dead in a hotel room with a needle in his arm. Two days after his funeral, Chuvalo's wife, Lynn, committed suicide with a pill overdose.

Teresa Guindon-Mader's website is www.mountainofhopefoundation. com.

CHAPTER 33: **Hospitality Industry**

They chose a different spelling for their camp than "Shan-gri-law," the spelling used in the James Hilton novel *Lost Horizon*.

Harley Davidson Guindon is a strong writer and many of his comments quoted here were written by him. I think he has the potential to be the next Roger Caron, writing-wise.

CHAPTER 34: **Nightmares**

Harley Guindon was a huge help here. The woman he considers his real mother (not his biological mother) helped a great deal too. She did not want her name made public and I have respected this. Also helping me was Maggie Pearce-O'Shea, a former friend of Guindon, and Angel from Oshawa.

CHAPTER 35: **Big Brother**

The biker world had forged more links with the mob since Guindon went behind bars in 1975. The family of Vito Rizzuto had replaced the Cotronis and Violis in Montreal, while in the Greater Toronto Area, power was shared between seven 'Ndrangheta, or Calabrian Mafia, families, although there was still a Sicilian Mafia influence. Hells Angels in the Montreal area were now off-loading planes carrying drugs for Colombian cartels. Some bikers were working toward building their own direct drug connections with South American suppliers.

Organized Crime Committee Reports, 1989 and 1990, Canadian Association of Chiefs of Police, gave general descriptions of numbers and growth during those time periods.

The Canadian chapters of Outlaws were a fresh force for Guindon to consider. On January 22, 1985, there were mass Outlaws arrests across Ontario. Ninety members were arrested and houses and clubhouses were hit. Guindon's old friend Sonny Lacombe was in the Outlaws now, and he was indignant the day of his arrest. Suspicions were everywhere, and a rival club was thought to be behind any misfortune except rain.

"The Hells Angels should be proud of you," Lacombe chided a police officer as he was taken into custody.

Maggie Pearce-O'Shea helped again here.

CHAPTER 38: **Moving On**

Guindon's sympathetic side also came out when he heard reports that an Oshawa Christmas toy fund had been robbed. Guindon and the club dipped into the bail fund box to make up the difference, but the charity turned down their offer, fearing it would be bad optics with the general public.

One year around 1990, Guindon rode 25,000 to 30,000 miles through Canada and the United States.

CHAPTER 39: **Unwelcome Guests**

Several articles provided information about the David Boyko murder. They include Paul Wiecek's "They'll Come to Bury a Biker: Real 'Dog's Breakfast' Expected in City," *Winnipeg Free Press*, May 15, 1996, A5; Tony Davis's "Biker's Funeral Draws Crowd," *Winnipeg Free Press*, May 19, 1996, A5; Doug Nairne's "'Vicious' City Biker Found Slain in Halifax," *Winnipeg Free Press*, May 14, 1996, A1; and "Establishment of Hells Angels a Bloody Tale," *Winnipeg Free Press*, March 15, 2005, B6.

CHAPTER 40: **Biggest Party Ever**

The Hamilton Red Devils were Canada's oldest outlaw motorcycle club when they suddenly gave up their name in November 2014. Their history could be traced back to 1949. They had thirty-one members and chapters in Hamilton, Chatham and Sudbury when they suddenly bcame members of the Maritime-based Bacchus Motorcycle Club. The move came as the Hells Angels ushered their support club—also named the Red Devils—into Ontario.

Guindon was with Suzanne Blais that spring at a Friday the 13th biker run in Port Dover, Ontario, when weekend riders and members of established clubs all take to the road and congregate in the Lake Ontario fishing town. Suzanne later recalled: "As I was being introduced to his friends, he said, 'Meet my lady friend Suzanne, who is my oldest friend. I'm going to give her a trophy one of these days. She was the only girl I knew while a teenager who managed to escape my clutches and keep her virginity.' At which point I piped up with, 'Yes, but I had to move to Toronto to do it.'"

On September 13, 2006, Mr. Bill was laid to rest in his Hells Angels leather vest in Peterborough after a fatal motorcycle collision with a truck. Guindon's suspicions about him being a rat were never proven, and some one hundred bikers gathered to pay their last respects.

Mr. Bill was sixty at the time of his death and had been saying some strange things in his final days, including that Gault was a police informer. Gault was among the mourners at the funeral, and would later deny in court that, after he filed by the open casket, he said to a fellow member,

"He's never smelled better." If he did make the remark, it would have been one time when he actually spoke the truth. Mr. Bill in life had been an assault to the senses. Guindon recalled his horror when Mr. Bill would peel off his socks. "Holy fuck. Jesus Christ. His nails had to be that much larger and they're black. Jesus Christ, this guy! Have you ever had a bath? . . . I almost got sick watching his feet."

Guindon was a little surprised by the turnout at Mr. Bill's send-off. "There was not as many people as I thought would show up." Perhaps the reason was the rumour circulating that he had been a rat. Guindon said, "If I would have known earlier, I would have done something about it . . . He didn't do drug transactions and he didn't work, but he always had money."

CHAPTER 42: Culture Shock

Harley left school after Grade 10 and then got his diploma as an adult.

Paul Gravelle was in a higher economic bracket than Guindon, and was of higher interest to the police. Gravelle pled guilty to a multi-million-dollar marijuana importation scheme but said he stayed away from moving what he considered to be hard drugs. He denied a role in the November 16, 1998, shotgun murders of Ancaster lawyer Lynn Gilbank and her husband. Gravelle told *The Hamilton Spectator* there was no truth to allegations his family took part in the murders to silence an informant working with Gilbank. "No," he said. "That's not true. Our family is not killers . . . That's beyond us to do a thing like that. That's a despicable act. That's a cowardly act."

Gravelle lived for five years in Mexico, where he said he performed magic tricks on the street for large crowds. He came home in 2010, once the murder beef had gone away. He leased a BMW X5, and not long after that, found some strange wiring under the hood. He took it back to the dealer, who responded with fear and called the Niagara Regional Police. When the bomb squad checked it out, they saw it was a hidden recording device, installed by Peel Regional Police.

CHAPTER 49: **Fathers and Sons**

Harley-Davidson motorcycles were under attack by demographics at the same time that Harley riding clubs were struggling to stay relevant. Articles on the aging of the Harley market include James B. Kelleher's "As Boomers Age, Harley Hunts for Younger Riders," Reuters.com, June 21, 2013; James R. Hagerty's "Harley-Davidson to Ramp Up Marketing, as Sales Skid," WSJ.com, October 20, 2015; and Trefis Team's "Harley-Davidson's European Fate Could Turn Around This Year," Forbes.com, April 1, 2014.

ACKNOWLEDGMENTS

O nce again, I'd like to thank editor Craig Pyette for his patience, good humour and considerable skill. Also, Suzanne Blais-Guindon, Lorne Campbell, George Chuvalo, Mark DeMarco, Shanan Dionne, Bill Dunphy, Verg Erslavas, Juliet F. Forrester, Rick Gibson, Paul Gravelle, Devin Guindon, Harley Davidson Guindon, Jack Guindon, Teresa Guindon-Mader, Daphne Hart, Paul Henry, Walter Henry, Franco Hobs, Sarah Hodgins, Chuck (Spider) Jones, Cecil Kirby, Richard Mallory, George McIntyre, Steve (Slick) McQueen, Mike Murphy, Maggie Pearce-O'Shea, Kathleen Power, Giovanni (John) Raso, Don Shebib, Vikki Sheldrake, Johnny Sombrero (Harry Barnes), Harley's stepmom, Ian Watson.

INDEX

Lobos, 102, 154, 209, 224

Loews Theatre (Toronto, ON),
124–25

London (ON) Road Runners, 55,
262, 280

Loners, 86, 210, 217, 219

Longo, Dominic, 280

Lorraine (Harley Davidson
Guindon's mother). *See* Angel
(Harley Davidson Guindon's
mother)

Los Bravos (Winnipeg, MB), 110,
217–18

Los Santos, 73

Lost Horizon (Hilton), 180

Lovely Larry (Choice member),
84

Lowe, Mick, 293

Lupin (NT), 221

MacDonald, Doug (Chicklet), 86,
94

MacDonald, Lauchlan (Lockey),
103–4

MacLeod, Rod, 43–44, 65–66,
70–71, 279, 287

Mafia, 72, 113, 135, 154, 161, 245,
261, 295

Magasztovics, Gabor. *See*
Dinardo, Joe (Ironman)

Magnusson, Donny, 218

Mak, Brendan, 236, 237

Mallory, Richard, 78, 104–5, 282,
284, 285

Maltz, Maxwell, 221

Marauders (Asbestos, QC), 290

Marciano, Rocky, 69

Maritimes, 64, 192

Markham police, 45–46, 48–49

Markopoulos, Athanasios (Tom
Thumb), 292

Marks, Ernie, 69

Marvin, Lee, 15

Matchless G80 motorcycles, 15,
49

Matiyek, Bill, 162–63

Mazzotti, John, 154

McDonald, Marci, 84

McEwen, Garnet Douglas
(Mother), 114–15, 134–35, 143,
145, 146, 148, 151, 152, 192,
219, 286

McIlroy, Larry, 117, 262

McIntyre, George, 158–59, 193–94,
290–91

McQueen, Lucy, 195–96

McQueen, Steve (actor), 94

McQueen, Steve (Slick), 192–93,
194–96, 262, 270

Melanson, Donald (Snorko),
208–9

Melo, Eddie (Hurricane), 124

Mike (Thunder Bay Choice
member), 95, 96

Millhaven Institution, 102–8, 144,
149, 153–56, 236, 243–46, 250,
251–56, 261, 284, 291

Missiles (Saguenay, QC), 290

Monarch Vending, 58

Moncton (NB), 215–16

PETER EDWARDS has written for the *Toronto Star* for more than thirty years, specializing in organized crime and justice issues. He is the author of twelve previous non-fiction books, including *The Bandido Massacre: A True Story of Bikers, Brotherhood and Betrayal*; *One Dead Indian: The Premier, the Police and the Ipperwash Crisis*; *Business or Blood: Mafia Boss Vito Rizzuto's Last War* (with Antonio Nicaso); and *Unrepentant: The Strange and (Sometimes) Terrible Life of Lorne Campbell, Satan's Choice and Hells Angels Biker*. Edwards was a member of a team that won a National Newspaper Award for spot news reporting. He has been awarded an eagle feather from the Union of Ontario Indians and a gold medal from the Centre for Human Rights.

www.peteredwardsauthor.com